Day care for young children

'Who will look after our children?' is a question that all working parents ask themselves. This practical and thought-provoking text looks at the issues raised by the increase in women's employment and the consequent greater need for childcare services. Adopting a unique cross-national approach, it focuses on five countries – the UK, the USA, France, Sweden and East Germany – where the provision of day care differs markedly.

The central theme is the child's environment, how it is shaped by the social context, and how it can affect the child's development. The contributors highlight the influence of social context on day care and emphasise the importance of understanding the wide range of factors which mould day care provision. They pay particular attention to one aspect of the social context – policy on childcare services – and explore how and why policies develop, and how they affect the type of care young children receive.

Day Care for Young Children will be of relevance to all professionals concerned with day care, and to students in the related fields of child development, psychology, family studies and social policy.

Day care for young children
International perspectives

Edited by

Edward C. Melhuish

and

Peter Moss

Tavistock/Routledge
London and New York

First published 1991
by Routledge
11 New Fetter Lane, London EC4P 4EE
29 West 35th Street, New York, NY 10001

©1991 Edward Melhuish and Peter Moss

Laserset by LaserScript Limited, Mitcham, Surrey
Printed and bound in Great Britain by Mackays of Chatham PLC, Kent

British Library Cataloguing in Publication Data
Day care for young children : international perspectives:
policy and research in five countries.
1. Working mothers. Children. Day care
I. Melhuish, Edward *1950-* II. Moss, Peter *1945-*
362.712

Library of Congress Cataloging in Publication Data
Day care for young children: international perspectives: policy and research in five countries/edited by Edward Melhuish and Peter Moss.
p. cm.
1. Child care services – Europe. 2. Child care services – United States. 3. Day care centers – Europe. 4. Day care centers – United States. I. Melhuish, Edward, *1950–* II. Moss, Peter, *1945–*
HQ778.7.E85D39 1990
362.7'12–dc20   90-8220
                                                                                 CIP

ISBN 0-415-01746-7
       0-415-01747-5 (pbk)

Contents

Contents

Illustrations

Contributors

Geneviève Balleyguier, Department of Psychology, Université François Rabelais, Tours, France

Anders Broberg, Department of Psychology, University of Göteborg, Sweden

Carollee Howes, Department of Education, University of California, Los Angeles, United States

C. Philip Hwang, Department of Psychology, University of Göteborg, Sweden

Michael E. Lamb, National Institute of Child Health and Human Development, Bethesda, Maryland, United States

Edward C. Melhuish, Department of Psychology, University College of North Wales, United Kingdom (formerly Thomas Coram Research Unit, University of London)

Peter Moss, Thomas Coram Research Unit, University of London, United Kingdom

Frédérique Leprince, Commissariat Général du Plan, Paris, France

Deborah Phillips, Department of Psychology, University of Virginia, United States

Christine Weber, Instituts für Hygiene des Kindes und Jugendalters, Berlin, GDR

Irina Weigl, Psychologisches Institut, Freie Universität Berlin, West Berlin

Editors' note

Chapters three and four on the German Democratic Republic were written before the momentous events in that country which began at the end of 1989, and which are likely to lead to the reunification of Germany. This process will affect many aspects of economic and social life in the GDR, including possibly the high level of employment among women with young children, and the extensive system of day care services for young children. Exposure to Western influences may affect how services are run. These chapters therefore should be seen in their specific historical context. However, the development of day care services in the GDR can make an important contribution to the development of day care in Germany as a whole. The significance of the chapters on the GDR is not eradicated by current political events. The continuous development of a day care system through the application of fundamental research in child development to the planning of a system, and the integration of research and policy, constitute a model which has lessons for all interested in day care for young children.

Introduction

Peter Moss and Edward C. Melhuish

Putting non-parental childcare in context

Parental employment and the care of young children

This book is about non-parental care for young children, in particular children under the age of 3. The effects of such care have been a concern of parents, scientists and policymakers for some time. But the issue has come increasingly to the fore, in both research and policy terms, because in many countries there has been an increase in the number of women with young children who are employed.

Employment rates among women with young children still vary considerably between countries. They are highest in Scandinavia, North America and France and lowest in the United Kingdom, Ireland and the Netherlands; moreover, in the last two countries, most employed mothers work less than 20 hours a week, whereas in other countries most work over 30 hours a week (Moss 1988). Even in these countries, however, employment rates are increasing and will continue to do so. The UK has recently entered a period during which employment rates among women with young children are likely to rise quickly (see Chapter 7), while in the Netherlands, the labour force participation rate among women aged 25–54 is expected to increase from 46 per cent in 1987 to 59 per cent by 2000, and much of this increase will include women with young children (OECD 1988).

The changes in employment rates described above refer to countries in Western Europe and North America. In many parts of Eastern Europe, however, maternal employment rates have been high since the end of the Second World War. Non-parental childcare has been a pressing issue for forty years or more, and countries such as the German Democratic Republic now have long experience of extensive non-parental care services for young children.

While the *issue* of non-parental care has come to the fore because of increased employment among women with young children, the *need* for such care is not the result of maternal employment. If it is assumed that fathers and mothers are equally responsible for the care of their children – a value-based assumption that we make – then non-parental care is a consequence of both parents being at work (or undertaking some other activity, such as studying, political work or involvement in community action). The amount of non-parental care needed, and when it is needed, is also determined by factors outside individual families – how employment is structured, the allocation of national resources and so on. If most employment is structured on the assumption that workers do not have family responsibilities, then non-parental care will be needed for longer periods than in a society which provides employment, at all levels, that is responsive to the family responsibilities of workers, and compensates consequent losses in earnings by increased income from social sources.

This point needs to be made because research about non-parental care and its consequences can, too easily, be used in a debate that still continues about whether mothers with young children should be employed. We want to make it clear from the outset that we reject the premises on which that debate is based, in particular that mothers should be primarily responsible for the care of young children. Having said that, we must also recognise current reality. In practice, there is a gendered division of work and responsibility for children and their care. Even in dual-earner households, mothers mostly continue to carry the major share of this work and responsibility; fathers, where present, mostly assume a subsidiary role as helper and assistant. This situation is a major contributory factor to the inequality experienced by women in income, employment and other areas of public activity; it also contributes to the anxiety, guilt, tiredness and other stresses experienced by many employed mothers.

The debate we would like this book to contribute towards concerns how satisfying and satisfactory parenthood and employment careers can be combined. 'Satisfying' implies that both careers are positive and enhancing for the men and women involved, and that each should complement the other; equality of opportunity is assumed to be an integral part of a satisfying employment career. 'Satisfactory' implies good performance in both areas of work, and in particular that the care of children, both by parents and others, is such as to ensure their well-being and healthy development – intellectually, socially and emotionally. This book concentrates mainly on one of the components needed to pursue this broad objective – good quality non-parental care. While this is a necessary condition, it is not, however, a sufficient condition; other components are needed, including changes in employment, associated income support measures and changes in men's behaviour.

Finally, by way of introduction, it should be recognised that non-parental childcare services, or at least publicly-funded services, also sometimes have a social work or social welfare role, providing for children with special needs (for example, handicaps) or whose parents are deemed unable to care for them adequately. In some cases this welfare role has extended to the provision of such services to provide care for children from low income or lone parent families while their mothers are out at work. Over the last 25 years or so, in a number of countries – such as Belgium, France, Italy and Denmark – publicly-funded services, which were originally based on this welfare model, have developed and expanded to provide a general service, to which any employed parents can apply for a place (Moss 1988). The welfare model of provision, however, still predominates among publicly-funded services in some countries, either as a matter of explicit policy or because shortage of provision imposes strict priorities on admissions, which are consequently limited to low income and other disadvantaged families. If, however, we include services that are not publicly-funded, the main reason why young children receive non-parental care, in all countries, is because of parental employment.

The 'first wave' of research

The increasing interest in the effects of non-parental care on children has led to what the American psychologist, Jay Belsky, has referred to as 'two waves of day care research'.

In the first wave, the principal issue was whether day care was bad for children. Prevailing cultural attitudes, many of which were influenced by scientific theory and research, contended that exclusive maternal rearing particularly during the early years was essential to healthy psychological development. This resulted in the principal organising question of day care research being 'Does rearing outside of the confines of the family in a group program adversely affect intellectual, social and, especially, emotional development?'

(Belsky 1984: 2)

Until recently, the prevailing view has been that there was no reason to believe that non-parental care for young children was inherently harmful – intellectually, socially or emotionally. In 1984, for example, Belsky concluded that 'the first wave of research revealed few, if any, inevitable deleterious consequences of day care rearing' (Belsky 1984: 3).

Recently, Belsky has qualified this earlier conclusion. He argues that evidence from a number of studies 'indicates that when formal classifications of attachment security are made, extensive nonparental care initiated in the first year of life is associated with heightened risk of insecure infant-parent attachment relationships' (Belsky 1988: 401). He further argues that such insecure relationships in infants may be associated with adverse behaviour patterns in older children, such as non-compliance, aggressiveness, social withdrawal and behaviour problems.

We return to the issue raised by Belsky in the concluding chapter. Three points should however be emphasised at this stage. First, all the studies referred to by Belsky to support his argument about the consequences of early non-parental care are American; as we shall argue later, results from one country do not necessarily generalise to other countries. Second, even within the United States, research results are not consistent, and American researchers have questioned Belsky's interpretation of the evidence (for example, Clarke-Stewart 1988).

Finally, the debate about the possible adverse effects of non-parental care has now become very tightly drawn. The view that non-parental care is necessarily harmful for children under the age of 3 is not supported by research in any country. The 'Belsky debate' is much narrower. He contends that there may be a *'heightened risk'* of insecure infant-parent relationships, if infants are admitted to non-parental care lasting *more than 20 hours a week, in their first year.* He further suggests that the size of this risk may be influenced by various other factors: that it may, for example, be increased where marital relations are stressed and be decreased where non-parental care is of high quality and stable.

The 'second wave' of research

Before this current controversy and resurgence of interest in the basic issues underlying the 'first wave' of research on non-parental care for young children, a second wave of research had begun and gathered momentum.

> This [research] addressed the issue, 'Under what types of rearing conditions do children fare best in day care? That is, what types of rearing environments prove most supportive of children's development'? ... [this] has led policy-minded students of child development to examine variation within day care milieus in recent years. In part this work has been motivated by the recognized limits of home care versus day care experience. It is also motivated by the realization that day care is here to stay and thus that policymakers need to know more about the conditions of day care,

especially those that can be regulated, and how they affect the child's development.

(Belsky 1984: 3, 18)

Much of the research has studied how features of the child's immediate environment – for example, type of care, or more specific features such as group size, caregiver: child ratios, or levels of training among caregivers – relate to her development or to her experience in that environment; or how experience relates to development. By comparison, less research has been done which links all three components – environment, experience and development. In his 1984 review, Belsky noted only one such study.

The social context

This 'second wave' of research offers a positive and constructive way forward, based on a better understanding of the implications of children's immediate caregiving environments, and of how these environments may be improved to maximise children's experience and development. But these caregiving environments are themselves the product of broader external forces, in particular what Bronfenbrenner has referred to as the exosystem and macrosystem.

In his model of the ecology of human development, Bronfenbrenner (1977, 1979) envisages the individual as situated within several nested levels of context – the micro-, meso-, exo-, and macrosystems. The 'microsystem' describes the immediate caregiving settings, for example the home, nursery or school. The 'mesosystem' is the interrelation of these immediate caregiving environments. The 'exosystem' refers to the 'formal and informal social structures that do not contain the developing person, but impinge on or encompass the immediate settings', for example employment and government policy. Finally, the 'macrosystem' covers 'the overarching patterns of ideology and organisation that characterize a particular culture or subculture' (Belsky *et al.* 1982: 99–100).

The exo- and macrosystems in Bronfenbrenner's model (and which together we refer to as the 'social context') can influence children's experience and thus their development through a variety of routes; for instance, through their impact on parents and parental caregiving, on children's experience in society at large – and on non-parental caregiving environments. Two important implications follow from this linking of social context and non-parental caregiving. First, it is not enough simply to identify what factors in non-parental caregiving environments have good or bad consequences. It is also important to understand what broader features of the social context facilitate the development of favourable factors and which support the continuance of unfavourable factors – 'social structure is influential (on day-to-day experience) because it ... influences whether certain experiences will be experienced' (Belsky 1984: 27).

Second, it is necessary to be extremely careful in interpreting the results from individual research studies. Most research into non-parental care, as most research in human services, is relatively small-scale and local in scope. This raises problems of generalisability within the wider society; for example, can the results of a study of childminders in one inner city area be assumed to apply to other inner city areas or to suburban or rural areas?

The same problem occurs, but with greater force, in assessing whether results from one country can be generalised to other countries. Differences in social context are likely to be greater between different countries, than between areas within the same country. Contextual differences, and their impact on non-parental care, may underlie some of the inconsistencies in research findings that have been observed between, for example, the United States and Sweden. One Swedish researcher, whose study showed that children who had entered non-parental care before 12 months of age 'achieved significantly better [than children who entered later or who had parental care only] on the aptitude tests and got more positive ratings from their teachers ... for school achievement as well as social-personal attributes' draws attention to the impact of contextual factors.

> When talking about daycare it is important to apply an ecological perspective and consider the whole culture and the cultural values which influence a country's daycare situation. The situation in Sweden and in other Scandinavian countries is quite different to the American scene. The standard and quality is generally high and the daycare is rather homogeneous. We do not talk about daycare for two or three month old babies as many Americans do but allow parents to stay home for a major part of the child's first year of life. We do not talk about completely untrained caregivers either. Therefore, one cannot translate this Swedish data without taking into consideration the child and family policy of [Sweden] as well.

(Andersson 1988: 27–28)

The Book

Taking a cross-national approach

The aim of this book is to explore the relationship between the social context and children's non-parental caregiving environments; and between these environments and children's experience and development. The central theme therefore is the child's non-parental caregiving environment, how it is shaped by the social context and how, in turn, it may shape the child's development. Particular attention is paid to one aspect of the social context – policy on childcare services, including how and why policies develop and how they affect the type of care that young children receive. Consideration is also given to another policy area, employment entitlements for parents, which can affect children's experience of non-parental care, for example by influencing the age at which children start to receive non-parental care.

The book adopts a cross-national approach, with contributions from five countries. Cross-national comparisons provide a valuable way of highlighting and assessing the influence of social context. Many local or national studies simply take contextual factors for granted; in cross-national comparisons they are impossible to ignore. And while it is not possible to evaluate precisely the impact of social context factors in the same way as other factors affecting non-parental care, through for example controlled comparisons, some attempt can be made to evaluate their likely impact by careful comparison between different countries.

Adopting a cross-national approach as an organising principle for the book also ensures some balance between the research and experience of different countries. Without such a deliberate device, there is a danger of American research and experience assuming a dominant position. This dominance would be a reflection not only of the sheer size of the United States, but also of the large volume of research undertaken there, proportionately greater than in any other country, and the strength and prestige of the American academic publishing system. We also recognise that as British researchers, the danger of American dominance is enhanced because we concentrate on English-language publications. European work – in German, Swedish, French or other languages – is unlikely to be widely known about in English-speaking countries such as Britain or the United States.

The five countries in this book – France, the German Democratic Republic (GDR), Sweden, the United Kingdom and the United States – appear on equal terms. While they vary considerably in population (Sweden: 8.3 million, GDR: 16.6 million, France: 55.4 million, United Kingdom: 56.7 million, United States: 241.6 million), all five countries are industrially developed and have relatively high levels of national income. In planning the book, we have deliberately sought societies that differ substantially in their political and economic systems, and on two other important parameters. The first concerns policy responses to the employment of parents with young children and in particular the extent and nature of government involvement. The US and UK represent one extreme, of minimal involvement and a consequent emphasis on parent and employer responsibility. Sweden and East Germany are at the other extreme, with major involvement by government, though that involvement takes significantly different forms. In this respect, France is in between, though nearer to Sweden and East Germany than to the US and UK.

The second parameter concerns the extent to which women with young children are in the labour force. Again, the UK is at one extreme, with relatively low employment levels, mostly involving short hours of work – though this seems likely to change rapidly over the next few years. At the other extreme again come East Germany and Sweden, where the great majority of women with young children are employed; indeed, in these two countries, most women are now in the labour force throughout their lives, with short breaks for maternity or parental leave. France and the United States come in between, with just over half of women with young children employed; in both cases, the employment rate has increased rapidly in recent years.

The structure of the book

For each of the five countries covered in this book, there are two chapters. The first chapter describes the employment entitlements available to parents with young children (such as maternity and parental leave), which have an important bearing on when children begin to receive non-parental care, and the current system of non-parental care for children under 3, both publicly-funded and private; examines usage of services, for example what proportion of children use different types of care and how far usage varies between families with differing socio-economic characteristics; and analyses some of the main factors which have shaped the system, with some reference to the historical development of policies. These chapters show how social context, and in particular government policy, affects the environments in which young children are cared for.

The second chapter for each country provides an overview of research on non-parental care with more detailed accounts of selected recent studies on the relationship between environments and children's experience and development. Two main types of research are reported – the implications for experience and development of different types of non-parental care, for example group care and childminding, and of different organisational features within the same type of care.

A recurrent problem in any form of cross-national work concerns terminologies, especially when this involves translating contributions from different languages into the common language to be used in a publication. The approach we have taken is to translate Swedish, French and German terms – for example the terms used to describe different types of childcare service – into English; but where the term appears first in each chapter, we give it in its original Swedish, French or German form alongside the English translation.

Finally, throughout the book, we have used the term 'day care' as shorthand for non-parental care; 'day care services' or 'day care provision' also refers to different types of non-parental care. 'Childcare' refers to the totality of caring, by parents and others.

References

Andersson, B.-E. (1988) 'The effects of public daycare – a longitudinal study', paper presented at a workshop on International Developments in Child Care, organised by the NAC/NAS Panel on Child Care, NAS Study Centre, Woods Hole, MA, 9 August 1988.

Belsky, J. (1984) 'Two waves of day care research: developmental effects and conditions of quality', in R.C. Ainskie (ed.) *The Child and the Day Care Setting*, New York: Praeger.

— (1988) 'Infant day care and socioemotional development: the United States', *Journal of Child Psychology and Psychiatry* 29, 4: 397–406.

Belsky, J., Steinberg, D.L. and Walker, A. (1982) 'The ecology of day care', in M.E. Lamb (ed.) *Nontraditional Families: Parenting and Child Development*, Hillsdale, NJ: Lawrence Erlbaum.

Bronfenbrenner, U. (1977) 'Towards an experimental ecology of human development', *American Psychologist* 32, 513–31.

— (1979) *The Ecology of Human Development*, Cambridge, MA: Harvard University Press.

Clarke-Stewart, K.A. (1988) 'The "effects of infant day care reconsidered" reconsidered: risks for parents, children and researchers', *Early Childhood Research Quarterly* 3: 293–318.

Moss, P. (1988) *Childcare and Equality of Opportunity: Consolidated Report of the European Childcare Network*, Brussels: European Commission.

OECD (1988) *Employment Outlook: September 1988*, Paris: OECD.

Chapter one

Day care for young children in France

Frédérique Leprince

Proliferating headlines in the newspapers in recent years reflect a problem facing French society: 'Finding someone to look after your children – a headache'; 'Who is looking after our children?'; 'Mum's working – go and see the local councillor'; 'One million balancing acts'.

In France today, 2.3 million children are under 3 years old, and more than half come from families where both parents, or the single parent, are in full-time or part-time employment. Allowing for some children who are cared for by a mother with an unpaid job or who works only a few hours a week, the number of children needing day care while their parents are employed is around one million. The problem is particularly acute for mothers with only one child and that child being under 3; 69 per cent of these mothers have a regular job. Moreover, increasing numbers of grandmothers are taking jobs these days, which makes the care of young children by their grandparents less available than in the past.

The French system of day care is faced with varied and increasing needs. On the positive side it provides a variety of services. On the negative side, services controlled and subsidised by the community are, in relation to demand, distinctly inadequate.

Employment entitlements for parents

For the first two children, maternity leave consists of 6 weeks before the birth and 10 weeks after, and for subsequent children these periods are extended to 8 and 18 weeks. During this period of leave, women receive benefit payments equal to 90 per cent of normal earnings. In addition, fathers are entitled to 3 days paternity leave at the time of the birth of their child.

There is also a system of parental leave (*conge parental*). A father or mother who has worked for over a year may, in the two years following maternity leave, ask for full-time leave or to work on a half-time basis until the child reaches the age of 3. In theory, at the end of this leave period the employee must be allowed to resume his or her previous work, otherwise the employer must pay compensation. Despite being available to both parents, parental leave is rarely taken by fathers.

In 1984, a benefit payment (*allocation parentale d'éducation*) was introduced for parents of three or more children, one of whom at least was under 3 years of age. Initially, this benefit could be claimed for two years by a father or mother who had been employed for 24 of the preceding 30 months, if they stopped work; alternatively, they could get half the benefit if they worked half-time. This measure had less success than originally expected, and it was amended in January 1987, so that parents qualified for the benefit if they had been employed for 2 of the preceding 10 years. At the same time, it was extended so that parents could claim benefit for 3 years, while the option of having reduced benefit for half-time work was dropped.

The benefit is a flat-rate payment (2,488FF per month in 1988 – by comparison, the minimum legal wage (*S.M.I.C.*) is 4,100FF per month, and average monthly earnings about 7,200FF). It provides parents on parental leave who have three or more children with partial compensation for lost earnings.

The current system of day care

Publicly-funded day care

Public funding for day care in France involves both demand- and supply-subsidy. The main form of demand-subsidy is tax relief on day care costs. This was first introduced in 1981, when it was fixed at 5,000FF for each child under 3 (that is, costs up to 5,000FF could be deducted from taxable income). The sum has since been raised to 10,000FF per child under 7; to qualify both parents must be employed. In addition, refunds or allowances are given to parents employing childminders or someone in their own home, to cover parents' share of the caregiver's social security contribution.

There are a range of publicly-funded day care services. Nearly all children between 3 and 6 (94 per cent) go to nursery school (*école maternelle*), which is free and provided by the Ministry of Education. In addition to this older age group, about a third of 2-year-olds attend these schools. The exact age of admission depends on the child's date of birth, stage of toilet training, local circumstances and parents' wishes, but in practice children do not start until they are 2 1/2. These schools are open from 8.30 to 16.30. Employed parents sending their children face the same problems they will encounter throughout the school system - arranging care after 16.30 (or 18.00 where the local authority (*municipalité*) provides an after-school care service), at lunch-time

11

where no school meals are provided, on Wednesdays (when schools close) and during school holidays.

For children under 3 not at nursery school there are a variety of publicly-funded services which provide specifically for this young age group. Some 85,000 children (4 per cent of under-3s) go to nurseries (*crèches collectives*) which offer full-day care. Most go to larger nurseries (the average number of children per nursery is 50); the more traditional divide children into three groups according to age, while others divide children into two age groups – under-2s and 2 to 3s, the latter in groups of 10-12 and with an educator (*éducatrice*) for part of the day. Some children however go to smaller nurseries; there are about 6,600 places in mini-nurseries (*mini-crèches*), which take less than 16 children and are usually sited in flats, houses or community buildings.

About 80 per cent of nurseries are solely for the use of the residents of a particular district. They are generally open for 8 to 12 hours a day, and are closed at night and weekends. The remaining 20 per cent of nurseries are attached to particular workplaces (mainly hospitals) and adapt their opening hours to suit the workplace. Hospital nurseries, in particular, have adopted timetable arrangements that fit in with the three-shift system (day, evening, night).

The great majority of publicly-funded nurseries (89 per cent) are run by public bodies, most by the local authority. A minority are run by private organisations, some by workplace committees but most (84 per cent) by associations regulated by the 1901 statutes; indeed most nurseries run by such associations seem to be 'para-public', largely subsidised from public funds. A distinctive group of association-run nurseries are mini-nurseries established and run by an association of parents (*crèches parentales*), which provided 2,600 places in 1987. These nurseries employ one or more permanent workers, but parents also work with the children; each family contributes between a half to a whole day per week according to the size of the nursery and the number of employed workers.

There are a further 41,400 places in other nurseries which provide part-time care (*halte garderies*) for children up to the age of 6 (though most attending will be under 3). These part-time nurseries were originally intended to serve the needs of non-employed women who wanted their children looked after for a few hours a week while they went shopping, followed sporting or other leisure interests etc. As nurseries providing full-time care will rarely take children part-time, and with the growth of part-time employment and the financial difficulties faced by some *halte garderies*, this provision is gradually turning into part-time *mini-crèches*.

The final form of publicly-funded provision consists of organised childminding schemes (*crèches familiales*). Under this system, children are looked after in childminders' (*assistantes maternelles*) homes; each cares for a maximum of three children under school age, including her own. In 1986, there were 46,400 places – about 2 for every 100 children under 3 – in these schemes, mostly administered by local authorities with the remainder run either by associations or, in a very few cases (2 per cent), by hospitals.

The function of publicly-funded services

Services such as nurseries, organised childminding and nursery schools are available to all families, though some places are reserved for cases of special need. The main objective of these services is to allow parents to go out to work, while ensuring the healthy development of their children. Even if the declared objective is to permit parents freely to choose their way of life, services are provided within the context of a public concern to increase the birth-rate and a preventive socio-medical policy intended to avoid or reduce handicaps among children.

Local variations in publicly-funded services

Publicly-funded nurseries and organised childminding schemes are practically non-existent in rural areas. Large towns (such as Paris, Lyon, Marseille, Bordeaux and Orleans) have the best supply of services, with the exception of Nord-Pas-de-Calais where, despite Lille being a large town, services are few and far between. Nearly half the places in nurseries (48 per cent) and over a third in publicly-funded childminding (37 per cent) are in the Ile-de-France area (in particular in Paris and surrounding communes), although this area has less than a fifth of the French population. These local variations are influenced not only by the population size of different local authorities, but by other factors such as cultural traditions, demographic structures, economic conditions and political control.

Private day care

The most common form of private day care is by childminders. By law, they are supposed to be approved and registered by public health and welfare authorities, and be officially declared by the parents who employ them so that social security contributions and income tax are paid. In 1986, there were 138,000 registered childminders (*assistantes maternelles agrées*) caring for about 200,000 children under 3 (about 9 per cent of the total).

But many childminders are neither registered nor officially declared. Unregistered childminders (*nourrices au noir* or *assistantes maternelles non-agrées*) are still numerous – some people even believe their numbers are increasing – and it is estimated that these caregivers look after at least 130,000 children under 3 (about 6 per cent). For parents, registration does not always bring satisfactory guarantees; the supervision and training of registered childminders varies widely from area to area. For the childminders, the registration procedures are an extra burden. If their work is officially declared, they may receive social security benefits; but most are already eligible though the social security contributions of their husbands and the benefits they receive when unemployed or retired are extremely low. Moreover, once registered they have to pay income tax. Overall, the risks of being penalised for not registering are very small, with the law rarely enforced except in cases of serious misdemeanour or complaint against the childminder. However, the increase in tax relief to parents for childcare costs should encourage an increase in registration, since this will only be available where a registered caregiver is used.

No registration procedure is required when a child is cared for in his or her own home. Such caregivers may also do domestic work and are normally paid the national minimum wage which in 1989 was 28FF an hour.

The final form of private day care is that provided by relatives, mostly grandparents. It has been estimated that as many as 270,000 young children may be cared for in this way. This practice is very widespread in Nord-Pas-de-Calais and Alsace.

Financing publicly-funded day care services

On average local authorities contribute about half the running costs of services and parents' fees a quarter. In most cases, parents' fees vary according to income and numbers of children; for example, the scale of charges for a nursery in 1988 fixed by the national family allowance office (*Caisse Nationale d'Allocations Familiale*, referred to as CNAF below) ranged from 12,5FF per day for a family with four children and earning less than 4,000FF monthly to 121,5FF for a one-child family earning more than 20,000FF a month. Parental contributions are similar in nurseries and organised childminding schemes, even though the running costs of the two services are very different – on average, about 220FF per child per day in 1988 for nurseries and 160FF for publicly-funded childminders.

The payment of a monthly fee by parents, irrespective of the number of days their child attends, is replacing payment on a daily attendance basis. The implementation of this monthly payment system varies. Some managing bodies allow only one month's absence per year when parents need not pay for their child's place, and only cease charging for children who are away because of illness after more than two weeks absence; while others allow six weeks absence per year and make no charge from the first day of a child's absence due to illness.

Finally, services receive subsidy from local family allowance offices (*Caisse d'Allocations Familiales*, referred to as CAFs below). The national family allowance office – CNAF – is one of the three parts of the social security system (the other two cover benefits for sickness and old age). CNAF comes under the Ministry of Social Affairs, but has its own Administrative Council, on which Trades Unions and employers are represented. There are local offices – CAFs – in each *département*, which must implement the policies laid down by CNAF, but which also have their own budget for supporting local social action and their own administrative committee; this allows them to adapt national guidelines to local circumstances. Funding comes from employer contributions.

Originally established to pay financial benefits to families with children, since 1970 CAFs have been increasingly involved in funding the capital and running costs of day care services, reducing the proportion of costs born by local authorities; day care provision for young children has become one of the main objectives of CNAF. CAFs provide subsidies equal to 30 per cent of a national figure for daily running costs (set by CNAF), and these go to all publicly-funded services except workplace nurseries where less than 30 per cent of children attending do not have parents employed at the workplace. The amount of subsidy, though not the proportion, is lower for parent-run nurseries and organised childminding schemes where the running costs are lower.

In 1983, CNAF initiated the nursery agreement (*contrat crèche*), as a means of increasing the amount of day care provision for children under 3, both in nurseries and in childminding schemes. These agreements were made between local authorities and their local CAF. They committed the CAF to raise its contribution to running costs from 30 per cent to 50 per cent for new services, and to raise the subsidy progressively (at the rate of 4 per cent a year) on existing places. The local authority committed itself to providing, within 5 to 7 years, 40 per cent of the local need for day care, need being calculated on the basis of the number of children under 3 and the local employment rate among women aged 24 to 34; an additional condition was that the number of places must increase by at least 50 per cent on current levels. Local authorities also agreed to improve financial efficiency by making sure that attendance rates neared 100 per cent (instead of 75 per cent that was usual due to children being absent), by changing parental payments to a monthly basis and by applying a standard scale for payments, based on income and with no upper ceiling so that the proportionate cost to low income families should be no greater than for high income families (CNAF suggested that costs for child care should be around 12 per cent of family income).

The objective was to create 20,000 new places each year. In fact, between 1983 and 1990, these agreements will have created only 15,000 new places. One reason for this limited progress has been the decentralisation of health and welfare services occurring at the same time, which has caused some upheaval among local authorities. Local authorities have also been discouraged from participating by the financial effort required of them at a time when they face other pressing concerns (for example, increases in the number of unemployed and old people). In some cases, too, local authorities and CAFs have made different assessments of the need for day care.

At the beginning of 1988, CNAF launched a new initiative – the childhood agreement (*contrat enfance*). The CNAF intends to allocate an extra 800 millions FF between 1988 and 1992 to this initiative. The agreements will again be made between local authorities and their local CAFs; CAFs will subsidise new services for the care of children up to age 6 and local authorities will commit themselves to increased expenditure during the 5 to 7 year period of the agreement. Increased local authority expenditure, subsidised by CAFs, is intended to benefit all families, and not just those where mothers are employed, and can cover a range of possibilities, including the running costs of day care services, financial help to families employing a caregiver in their own home, co-ordinating services, information for families and training for workers in day care services.

The division of responsibility between national, regional and local authorities

A wide range of official bodies have some responsibility and interest in day care services. Nationally, the Ministry of Education provides nursery schools, while the Ministry of Social Affairs is concerned with nurseries and childminders, though not making provision directly, and supervises the CNAF. There are ninety-five *Départements*, each with a *Conseil Général* which is directly elected and has its own budget. Under the process of government decentralisation, this body is being given a decisive role in social services and has taken over responsibilities for maternal and infant welfare services in its *Département*, including the approval of nurseries and childminders; it is also able to give subsidies to day care services.

Local authorities are the main managers of day care services, although they are not obliged to provide any at all. It is at this level that policies on day care services are really worked out. Their responsibilities are not directly affected by decentralisation, but even if they are by law autonomous, their policies are closely linked to those of the *Conseils Généraux*. Local authorities are the main partners of the

CAFs, which operate at *Départemental* level.

This structure explains why CNAF and CAFs can only intervene in day care on a contractual basis and in agreement with local authorities. It is also important to note the frequent absence of consultation between the parties involved in policy on day care provision: CAFs, *Conseils Généraux* and local authorities are not always well co-ordinated, nor is consultation always smooth between the Ministeries of Education and Social Affairs.

Staffing and staff training

Nurseries

The directors of nurseries must be doctors (which is rare) or qualified children's medical nurses (*puéricultrices*) and have worked for at least five years in the profession. The training leading to the *puéricultrice* qualification involves a one-year course on top of basic nursing training. The director deals with administrative duties, appoints staff or advises on appointments and is involved in decisions about admissions. She supervises health, safety and the children's development and deals with parents.

When nurseries have more than forty children, they have to employ educators (*éducatrices de jeunes enfants*), whose task is to stimulate the psycho-affective development of children over 18 months and advise other nursery workers. They trained in special colleges to which admission is gained via competitive examination for young people who have reached Lower Sixth Form standard at least (that is the year before the *Baccalauréat*, the diploma obtained at the end of secondary schooling between 17 and 18 years of age). Half the staff in a nursery must have the diploma of *auxiliaire de puériculture*, which is gained after a one-year course in a specialist institution; entrance is obtained via competitive examination at the end of the fourth year of secondary schooling. *Auxiliaires* care for children, supervise their play and cope with domestic work. Similar tasks are undertaken by *agents de service*, though some specialise in domestic work such as cooking or washing. No training is required for *agents*.

Parents running their own nursery (*crèche parentale*) often employ an *éducatrice*, preferring someone trained mainly in psycho-affective development rather than in children's physical care and hygiene. Altogether, 40 per cent of permanent staff in these nurseries are *éducatrices* and only 12 per cent are *auxiliaires*.

In 1988, the salary of nursery directors was between 7,000 and 10,000FF per month, according to length of service. *Puéricultrices* working in nurseries, but who were not directors, received

6,000–9,000FF; *éducatrices* and *auxiliaires* between 5,500–6,600FF; and *agents de service* 5,000 to 6,000FF. The national minimum wage at the same time was 4,300FF a month.

There must be 1 adult to every 5 children, for children who are not yet walking, and 1 to 8 for other children. By contrast, nursery schools which take a large number of older 2-year-olds, have class sizes up to 35 children, with each class supervised by a teacher and an *agent de service*. Nursery school teachers receive a two-year college training which they enter via competitive examination after obtaining the Diploma of General University Studies two years after the *Baccalauréat*. Their monthly salary, paid by the Ministry of Education, is between 6,000–9,000FF. *Agents* are appointed and paid by local authorities.

Organised childminding schemes

Directors of organised childminding schemes must have the same qualifications as directors of nurseries or, by special dispensation, they may be qualified midwives or nurses who have worked for at least two years on paediatric wards. The director looks after administrative and financial matters, is responsible for selecting childminders and placing children and must pay weekly visits to the home of each childminder. By law, there must be a director for 40 childminders, and if the scheme has more childminders there must also be a deputy, who is a *puéricultrice* or qualified midwife.

Childminders in organised schemes have a lower salary than workers in nurseries and must meet all equipment and upkeep costs. Childminders do not need to have any training, but may take advantage of training arranged by local authorities; however, such training does not always exist and where it does, it is not always well publicised. Childminders often find it difficult to get to training courses and do not always see its point when caring for children seems to them to be such a natural activity.

Whether they work in schemes or independently, registered childminders must be able to contribute to the affective and intellectual development and the education of children in conditions suited to their age. They must pass a medical examination and live in suitable accommodation. Registered childminders, outside a scheme, should sign a contract with parents which guarantees them compensation in the case of unforeseen absence by the child and in case of redundancy and allows them to claim social security benefits. Their pay must not be lower than two hours of the national minimum wage per day per child, excluding expenses necessary for the child's maintenance. As the demand for places is usually high, especially in large cities, parents often pay more than the minimum required.

Childcare arrangements for children under 3

It is difficult to know precisely how children are cared for and to do so it is necessary to make cross-references to different statistical sources dating back to 1982 and 1983 (INSEE 1982a, 1982b; Ministère de l'éducation 1983; Ministère des affaires sociales 1983). At that time, 59 per cent of children under 3 were looked after by their mothers, though 14 per cent had mothers who were employed. This high proportion of children looked after by their employed mothers covers a diversity of situations. Some mothers work at home or at other people's homes, where they can take their child to work. Almost all women who work on the land look after their own children, as do many shopkeepers, people in the service of others (such as domestic cleaners and childminders), workers in small workshops and those in certain professions.

Among the remaining children under 3, 11 per cent attended nursery school, 5 per cent went to other publicly-funded childcare services (3 per cent to nurseries, 2 per cent to organised childminding schemes) and 8 per cent were with registered childminders. The remaining 17 per cent were divided between care by family members (11 per cent), mainly grandparents (though many children are reported to be cared for by the family when in reality they are cared for by unregistered childminders) and care by unregistered childminders, who provided for more children than publicly-funded nurseries and childminding schemes.

Socio-demographic variations in usage of different types of care

As already noted, women in certain sorts of employment are more likely to care for their own children while at work. Non-parental care also varies according to parental socio-occupational status. Care in the child's own home by a paid person is more common for children with parents in high status occupations – 18 per cent of executives and 13 per cent of managers, shopkeepers and artisans compared to 6 per cent of the intermediate professions (middle managers, primary school teachers, etc.), 5 per cent of factory workers and 3 per cent of clerical workers. Care by a relative is widespread among artisans and shopkeepers (52 per cent), shop assistants (56 per cent) and factory workers (52 per cent), but is much less common among managerial staff and executives (21 per cent) and intermediate professions (26 per cent) (INSEE 1982b).

Excluding unpaid care by relatives, publicly-funded services provide the cheapest day care for parents, especially as parental financial contributions are income related; but it is the most expensive system for the community. Yet it is used more by parents in higher income jobs (16 per cent executives, 15 per cent of middle managers) than by parents in lower income jobs (for example, 5 per cent of factory workers). The

level of education among parents whose children are in publicly-funded
services is also relatively high: 20 per cent of all children under 3 have
a mother who has gained the Baccalauréat or a higher diploma
compared to 40 per cent of children in publicly-funded nurseries or
childminding schemes.This social differentiation cannot be explained
simply in terms of the cost of infant care. Communication problems
between professional day care workers and families in lower
socio-economic groups – such as those who due to lack of information
put their names down too late on waiting lists that are often very long –
may also contribute.

Attitudes to employment affect decisions concerning care for young
children and these attitudes are also closely linked to socio-cultural
background. For instance, North African and Turkish women rarely go
out to work and almost all of them look after their children themselves
– though their children go to nursery school at a relatively younger age
than French children. The proportion of Portuguese women who look
after their own children is similar to the proportion for French women
who left school with the lowest level qualification in the French
education system (*Certificat d'Etudes Primaires*). This probably
reflects the sorts of jobs they are most likely to do, for example
concierge, domestic cleaner, childminder.

Supply and demand

According to the criteria used, the number of children who could be in
need of some form of day care provision ranges from 700,000 (if
children at nursery school or looked after by their mother while she
works are excluded) to 1.2 million (if all children with employed parents
are considered). The increase in the number of children needing some
form of care can be estimated at about 250,000 between 1975 and 1982
(the last two years when the national census was carried out). During
this period the number of places in publicly-funded nurseries and
childminding schemes grew by 50,000, while the number of 2-year-olds
at nursery school went up by 34,000. Some children go to nursery school
when their mothers are not at work and the practice of part-time
employment is spreading, both of which increase recourse to unofficial
care arrangements; while the steady increase in the number of
unemployed people has brought with it different kinds of need. So, it can
be estimated that the number of children who are neither looked after by
their parents nor cared for in publicly-funded or regulated services
increased by 100,000 between 1975 and 1982. Long waiting lists,
especially for nurseries, indicate a continuing high level of unsatisfied
demand for publicly-funded services.

Surveys of parents with young children show a clear preference for care provided by mothers, with nursery care clearly ahead of that offered by childminders or relatives. For example, a 1980 survey in Lorraine of 2,000 employed mothers showed a discrepancy between their preferences and what they did; 39 per cent said they wanted to look after their own child compared to just 3 per cent who actually did so (Wagnon 1983). This finding is certainly ambiguous, being heavily dependent on the way the question was asked: should it be regarded as the expression of a real desire or of the need to give a socially acceptable reply? Slightly more mothers wanted their child cared for at home by a paid caregiver or at a nursery than actually used these types of care; but the preference for care by grandparents (26 per cent) and by childminders (10 per cent) was well below the proportions actually using them (40 per cent and 31 per cent respectively). Discrepancies between preference and actual arrangements narrowed as the level of parental income rose; factory worker, clerks and employees reported the greatest discrepancies. National surveys between 1978 and 1980 also show satisfaction highest with maternal caring (97 per cent) and nurseries (76 per cent), and lowest amongst parents using relatives and childminders (51 per cent and 52 per cent respectively) (CREDOC 1981).

The gap between use of and preference for childminders reflects shortages of public day care, and especially of nursery places. Many parents would prefer their child cared for in a nursery, but find there are no places, often at a very late stage. They then have to use a childminder, registered or not, whose services are often considered a stop-gap measure.

Lack of choice for parents can affect the birthrate, increase inequalities and harm the development of a child.

> Changes in care arrangements are in every case damaging for the child, especially if he is cared for outside his family home. To prevent the possibility of serious disorders it is vital that a child should have, apart from a reassuring and reliable person to care for him, stability in the chosen form of care. That is why it is very important that this choice be made in accordance with the mother's wishes, her way of life and the fundamental needs of the child.

> (Davidson 1977)

A study in the late 1970s found that changes in care arrangements were four times more frequent among children cared for by childminders, than for those cared for in other ways (Davidson 1977). This said, many parents appreciate the more personal care given by a childminder, who is more likely to take the child into her home when he or she is sick, may offer more flexible hours than a nursery and can provide out-of-school care for a child once he or she has started at *école maternelle*. The great problem is that the childminder's wage is mainly paid by the parents.

The development of the system for day care provision

As far back as the Middle Ages, it was common practice for childminders in the country to care for town children. From the twelfth century, this work was organised by a charity, and in 1350 a royal decree fixed the payments for childminders and *recommanderesses*, who were the intermediaries between childminders and parents. However, until the eighteenth century, French society showed considerable indifference towards young children.

The eighteenth century was a turning-point. Society became aware of the importance of young children and increasingly concerned about their well-being. The population came to be seen as a source of wealth, and anxieties about a fall in population coincided with the views of doctors and philosophers (such as Rousseau) who glorified motherhood and denounced the dangers of placing children with childminders. A series of measures were taken then to control the activities of childminders, but it was not until 1773 that the transport of children had, by law, to be in carriages with 'the bottom made of planks not too far apart and padded with sufficient quantities of fresh straw' and childminders had to remain with children to ensure that none fell out. At about the same time, Pastor Oberlin created the very first nursery and nursery school in the Vosges, to enable women to work in the local timber industry.

It was in the nineteenth century that local systems for the care of young children developed. Industrialisation, requiring more women workers, combined with concerns about the population to highlight the contradiction between women's 'productive' and 'reproductive' roles. The first *salle d'asile* (now called *école maternelle* or nursery school) was opened in 1826 by a charitable organisation, and a decree from the *Assistance Publique* in 1829 placed these institutions under its authority and granted them subsidies. From 1836, the Ministry of Public Instruction increasingly took control of them, while preserving their function of helping children from the working class. In 1881, with the introduction of free primary schooling, the *salles d'asile* were fully integrated into the education system, becoming known as *écoles maternelles*. From 1921, they were no longer open 12 hours a day and local authorities who wanted these longer hours had to provide a supplementary system of care outside school hours.

Nurseries evolved in a different way. They first appeared in 1844, after which their numbers rapidly increased, and were intended for children from 15 days to 3 years old whose mothers 'went out to work and were of good behaviour'. Firman Marbeau, who established nurseries, wrote several books, one of which had the significant title of *Nurseries – or the means of reducing poverty while increasing the birth rate*. From 1862, nurseries could receive state subsidies, as long as they were licensed by the *Préfet du Département*. In 1867, workplace nurseries appeared for the first time, but did not develop much despite the demands of Trades Unions. Unlike nursery schools, for a long time nurseries were considered to be welfare institutions, primarily concerned with health and hygiene.

It was also at the end of the nineteenth century that the activities of childminders came under proper control. The *Loi Roussel* of 1874 required every child under 2 left with a childminder to be 'under the surveillance of the public authorities to protect its life and health'. However, no controls were placed on care provided in the child's own home, a distinction which continues until today.

A second turning-point came after the Second World War. Demographic and child welfare concerns, apparent since the nineteenth century or earlier, became more influential. The present system of mother and infant welfare was created in 1945, together with the social security system which incorporated the child benefits (cash allowance for parents) in existence since the nineteenth century and made compulsory in 1932. Among the objectives of the social security system was the reduction of infant mortality and supporting optimal child development. A decree in 1945 strictly regulated nurseries, though it dealt exclusively with health and hygiene. After post-war reconstruction was completed, labour shortages affected the economy, especially the tertiary sector, and female employment was encouraged.

From the 1970s, greater attention was given to child psychology and development. The early socialisation of children was put forward as a contributing factor in child development and in tackling disadvantage. At the same time, the trend towards female employment increased, and the socio-educational function of day care services was emphasised. In 1974, a decree regulating nurseries stressed their role in the mental development of the child, and within the Ministry of Social Affairs a group of experts in this field was transferred from the General Health Department to the Social Action Department. A series of measures were also taken to increase the supply of day care provision – for example, the involvement of CNAF in subsidising capital and running costs and official recognition of organised childminding schemes (which had first appeared in 1959).

Since the mid-1970s, new economic and social developments have emerged – increased unemployment reflecting the diminishing labour needs of manufacturing industry and a drop in the birth rate. Concern about the population led to further pro-natalist measures, with particular emphasis on encouraging more women to have three or more children (for example through increased financial benefits). Birth-rate and day care facilities were seen to be connected: might not women, rather than leave employment, decide not to have another child? Or alternatively, they might seek a form of care outside state regulation, running counter to a policy of socio-medical protection for children.

Faced by these dilemmas, the state has concentrated on developing childcare systems which, in the main, cost as little as possible – organised childminding, *crèches parentales* and unpaid parental leave. The aim of current policy is to reduce the gap between supply and demand by making services more flexible and efficient in operation. The Socialist government in 1981 set out to develop a real policy for young children and the national priorities in the Ninth Plan included an increase in day care services and their better adaptation to parents' demands. A target was set of 300,000 new places for children under 3. This has not been achieved because of the failure of *contrat crèches* and because expenditure in this area was not made compulsory for local authorities or the state.

Political positions

In their public statements, political differences appear clearly between Right and Left. The Right has a more conservative concept of the care of young children, favouring care by the mother or her nearest substitute, a childminder. It is however less usual to openly criticise women for going out to work these days; so the talk is now mostly about 'enabling' women, who wish to do so, to look after their own child. Economic liberals argue that the state should not be involved in funding or managing institutions, while making sure that individuals have equal opportunities in the day care market through the payment of grants.

The Left have a more 'socialising' view of childcare, and do not think that care by the mother is necessarily the best solution for children or their parents, especially the mother, who will find it difficult to get back to employment when she wants to, especially in times of high unemployment. The Left therefore gives more backing to local authority and state provision, such as nursery schools, nurseries and organised childminding, which is publicly funded and provides early socialising for children in keeping with the wishes of a growing number of parents.

In practice, however, the positions of politicians are not so clear-cut, and are influenced by a certain pragmatism in the face of economic problems and other developments in French society. For instance, a Socialist government introduced the *allocations parentales d'éducation*; while a Left-wing local authority may provide fewer day care services than a Right-wing authority (for example, Paris), depending on its budget and local traditions. There seems to be general agreement that it is necessary to develop a system which combines financial support for families with the provision of services, to allow parents choice in their way of life.

This objective, however, runs up against financial constraints. The lack of choice between different types of day care provision has already been mentioned. The CNAF (1980) emphasises the absence of real choice for a mother between looking after her own child and having it cared for:

> If no [day care] place is made available, there is no choice, only chance or luck. With no qualifications and a saturated labour market, there is no choice, only the possibility to stay at home. When a single income is insufficient to meet the needs of a family, there is no choice – a working mother has to carry on working if she has a job. For single mothers, it is often a vital necessity for them to work and find some form of child care – whatever it may be. In the end, real choice is only available to a minority of women at the top end of the social scale.

Finally, it is important to note that CNAF contributes to maintaining a certain continuity of policy. It plays a major role in the field of day care, and though it comes under the Ministry of Social Affairs, it has its own administrative committees.

Conclusion

France has a long tradition of public involvement in childcare. Today that involvement takes a variety of forms – parental leave and other employment entitlements, regulation of private day care, subsidies for parents' day care costs and the provision of a range of services. Government involvement is at various levels – national, *département* and local – but also increasingly through the national and regional role of CNAF and CAFs, which provide cash benefits for parents and financial support for the development of services. Public involvement in day care has been influenced by concerns about population (reflected in policies concerned to encourage the birth rate and protect the health and welfare of mothers and young children), the labour force and increasing choice for parents.

In practice, though, choice for parents is limited. Parental leave is either unpaid or paid at a low level. Funding services has never been made compulsory for local authorities, so that there are large local variations in provision and the overall supply of publicly-funded services falls well below demand. As a consequence, though also because of the preferences of some parents, many young children continue to be cared for privately, sometimes by caregivers employed in the child's home, but most often by childminders (both registered and unregistered) and relatives.

References

Benjamin, R. (1981a) 'L'enfant dans la famille et dans la société', *Recherche Sociale* 80, Octobre-Decembre.
— (1981b) 'La crèche parentale: une réponse adequate à un besoin nouveau?', *Recherche Sociale* 80, Octobre-Decembre.
Bouyala, N. and Roussile, B. (1982) *L'enfant dans la vie: une politique pour la petite enfance: rapport au Secrétariat d'Etat à la famille*, Paris: La Documentation Français.
CNAF (1980) *Consacre aux jeunes parents et la garde de leurs enfants: Revue informations sociales, no. 3/1980*, Paris: CNAF.
— (1987) *Entre vie familiale et vie professionnelle: Revue informations sociales, no. 3/1987*, Paris: CNAF.
CREDOC (1981) *Enquêtes annuelles sur les besoins et les aspirations des familles et des jeunes*, Paris: CREDOC.
Davidson, F. (1977) *Enquête sur les besoins differentiels de mode de garde des jeunes enfants dans une population urbaine*, Paris: Institut National de Santé, d'Epidemiologie et de Recherche Medicale.
Desplanques, G. (1985) 'Modes de garde et scolarisation des jeunes enfants', *Economie et Statistiques* 176: 27–40.
INSEE (1982a) *Recensement de la population*, Paris: INSEE.
— (1982b) *Enquête sur les familles*, Paris: INSEE.
Leprince, F. (1986) *Les structures d'accueil de la petite enfance*, thesis Université de Paris 1.
Leprince, F. and Fenet, F. (1985) *L'accueil des jeunes enfants: les actions des comités d'entreprise et des associations parentales: rapport intermediaire*, Paris: Laboratore d'economie.
Ministère de l'éducation nationale (1983) *Statistiques du Ministère au 1/09/83*, Paris: Ministère de l'éducation.
Ministère des affaires sociales (1983) *Statistiques du Ministère au 1/01/83*, Paris: Ministère des affaires sociales.
Mozere, L. (1978) *Analyse des expériences d'ouverture et de decloisonnement dans la secteur de l'enfance: rapport pour la CNAF*, Paris: CNAF.
Soule, D. (1981) *Les modes de garde des enfants de 0 à 3 ans*, Paris: Editions ESF.
Sullerot, E. (1981) *Les modes de garde des jeunes enfants: rapport présente, au conseil économique et social*, Paris: Conseil Economique et Social.
Wagnon, M.D. (1983) *Femmes, métier et foyer: dossiers d'économie lorraine*, Nancy: INSEE.

Chapter two

French research on day care

Geneviève Balleyguier

Overview of research in nurseries

Nurseries occupy a privileged place in research on the young child. French mothers or childminders do not like to bring their child to a laboratory, and it is difficult to enter their home when one is not a friend or relative. Therefore, institutions like maternity wards, nurseries and nursery schools are often used for undertaking research on various functions of the young child's personality: e.g. the beginning of the symbolic function (Inhelder, Lézine, Sinclair de Zwart and Stambak 1972), the infant's perceptions (Vurpillot 1973), manual co-ordination and lateralisation (Flament 1975), facial expression (Rouchouse 1980), the language of parents to their child (Josse and Robin 1981), the infant's imitative skills (Fontaine 1984), the development of intelligence through games with toys (Sinclair de Zwart, Stambak, Lézine, Rayna and Verba 1982), etc. These places were also used for standardising baby-tests (e.g. Casati and Lézine 1968; Balleyguier 1979), although home-reared children were also included in such studies.

Research has also taken advantage of the situation created in the nursery (especially when it is organised in groups of children of the same age) for studying the development of relationships amongst children. For example, Montagner (1978) studied non-verbal communication (affiliative and agonistic relationships, and dominance/submission) in group interaction. Nadel (1986) demonstrated that imitation is the preferential mode for communicating between children in their third year. In the same laboratory, Legendre (in Baudonnière 1985) showed how the organisation of available space influences the type of relationships between children. Legendre found that when fifteen 2–3-year-olds were in a large room with many toys scattered around, they often quarrel and cry; but when 'corners' were organised with specific games (dolls' house, garage, etc.) the children form small groups in these places and play with more interest. Finally, Stambak et al. (1983) studied how young children, when in small groups, communicate amongst themselves in order to explore the physical properties of things and develop their capacity for logical thought and imagination. These group activities with familiar children help them acquire a comprehension of social interaction and develop sophisticated social strategies. However, such research was not intended to evaluate the influence of type of care and they were done in traditional nurseries, with same-age groups.

Research comparing different day care settings

In comparison, little research has been done on the consequences of the various types of day care for child development. This is probably due to the strong emotions aroused by this issue. The social stereotype of the mother's unique role for her child's normal development – a role which was not always recognised, as the previous chapter has shown – leads mothers to feel guilty about placing their child in day care and they justify their actions by having a good opinion of the day care they use. In surveys asking mothers and caregivers what is the best type of day care for young children, the first choice is home-rearing, and the second choice the day care they have chosen. Specialists also disagree: private paediatricians often recommend a childminder rather than a nursery, where they think that the child will suffer from emotional problems. However those working in public institutions favour the nursery because of its medical supervision. Opinions are also ideologically oriented. People to the Right of the political spectrum favour home-rearing and, when it is not possible, the childminder's home, because it resembles family life more. Those to the Left think that collective education gives the same chances to every child to develop his capacities and therefore prefer nurseries.

A few researchers have tried to evaluate objectively the consequences of the various modes of day care on the child's development.

The pioneer work of Irene Lézine

Being of Russian origin, Lézine was acquainted with the highly developed nurseries of eastern Europe. Brunet and Lézine (1951) produced a developmental assessment inspired by the work of Gesell and Buhler. Lézine (1951) used this assessment to compare the psycho-motor development of children cared for in their family (1,500 children) with those cared for in nurseries (200 children). She found that the latter showed slightly delayed development for talking, cleanliness and play with toys; their verbal development was the most delayed (verbal D.Q.: 103 for girls and 100 for boys brought up in their family; 91 for girls and 88 for boys cared in a nursery). Having observed that caregivers tend to chat between themselves and not to the children, Lézine and Spionek

(1958) recommended that caregivers talk more to the child to facilitate language development.

In her studies Lézine (1951, 1974) put forward ways for improving nurseries, such as more toys adjusted for the child's age, more conversation and play with children, introducing them to the nursery before the age of six months when adaptation is easier, being sensitive to their individual needs and rhythm of development and establishing a good relationship between parents and caregivers. Lézine's work has given a great impetus to the improvement of nurseries, but she did not question this mode of care. She thought that it may be as good as the family when the caregiving environment was improved.

Consequences of different modes of care at 4 years

The debate over what is the best mode of care motivated the French Health Department (Mermilliod and Rossignol 1974) to compare the development of children who were previously cared for in one of five ways:

1 by their mother (66 per cent of the population studied),
2 in their home by an employee (who cares for the child while doing the housekeeping) (3 per cent),
3 in a childminder's home during the day (10 per cent),
4 or on a weekly or monthly basis (4 per cent),
5 in a nursery (10 per cent), or
6 where children changed mode of care many times during their first three years (7 per cent).

Mermilliod and Rossignol analysed the records of 982 Parisian children. These records were established during the many compulsory health visits of the first three years, and at the age of 4, when all the children were at nursery school. Twenty-four items concerning the child's development were investigated. They were divided into three groups: previous health development; physical development at 4 years; psychological development at 4 years (psycho-motor test results, and signs of behavioural adjustment such as quality of sleep, appetite, autonomy, cleanliness, language development, behaviour during the examination).

Each of the 24 items was scored as low, medium or high. Priority items were weighted and global scores calculated.

The results revealed that no mode of care – not even mother only care – was always the best. It depended on the socio-economic class of the family. In the upper and middle classes, the mother's care gave the best results, but in the lowest socio-economic groups, the use of a child-

Geneviève Balleyguier

minder or nursery during the day appeared more satisfactory. In general, care by an employee (nanny) – which exists only for mothers of the highest socio-economic groups – gave poor results. Care in a child-minder's home on a residential weekly or monthly basis, which was only used by middle and low socio-economic groups, gave rather unsatisfactory results; multiple changes of care disturbed the child. Children from all socio-economic groups brought up in a nursery appeared to be in good condition at 4 years; therefore, this option was recommended by the authors.

These results need some explanation. The home employee was often poorly qualified for the work and tended not to stay for long; it was therefore an unstable mode of care. The nursery was associated with poor health for upper and middle-class children; but for children from lower social classes, health appeared better when they were cared for in a nursery than when they stayed with their mother. This may be explained by the medical supervision, from which such children would not otherwise benefit.

However, these results relied mostly on medical data, with only partial evaluation of psycho-motor development; and affective development was only indirectly appraised (through the quality of sleep, appetite, etc.). Do the different types of care have specific consequences for affective development?

A study of affective development and childrearing

Having devised a test ('The Baby's Day', Balleyguier 1979) for measuring the affective components of the young child's personality, it was applied to 262 children who experienced the most common types of day care: at home, in a childminder's home or in a nursery. All children were of French origin, living in two medium-sized towns. Their parents were married, both lived with the child, and were lower or middle class (since few upper-class children are cared for in a nursery). There were as many boys as girls in each group. All children were in good physical condition at birth and had current good health status. The designated mode of care had begun at least six months previously (three months for the youngest). Children were in day care because both parents were employed.

Three child ages were investigated. At 9 months there were 76 children – 34 home-reared, 9 with a minder and 33 in a nursery; at 2 years 98 children – 35 home-reared, 32 with a childminder and 31 at nursery; and at 3.5–4 years 88 children, currently all in nursery school, of whom 44 had previously been home-reared, 31 had been with a childminder and 13 at a nursery.

Procedures

The test consists of a structured interview asking about the child's behaviour, and observations made by the examiner. The questions also provide information about the behaviour of the persons interacting with the child. The test thus evaluates a child's temperament and social relationships and the childrearing style of the caregivers.

Temperament is measured by coding the child's behaviour in 50 everyday situations, to produce three dimensions: 1 tension or excitation (level of activity and emotional participation); 2 control (restraint of muscular and emotional manifestations); 3 orientation of the behaviour (non-oriented like restlessness or crying, self-oriented, thing-oriented, person-oriented or defensive reactions).

Social relationships refer to the ways children relate to the members of their family (or their caregiver and playmates). They are measured with thirteen scales, some of which are the same for different members of the family: affection for, imitation of, aggression toward the father, mother (or her substitute) or sibling; obedience toward the mother or father; autonomy, cleanliness.

Six scales of *negative reactions* based on situations involving unpleasant sensations, separation anxiety, resisting maternal care (being fed, clothed, etc.), reaction to maternal frustrations (object taken off, etc.), reaction to paternal or fraternal frustrations and fear of a stranger.

The childrearing environment is measured by asking whether the caregiver acts in specific ways towards the child. These acts are grouped into the following scales: mother's (or her substitute's) affection, indulgence, bond loosening, rigidity, education, strictness, toilet training; father's affection and strictness; sibling's (or playmate's) affection and aggression.

The Baby's Day test was administered to all mothers while the children were being observed in their homes. For children aged 9 months and 2 years who were cared for in a nursery or a childminder's home, the same test was also administered to the caregiver while the child was observed in this setting. A 'Questionnaire for the Teacher' was devised for the older children. It consisted of questions about 100 behaviours that might occur in school and the teacher recorded if the child showed such behaviours. These behaviours were then grouped into the following eleven scales: activity, rigidity, inhibition, autonomy, self-stimulation, sociability, aggression, dependency on other children, leadership, dependency on the teacher, and obedience.

The children's results were analysed through a principal component analysis (for more details, see Balleyguier 1988). The gender, birth-order, socio-economic level and types of childcare were correlated with the principal components. This analysis was performed at each age, on the Baby's Day results obtained at home and at 9 months and 2 years (separately) on the results of this test obtained both at home and at the place of care, for children cared for outside the home. Since each child had two sets of results, these were treated as belonging to separate children.

The first two principal components found with the Baby's Day results were the same for the three ages. They are called: *the tension factor* – at one extreme high tension (frequent crying and tantrums, mostly negative reactions to situations and aggressive relationships) and low tension and passivity at the other extreme; *the developmental factor* which comprises at one extreme moderate tension, high control, strong autonomy and many positive relationships with familiar persons, to their opposite at the other extreme.

The results concerning the social environment were analysed with the same statistical technique. Four predominant types of childrearing style were identified:

A: *The over-stimulating environment:* the main caregiver (mother or her substitute) was very affectionate, very indulgent (responds quickly to his cries and demands) but also very anxious; she set high standards for the child's education and insisted strictly on attaining them. Toilet training was early and insistent. The father participated much in child care but was also quite strict.

B: *The affectionate environment:* the main caregiver was also very affectionate and indulgent, but she was self-confident (not anxious), and therefore her childrearing style was more relaxed. She was not rigid, and the mother-infant bond may be loose. The father was also very affectionate and liked to care for the baby but was not strict.

C: *The strict environment:* the main caregiver was very concerned about giving a good education to her child: she insisted on good manners, was relatively rigid, forbade many things, scolded and slapped often. She cared for the child only when necessary. The father was also strict.

D: *The under-stimulating environment:* the main caregiver was not very interested in the child. She did not spend much time caring for his needs and had no time to play with him or respond to his demands. She was not at all anxious about him and often left him alone or in somebody else's care. She did not put a lot of effort into his education and was not strict. The father did not care at all for the baby.

When comparing results obtained at home, the childrearing style was evaluated according to the mother's and father's scales. When comparing childrearing at home and in the place of care (for the outside-reared children), only the mother's (or her substitute's) scales were retained, since there was no father substitute in day care.

Results

Statistically significant results are reported here, unless otherwise indicated. For more details on statistical methods see Balleyguier (1988).

Nine months

Family-reared children were more tense than children cared for in a nursery or by a childminder when examined in their home. They cried more often and were more restless in everyday situations, they demanded more attention when they could not do something, when mother did not look after them or when left alone (stronger separation anxiety).

Nursery children looked more passive and less well-developed when they were in the nursery than with their mother. In the nursery, they were less autonomous and indulged less often in activities requiring a moderate degree of tension and good control (e.g. playing with toys, adapted activity) than at home. So, they looked quite different in both settings. These differences came from behavioural descriptions in definite situations and not from judgements; they reflect the child's behaviour, even if the caregiver's perception cannot entirely be ruled out.

Children cared for by a childminder appeared intermediate between home-reared and nursery children. At home, they were not as tense as family-reared children. But, compared to nursery children, they showed better development with similar results from home and their place of care. They were also characterised by precocious development of imitation and obedience when they were in their home and in their place of care, compared to nursery children.

The condition which differentiated infants most was the type of care, but gender (boys cry more than girls) and birth-order (first-borns were better developed than later-borns) also had an influence, although these differences were not significant. Social class did not make any difference, in contrast with what was found at 4 years.

Do these differences in the child's behaviour reflect any difference in the childrearing received? Some relationships existed with parental childrearing. When parents were predominantly oriented towards socialising their child, the child was more controlled and moderately tense, and therefore looked more advanced. On the other hand, when parents were less involved with their child, the child was more likely to appear passive.

Table 2.1 Childrearing of 9-month-olds and type of care

| Type of care | Childrearing style | | | | | |
---	A	B	C	D	E	Total
Home care	2	7	14	9	2	34
Childminder						
Mother's rearing style	0	2	4	2	1	9
Childminder's rearing style	1	2	4	2	0	9
Nursery						
Mother's rearing style	3	13	12	4	1	33
Caregiver's rearing style	5	8	16	3	1	33

Note: Childrearing style: A – overstimulating; B – affectionate; C – strict; D – understimulating; E – atypical.

Childrearing style did not differ much between day care settings. The most frequent type of childrearing was the strict one (Type C), be it in their family or in day care (see Table 2.1). The only difference (although statistically non-significant) was more strict childrearing (Type C) in the nursery and more affectionate childrearing (Type B) with the parent of these children. There was more similarity between the type of childrearing given by parents and childminder.

Summary of 9-month results

Children entirely brought up in their family generally showed good development and the attachment to the mother was already well established. But they also cried often in unpleasant situations, and particularly when separated from the mother or when she did not give them attention. They showed a strong fear of strangers, perhaps because of limited experience of unfamiliar people. A possible interpretation was that they expressed themselves more vigorously, being already more assertive than children cared for outside the home.

Children cared for by a childminder generally showed good social and psycho-motor development (social relationships well developed, good autonomy and control). They mostly behaved in the same way in the two environments, which were not very different especially when both caregivers co-operated to ensure good childrearing. Mothers found that, at home the child was a relatively easy child (compared to family-reared children).

Children cared for in a nursery, on the other hand, were very different in the two settings. In their home, they showed good social and psycho-motor development; they were less irritable than family-reared children, but were still very interested in the environment. In the nursery, their development looked rather slow (weak autonomy, few adapted activities). Some children cried a great deal but most of them were rather passive. Their relationships were poor, they did not show much attachment to their caregivers and were not afraid of strangers.

These differences were likely to be due to different childrearing styles. Many mothers have a more emotional attitude than the substitute caregiver. Often they felt guilty about leaving their child while they worked and they may have tried to compensate at home with more affection and indulgence. In the nursery, time schedules were more rigid, caregivers had less time for playing with the baby, and they left the child alone more. The children's passivity reflects this lack of stimulation. but the babies reacted more intensely when they met with their mother at the end of the day; they made vigorous demands on her. It was frequent to see a quiet and submissive child in the nursery become very demanding as soon as the mother arrived. They were more active and responsive at home.

Let's see how a child, Brice, aged 8 months 22 days, behaved in the same situations, according to the descriptions given by his mother or a nursery's caregiver:

Situations	At home	At the nursery
Wakes by himself	Calls	Plays by himself
Time to eat	Restless	No reaction
Interrupted meal	Cries	No reaction
Caregiver passes by	Looks at her	Did not care
Being dressed	Grumbles	Lets her
She refuses to take him	Cries	Accepts
Hindered to take something	Cries	Accepts
Mother/caregiver arrives	Laughs	Indifferent
Brother/child comes	Laughs	Indifferent
In bed	Tries to sit up	Did not try to sit

Two years of age

With increasing age, similar differences due to the childcare settings were found, and they were more clear-cut. Home-reared children were again very irritable. They were now in the 'tantrum period' (Balleyguier 1982), where they try to impose their will by opposing the mother's demands. She, in turn, tries to restrain this intense activity and to socialise the toddler's manners. So, her childrearing was still predominantly of the strict type (see Table 2.2).

Geneviève Balleyguier

Table 2.2 Childrearing of 2-year-olds and type of care

Type of care	A	B	C	D	E	Total
Home care	5	7	13	7	3	35
Childminder						
Mother's rearing style	5	6	13	3	5	32
Childminder's rearing style	4	8	14	4	2	32
Nursery						
Mother's rearing style	9	13	4	2	3	31
Caregiver's rearing style	3	6	9	12	1	31

Column header: *Childrearing style*

Note: Childrearing style: A – overstimulating; B – affectionate; C – strict; D – understimulating; E – atypical.

The behaviour of children cared for by a childminder was intermediate between that of the two other groups. In their own family, they looked less tense than home-reared or nursery children, but generally well developed. They were less afraid of a stranger than children of the two other groups. However, their behaviour changed from one setting to the other. They were much more passive in the childminder's home than in their own family although mothers and their substitutes generally showed similar childrearing styles, centred on socialisation (strict type predominant).

The behaviour of the nursery children was very different between settings. In their home, the toddlers were now more tense (frequent crying and tantrums) and their reactions were rather negative; the same children, when in the nursery, showed a more passive behaviour with poor social relationships. This contrast may again be explained by the difference in environments. Their mothers were tender and indulgent, and did not try to socialise them much (affectionate type predominant), while in the nursery, the children received less stimulation from the caregivers.

Table 2.2 also suggests that the chosen method of day care may influence maternal rearing as well as toddler behaviour. Mothers who put their toddlers in a nursery showed a more stimulating and affectionate rearing style than those who cared for the toddler themselves or entrusted him to a childminder, where mothers' childrearing style was more strict or understimulating.

Summary of 2 year results

At 2 years of age, there were not many differences in developmental factors (autonomy, control) for these three groups of children. The main differences were seen in the intensity of behaviour revealed by crying, tantrums and strong negative relationships (e.g. aggression).

The family-reared children were still very tense. This may be interpreted as showing that the child had a strong attachment to the mother while also wanting to impose his will. This ambivalent period has been described (Balleyguier 1982) as one of conflict between mother and child, and interior conflict between dependency on the mother and opposition to her in order to become autonomous (Mahler, Pine and Bergman 1980). The strong socialising tendency of these mothers was meeting a relatively strong ego.

The childminder-reared children look much easier to handle, in their home and in their place of care. Were they better adapted to their environment, more secure as the slight anxiety towards strangers suggests? But, in their place of care, they often appeared very passive and submissive. Let's see the example of Guillaume, aged 21 months.

In his home, he was moderately tense and rather person-oriented. He was very attached to his parents and sought contact with them but did not imitate much. When frustrated, he withdrew but sometimes cried when hungry or tired and when his mother imposed some constraint. He was a little bit afraid of strangers. He was not very autonomous but already very clean. In his childminder's home he appeared much more passive. He played very little with toys and mostly sucked his thumb. He showed some affection towards his childminder but did not imitate her. He had almost no negative reactions, did not seem hungry, nor ask to be held, and never cried. The childminder did not have to scold him and found him very easy. He was very quiet during meals, did not touch forbidden things, and never made a mess.

The observation of his behaviour confirmed the child's strong passivity reported by his childminder. Did he find it impossible to insist on sometimes having his own way?

The nursery children showed the same kind of differences found at 9 months, but now even more clearly. In the nursery, the children received little stimulation, moreover, they lacked relationships with men and older children, and could not imitate household activities. The schedule was rather rigid; their daily life was therefore very monotonous. In this environment, they appeared submissive and waited until their mother came. With her, they tried to impose their will by crying and fussing until she yielded, a strategy sometimes successful. In their home, they were very tense, and reactions were mostly negative. Their mother tended to be affectionate and gave in easily to their demands, while leaving their socialisation to the nursery's caregivers. This childrearing style may strengthen the child's insistence on his demands, while his irritation may reveal an insecure attachment.

At 2 years of age, the type of care was still the condition which had the greatest impact on the child's behaviour. Other conditions had a lesser role. In their family, boys were still more tense than girls; but now first-borns were less tense than later-born children. This was probably due to the increasing interactions of children with older siblings. Socio-economic level still did not make much difference. Do we find the same trends when children were cared for in the nursery school?

Three-and-a-half years of age

At this age, data were collected in different ways at home and at school; they cannot therefore be directly compared. The results obtained with the mother will be presented first, and then those obtained from the teacher.

Mothers' reports of children's characteristics did not vary much between groups who had received different day care previously, nor did social class affect the results significantly. They varied slightly for boys and girls in that boys were reported to be more tense. Concerning children's control and social development, the previous type of care did not make a great difference. What differentiated the children most was gender combined with birth order. Later-born girls were very well developed (good autonomy, good control) and very sociable, while first-born boys were described as passive, inhibited, and with slow development.

Table 2.3 Childrearing at home for 3.5 to 4-year-olds related to previous type of care

| Previous type of care | Childrearing style | | | | |
	A	B	C	D	Total
Home care	2	9	18	15	44
Childminder	7	12	8	4	31
Nursery	1	1	6	5	13

Note: Childrearing style: A – overstimulating; B – affectionate; C – strict; D – understimulating.

At this age, there was a great difference in maternal rearing style related to previous day care (see Table 2.3). Mothers who had entrusted their child to a childminder gave a more stimulating or affectionate up-bringing to their children, compared to the other mothers. This may be because, very often, the childminder still looked after these children after school or during the weekly free day, while the other mothers were not helped outside school hours. So the difference in support may account for the mother's rearing style with her pre-school child.

The results of the teacher's questionnaire again gave two main components, which were not very different from those found with the test. The first component revealed, at one extreme, high activity, high autonomy, domination and aggression towards peers, and at the other strong passivity, inhibition and docility; so, this referred mainly to the style of reaction. The second component had high sociability, high dependence towards the teacher and submission to her at one extreme, high aggression and domination over peers at the other. This factor was based on differentiation of social relationships.

For the teachers, gender was what most differentiated the children. Boys were more active while girls were more inhibited and submissive. Social class also differentiated them; children from a low status family were more active than those of higher status families, who were more passive and docile. Finally, birth order was also a condition which differentiated them; first-born children were more active than later-born. Social class and birth order interact, when they were first-born in a lower status family, they were more active and less submissive than others.

The previous type of care made some difference; children brought up in their family were less active and more inhibited in school than children who had had non-parental care. This was probably due to the fact that they missed the contact with other children; so, even after 6 months, they were still uneasy in the collective world of the school, as Zazzo (1984) also found. In contrast, children who were cared for by a childminder were described as more sociable and less aggressive than the children cared for either in their family or in a nursery. These children, and those cared for in a nursery, came more often from lower status families, and were more often first-born. At any rate, the type of day care, which appeared previously to have had a great impact on the children's behaviour, seemed to have lost some impact when they were all cared for in the same way.

Overall summary of results

When at home, the children's behaviour was influenced by type of care. Home-reared children appeared more difficult at 9 months and at 2 years; but they were also more autonomous, and had more intense relationships with the members of their family. They developed a stronger will, which entered into conflict with the mother's socialising aims. Mutual adaptation seems to occur by the fourth year.

Children reared by a childminder appeared, at all ages, easier to manage when in their home. They were more compliant than home-reared children and less irritable than nursery children. They looked well developed. In the nursery school, they were described by the teacher as more sociable and less aggressive than other children. The nursery children looked more passive at 9 months. But afterwards, mothers found them more tense, crying easily and reacting negatively. Their attachment looked insecure and they appeared slightly less well developed. But these peculiarities did not persist when they went to nursery school, where they adapted easily, being used to a collective environment.

Differences in behaviour existed also for the same children when they went from one setting to the other. Apart from some babies (9 months old) who cried more in the nursery, up to 2 years of age, children were generally found to be more passive, more submissive, and with a more restricted range of relationships in the nursery than in their own home. They appeared much more attached to their mother than to their caregivers. It looked as if the children waited and did not ask for what they wanted at their place of care but made vigorous demands when reunited with their parents, who generally were more responsive to them. So, their style of emotional expression was quite different from one environment to the other.

Children cared for by a childminder were less markedly different when moving from one setting to the other, but the discrepancy in their behaviour grew with age (it was greater at 2 years than at 9 months). During their fourth year, the children's behaviour often appeared quite opposite in their home and in the nursery school. For example, the behaviour of home-reared girls was described by their mother as active and sociable, while the teacher found them passive, rigid and very submissive; these were not judgements, but answers on a descriptive level (e.g. did not leave during an imposed task, obeys immediately at command, etc.). The sudden shift from a family environment to a collective one probably explains their difficult adaptation to school.

The influence of type of day care did not have a long-lasting effect once the child had moved on. Although this was the condition which best differentiated the children at 9 months and at 2 years, this was no longer true when they were all cared for in the nursery school. The effect seemed strong when the day care was present, but it did not mark the child definitively. On the contrary, this study revealed how resilient infants are, and how much the young child adapts itself, changing behaviour when there is a change of environment. Other more lasting conditions, like social class, which seemed unimportant during the first two years, gender and birth order, better differentiated children when they were at nursery school, whatever their previous type of care may have been.

Finally, we did not find any pathological cases in the whole population. This was probably due to the fact that the conditions which generally produce them were eliminated. These children were in complete and stable households. So, the fact that the mother worked and placed her child to be cared for outside her home was not, taken alone, a condition which might produce pathological results in the child.

A comparison of children in two nurseries

The study just reported shows children behaving differently in different settings. But are there differences within the same type of care, for example, nurseries? Are the differences in the child's behaviour due to the organisation of the setting (number of children for one caregiver, groups of same age opposed to different age children) or rather to the caregiver's attitude and behaviour? A piece of exploratory research based on observations of four children in each of two nurseries has looked at this question.

Procedure

The 'Baby's Day' test was carried out in the nursery (questionnaire to the caregiver and child observation). For this study, only the results concerning the intensity of the tension and the orientation of the behaviour will be considered: for more details, see Patry (1986). The child's behaviour was noted every minute according to a prepared list of 33 activities (the same list as that of the test described in 'The Baby's Day', pp. 30–2). The observations took place at the same time of day (in the morning). The children were 6 to 8 months old. They were observed during a standardised set of ten situations, including naturally occurring events (a meal, washing, etc.); the observation lasted an hour. The activity scores were then weighted as they were for the test according to the intensity of tension (weak, moderate, high) and the orientation of the behaviour. A previous study on 15 children of the same age cared for in a nursery had shown that these measures were stable over a one-week period.

The nursery environment was also observed, and globally rated as Stimulating (S) or Non-stimulating (NS). As an illustration, here are some data concerning two 6-month-old children, one in each nursery, observed over a period of 140 minutes (see Table 2.4).

Table 2.4 Characteristics of stimulating and non-stimulating nurseries

	Stimulating	*Non-stimulating*
Number of children in group	9	10
Number of caregivers	3	4
Number of toys given	2	0
Number of words spoken to child	105	10
% time without contact	81	91
% time with contact	19	9

Note: Data recorded in 140 minutes of observation of a child in each nursery.

The language addressed to the children also differed qualitatively. The caregiver in the NS nursery used abrupt language with little opportunity for child response, e.g. 'Stop fussing! Will you stop fussing?' while the child in the S nursery was addressed in a more varied and gentle way: 'Oh don't cry, little one! Were you cold, Caroline? Let's eat a little more.'

Results

The children of the NS nursery showed weaker tension, in the test results and in the observations. Their control was also weaker. At this age, spells of high tension were rare. Their modes of reaction were more passive and less object-oriented, which was understandable since they were given very few toys (which generally stayed in the cupboard), contrary to what was found in the S nursery. All these results were statistically significant. They also showed less person-orientation, more self-oriented behaviour and more aimless activity, but differences for these behaviours were not statistically significant.

These results show in a very dramatic way that, in the same kind of setting, the environment can be quite different. The very young child reacts to the lack of stimulation, which may be due to a caregiver's negative attitude towards him, with a more passive behaviour and lack of interest in the outside world.

Conclusions

All this research points in the same direction. The young child was very sensitive to the quality of the environment. It influenced psycho-motor development – as Lézine has shown – and also 'style of reaction'. The more stimulated the child was by a positively oriented caretaker, the more interest was shown in the outside world (things and people); the child also reacted more vividly, showing joy and anger, to daily events. In contrast, the less stimulated the child was, with little affection from the caregiver, the quieter the child was and this passivity was accompanied by a relative slowness of social and psycho-motor development. However, the child adapted very rapidly to another environment, changing behaviour the same day when going from one setting to the other. Also, the influence of the kind of care during the first three years did not mark personality definitively.

Parents were generally very much emotionally involved with their child, so they greatly stimulated their child but were also very demanding (especially with their first child); this may explain why children are more tense in their family than outside; but the children also had good social and psycho-motor development. Childminder rearing was not so bad as many 'specialists' have maintained, especially when this placement was stable. The caregiver acted very much like the mother when they had good communication, but had a weaker attachment to the child. The child often looked quieter and more submissive than family-reared children, but better developed than children in nurseries. The relationship with the childminder may persist after the third year, which helped mother and child adapt to the new world of the school. Finally, the nursery was still often a place where children were not stimulated very much; caregivers talked more between themselves than with the children. The children were therefore found to be more passive and with fewer social relationships than in the two other settings.

However, great differences may be found in each kind of setting. The third piece of research showed that, with the same general organisation, the quality of the environment may be quite different, which has a strong impact on the child's behaviour.

Nurseries may be improved by giving child development training to the caregivers, and helping them better to understand every child's individuality (by facilitating contacts with parents, by organising the groups into 'small families' where the children keep the same caregivers during the three years, etc.). Childminder care was improved when it remained stable and the communication with the parents was good. These are the aims of the supervisors (*puéricultrices*) who select and supervise childminders in the organised childminding schemes (*crèches familiales*). Finally, parental care also needs to be improved in many cases; adolescent education in child upbringing would be helpful; and group workshops for parents might be offered at the maternity ward.

References

Balleyguier, G. (1979) *Test pour l'évaluation du caractère du jeune enfant et des attitudes éducatives de l'entourage*, Issy-les-Moulineaux: Editions Scientifiques et Psychologiques; English trans.: *The Baby's Day*, available from the author, Université de Tours, France.
— (1981) *Le caractère de l'enfant en fonction de son mode de garde pendant les premières années*, Paris: Centre National de la Recherche Scientifique.
— (1982) *La formation du caractère pendant les premières années*, Issy-les-Moulineaux: Editions Scientifiques et Psychologiques.
— (1988) 'What is the best mode of day care for young children: a French study', *Early Child Development and Care* 33: 41–65.
Baudonnière, P.M. (1985) 'Etudier l'enfant de la naissance à trois ans', *Comportements* 3.
Brunet, O. and Lézine, I. (1951) *Le developpement psychologique de la première enfance*, Paris: Presses Universitaires de France.
Casati, I. and Lézine, I. (1968) *Les étapes de l'intelligence sensori-motrice*, Paris: Centre de Psychologie Appliqué.
Flament, F. (1975) *Coordination et prévalence manuelle chez le nourrisson*, Aix-Marseille: Centre National de la Recherche Scientifique.
Fontaine R. (1984) 'Imitative skills between birth and six months', *Infant Behaviour and Development* 7: 323–33.
Inhelder, B., Lézine, I., Sinclair de Zwart, H. and Stambak, M. (1972) 'Les débuts de la fonction sémiotique', *Colloques internationaux du CNRS* 1972: 133–47.
Josse, D. and Robin, M. (1981) 'Qu-est-ce que tu à dis Maman? Ou le langage des parents adressé à l'enfant de la naissance a dix mois', *Enfance* 3: 109–32.
Lézine, I. (1951) *Psycho-pédagogie du premier age*, Paris: Presses Universitaires de France.
— (1974) *Propos sur le jeune enfant*, Paris: Mame.
Lézine, I. and Spionek, H. (1958) 'Quelques problèmes de développement psychomoteur et d'éducation des enfants dans les crèches', *Enfance* 3: 245–67.
Mahler, M., Pine, F. and Bergman, A. (1980) *La naissance psychologique de l'être humain*, Fr. trans., Paris: Payot.
Mermilliod, C. and Rossignol, C. (1974) 'Le développement de l'enfant à 4 ans est-il significatif des modes de garde antérieurs?' *Bulletin de Statistiques 'Santé-Sécurité Sociale'* 2: 105–31.
Meudec, M. (1986) *Direct Observation of the Behavioural Stability of Six-month-old Babies*, Second European Conference on Developmental Psychology, Rome: Istituto di Psicologia, 227.
Montagner, H. (1978) *L'enfant et la communication*, Paris: Pernoud/Stock.
Nadel, J. (1986) *Imitation et communication entre jeunes enfants*, Paris: Presses Universitaires de France.
Patry, S. (1986) *L'influence des stimulations sociales de la crèche sur le tempérament du jeune enfant*, Mémoire manuscrit, Equipe de Recherche sur la Première Enfance, Université de Tours.

Rouchouse, J. C. (1980) 'Ethologie de l'enfant et observation des mimiques chez le nourrisson', *Psychiatrie de l'enfant* 23, 1: 203–49.

Sinclair de Zwart, H., Stambak, M., Lézine, I., Rayna, S. and Verba, M. (1982) *Les bébés et les choses*, Paris: Presses Universitaires de France.

Stambak, M., Barrière, M., Bonica, L., Maisonnet, R., Musati T., Rayna, S. and Verba, M. (1983) *Les bébés entre eux. Découvrir, jouer, inventer ensemble*, Paris: Presses Universitaires de France.

Vurpillot, E. (1973) *Les Perceptions des nourrissons*, Paris: Presses Universitaires de France.

Zazzo, B. (1984) *L'école maternelle à deux ans: oui ou non?* Paris: Stock.

Chapter three

Day care for young children in the German Democratic Republic

Irina Weigl and Christine Weber

Nurseries (*krippen*) are part of daily life in the German Democratic Republic (GDR). It is very common to find the well-known flat-roofed building, with its large windows, terraces and a garden with toys and climbing frames, situated between new houses in a residential development. Anyone who passes recognises this as a new nursery. A nursery worker pushing a large pram, seating a number of children, or a small group of happy toddlers strolling the roads with their nursery workers, are common sights in towns and villages.

Employment entitlements for parents

Although nurseries may admit children from a few months old, most children now enter the nursery system at the beginning of their second year. The proportion of infants in nurseries has very much reduced and only a few nurseries now have special care facilities for very young infants; such children are only admitted in exceptional circumstances (for example, where the mother is currently studying or cannot interrupt her employment), and then usually from the age of 5 months. These changes follow the introduction in 1986 of the so-called 'baby year'. Until then, fully-paid maternity leave was available for 26 weeks; women usually took 3 or 4 weeks of leave before their baby was born and the rest afterwards. In 1986, a further 7 months of leave was introduced, paid at 90 per cent of earnings; this leave can be taken by either parent, or indeed by grandmothers.

The current system of day care provision

Nurseries in the GDR provide care and education for children up to 3 whose parents are in full-time employment or studying. They are the responsibility of the Ministry of Health, which has an organisation at national, regional and district level, with a separate department for nurseries at each level. The regional level decides about the allocation of resources, both between different districts and different services; the district level is responsible for providing services. In larger districts, with more than 500 nursery places, nurseries are organised into co-operatives which are structured like commercial enterprises, for example with a Director, Co-director, Finance and Administrative Departments, expert advisors and so on.

Admission to nurseries is based on catchment area; children go to the nursery they live closest to. Most nurseries (89 per cent) are community-based, while the remainder (11 per cent) are attached to factories or other commercial enterprises; in the latter case, the costs are divided between the company and the state, the former for instance funding the building and its maintenance while the latter pays for materials and the wages of the nursery workers. An increasing number of nurseries – currently 20 per cent – are part of a combined day care institution (*kindereinrichtungen*), sharing the same building with a kindergarten which takes children between 3 and 6 (in 1987, kindergartens provided for 94 per cent of children in this age group).

The education and care provided in nurseries is free to parents, who do however make a small contribution towards the cost of food; the maximum contribution is 1.40 marks a day, though it can be less, while the total cost for food is 1.90 marks a day or more (in 1987, the average monthly income for full-time employees in industry was 1,233 marks). A new nursery place costs about 12,800 marks, and is provided by the state, which also funds annual running costs averaging 3,200 marks per place. The 1989 economic plan for the GDR included a budget of 1.44 billion marks for the building and running of nurseries, and a further 1.84 billion marks for kindergartens; these two services are part of a planned health and education budget for 1989 of 30.1 billion marks.

In 1987, there were 7,559 nurseries with 348,422 places, sufficient to cover 81 per cent of children eligible for admission (the number of children in the GDR aged 12 to 35 months was 446,800). The network of nurseries is still expanding; 45,600 new places will be created by 1990, when it is intended to provide a place for every child. This means that every child will be able to start his or her education in a nursery if the mother wants this.

Most of the children not in nurseries are looked after by their mothers. There are childminders (*pflegemutter*), but they care for very few children – less than 2 per cent of under-3s. Childminders are not officially registered or regulated and are paid entirely by parents. They are very expensive, and usually only take children for a few months. (For further details on the day care system, see Weigl and Niebsch 1983; Weigl 1987).

The function of nurseries

The pedagogical function for children

Nurseries have a number of pedagogical and social functions. There is a pedagogical role, to secure the physical, emotional and cognitive development and the health of children. Nurseries provide education, care and hygiene. Although they are an integral part of the health service, and the responsibility of the Department of Health, they are also regarded as a part of the integrated socialist education system, which consists of a series of educational institutions, from nursery through to university. The institutions for children under compulsory school age consist of nurseries, followed by kindergartens. The development of the educational role of nurseries is discussed further below.

The nursery supplements education in the family: the nursery and the family provide important specific contributions to the development of children. The family, the smallest and first micro-social grouping for a child, provides a secure basis for the child's development; it ensures stability and continuity of emotional relationships between different family members. Parents and siblings provide the child with deep affection and security. The child feels he is loved and cared for and develops feelings of belonging and love. The education of children is integrated in these daily routines, leisure activities, the organisation of daily life and family relationships. This is a particular feature, only found in families, which cannot be substituted by state institutions.

Like the family, the nursery provides a very specific contribution to the education of children. The pedagogically trained nursery worker or educator (*krippenerzieherin*) guides the education of children, promotes their independence and the acquisition of social experiences. The nursery operates within a clearly defined time framework and creates special environmental and educational conditions. A loving relationship between nursery educator and child and respect for the individuality of the child provide the framework in which the educational work is conducted. (For further details on the pedagogical function of nurseries, see Küchler 1979; Weigl 1987a.)

Women and employment

Most women (92 per cent) in the GDR are employed or studying; 49 per cent of the working population are women. The full-time education and care provided for children by nurseries enables mothers to participate fully in employment and society, and so contributes to the emancipation of women.

These functions of the nursery – for children and women – are closely interlinked. The education and care of young children at nurseries influences the children directly. This direct influence is transmitted through the children to the mothers, who can live and work in the knowledge that their children are well educated and cared for. Nursery facilities are thus not provided only for children or only for the benefit of their mothers, but for the children and the mothers – and the society as a whole.

Regulations and quality

In May 1988, the Recommendations for the Education and Health Protection of Children in Nurseries and Residential Homes – Nursery Directive (*Die Anweisung Uber die Erziehung, Betreuung und den Gesundheitsschutz der Kinder in Krippen und Heimen – Krippenordnung 1988*) became law. This directive, as well as additional guidelines, provides a legal framework for the pedagogical, medical, social, hygienic and nutritional aspects of daily work in nurseries. It is also intended to provide measures for the prevention of accidents. Some readers may consider these to be unnecessary regulations. However, they are a way of making available to every nursery, even in the most remote village, the results of many years of research and practical experience; they are seen not as a constraint, but as an immense help in the care and education of more than 350,000 children. Indeed, we cannot consider these guidelines as regulations, since they provide ample scope for individual and creative application.

There are three main principles in the Recommendations:

1 Nurseries are pedagogical institutions – 'institutions of social pre-school education and the first step of an integrated socialist education system'.
2 The nurseries are places for happy child experiences and the role of the educators is to promote the physical, cognitive and emotional development of children, in close co-operation with the parents.
3 The basis for the education and care of children is the confirmed programme for educational work in nurseries.

The directive includes criteria concerning the admission of children to nurseries and about education in groups, with an interesting section about the arrangement of daily routines in the groups within nurseries. There are recommendations about how to ensure the healthy physical, cognitive and emotional development of children by providing an educational and age-appropriate daily curricula, involving play and other activities. It is emphasised that play has an important place in the education of children, and that every child must get the opportunity to play actively, independently and in an age-appropriate way. Other

49

recommendations cover the development of independence, hygienic conditions, daytime sleep, outside activities, health checks for children, the role of the nursery director and educators, and co-operation with medical and dental staff, the Mother Advice Centre and, last but not least, with kindergartens and parents.

The nursery directive includes a number of specific regulations about the education, care and health protection of children in nurseries and residential homes. The first covers the work of medical officers. Their responsibilities are outlined, ranging from regular medical check-ups for every child and vaccinations, which are carried out in the nurseries, to supervising a number of areas of daily routine, such as daily sleep, appropriate ventilation and nutrition.

The second set of regulations is in two parts. The first part covers the environment, to ensure it is healthy; there are standards and guidelines, for instance, on the furnishing of group areas (for example, the furniture has to be appropriate to the size of the children), how the kitchen and milk kitchen are to be furnished and the design of the group bedrooms, the hand-over rooms, the washing areas, the isolation and pram rooms, and the free activity areas. In addition, based on research findings, detailed norms regarding room temperature, ventilation, lighting and noise protection are given. The second part is concerned with the organisation of daily routines. Particular emphasis is given to daytime sleep, with exact recommendations provided; in the first year of life, there should be two or three daily naps, in the second year two and in the third year one. It is recommended that children spend at least 3–4 hours daily in the fresh air except in winter, when the period should be at least 2 hours.

A third area of specific regulations covers the prevention of accidents, while the fourth deals with nutrition. Nutritional guidelines for pre-school children are outlined. The fifth area deals with support for infants and pre-school children with disabilities, and is discussed further below.

Staffing and staff training

By the end of 1987, there were 98,877 nursery workers, of whom 25,467 had no professional qualification, a proportion which is still slightly too high; there are however possibilities for these unqualified workers to qualify as nursery educators (*krippenerzieherinnen*), by studying part-time at special institutions. The remaining 73,400 nursery workers are qualified nursery educators, who have been trained in one of 39 medical colleges in the GDR. The entry qualification for the three-year course is successful completion of high school (*oberschule*), at 16 or 17. The course covers educational theory, psychology, anatomy, physiology, hygiene, preventive health, nutrition, paediatrics and general knowledge. Theory and practice are closely integrated in the training programme: in the first two years of study, half the time is devoted to theoretical instruction, while in the third year, the emphasis is on practical training. Special training nurseries exist in every region and district, where instruction and practical work are systematically supervised. Nursery educators also acquire experience in a variety of other settings, such as kindergartens, child clinics and advice centres for mothers.

Further training is provided at the Humboldt University in Berlin for workers who will have supervisory and managerial positions in nurseries or who will train nursery educators in medical colleges. Since 1984, psychologists have also been specially trained for work in nurseries at the Karl Marx University in Leipzig.

Nursery educators are paid an initial starting salary of 825 marks per month (or 845 in Berlin), with subsequent increments. The top of the salary scale is 1,095 marks, below average earnings for workers in industry. Comparison with workers in kindergartens and primary schools is impossible because of differences in bonuses, pensions and other conditions. (For further details on staff training, see Schmidt-Kolmer 1989.)

Staff ratios

In nurseries the staff to child ratio is 1 to 5. In some nurseries there are special and separate groups for children with minor to moderate handicaps. The Nursery Directive provides guidelines about which children should be considered for admission to these groups. The number of children in a special group should not exceed 8, with at least one educator to every three children. Severely handicapped children are cared for at home, in hospitals or in other institutions.

The development of the day care system

The first phase

There is a long tradition of kindergartens in Germany (public kindergartens already existed in the nineteenth century). By contrast, the systematic development of nurseries in the GDR only started in 1945, after the Second World War and the destruction of fascism. The main function of nurseries in these early post-war years was to look after children with single employed mothers who were engaged, under most difficult conditions, in the rebuilding of the economy and of destroyed cities and villages. One of the first achievements of the government of the newly created German Democratic Republic was to incorporate equality for women in the Constitution (in 1949) and, a year later, to pass the law for the Protection of Mother and Child and the Rights of

Women (*Das Gesetz zum Schutz von Mutter und Kind und die Rechte der Frauen*). This law guaranteed equality for women, and outlined how this could be put into practice by the introduction of institutions for the care of children. At that time, in 1950, there were only 8,542 places for children under 3, and half of these were in residential orphanages and homes. Only a small proportion of children could be provided for in these institutions, and priority was given to children who could only be cared for partly or not at all by parents and relatives or whose mothers worked in essential jobs (such as teachers or doctors).

The protection of children's health, in particular the prevention and fight against such dangerous infectious diseases as diptheria, whooping cough, measles, tuberculosis and polio, was the most urgent task in this first phase of the development of nurseries. This required great efforts by doctors and nurses, as no safe vaccinations had been developed for many of these illnesses at that time. Similarly, nutritional problems had to be solved to guarantee the children's healthy physical development.

The work of these new institutions was guided by clinical paediatric experience in the care of sick children. Nursery workers were mainly paediatric and nursery nurses; many women took up this work without any professional training, but with the intention of obtaining a qualification. There was a lack of programmes and guidelines for the education of healthy infants and toddlers in institutions, and a lack of curricula for the appropriate training and education of nursery workers. There were no adequate projects, programmes and guidelines for the design and construction of nurseries. Overall, the issues raised by the education and development of toddlers in peer group settings had been little researched.

Table 3.1 The development of nursery provision, GDR, 1960–87

	Number of nurseries	*Number of places in nurseries*	*Places in nurseries as proportion of children eligible for places (%)*
1960	2, 517	81, 495	14
1965	3, 317	116, 950	19
1970	4, 323	166, 700	29
1975	5, 576	234, 941	51
1980	6, 415	284, 712	61
1985	7, 315	338, 676	73
1987	7, 559	348, 422	81

Later phases

Since the end of the war, the number of nurseries in the GDR has increased greatly. By 1960, there were 81,500 children in nurseries, or 14 per cent of the age group. Since then, there has been a continuing expansion of provision, with the number of children in nurseries increasing more than fourfold and places now available for the great majority of children (see Table 3.1). At the same time as increasing quantity, the quality of educational work in nurseries has developed enormously, especially since the 1960s.

Experimental investigations and subsequent changes in the physical and hygiene arrangements in nurseries played an important part in the second phase of the development of the nursery system, from the end of the 1950s up to the middle of the 1960s. Research findings showed that the average physical and psychological development of children living with their families and receiving care in nurseries was better than that of children in *wochenkrippen* (where children received residential care for most of the week, going home only for two days) or in permanent residential care in orphanages and children's homes. The rate of illness was also lower in ordinary nurseries than in *wochenkrippen*. As a result, places in nurseries continued to increase, while places in *wochenkrippen* and residential care institutions were reduced from 32 per cent of all care places in 1965 to 3 per cent by the end of 1987.

In the early post-war years, the care of children in nurseries and their daily routine was primarily concerned with keeping children healthy by providing adequate hygiene. This changed in 1965, when the Parliament of the GDR (*Volkskammer*) passed the Law of Integrated Socialist Education (*Das Gesetz uber das Einheitliche Sozialistische Bildungssytstem*). This introduced a new stage in the development of nurseries.

The law redefined the role of the nursery as the first stage in an education system from birth to adulthood, for every citizen. The integration of nurseries into this system was a major step towards the recognition of nurseries as pedagogical institutions. The Department of Health, which was the ministry responsible for nurseries, was required to develop plans to realise this new role. This task was assisted by developments in staffing for nurseries; two new groups of professional nursery workers were established – child care worker (*kinderpflegerin*) in 1961 and nursery educator (*krippenerzieherin*) in 1969 – who were quite different to paediatric nurses. Special training courses for personnel dealing with the needs of healthy children were also implemented.

In 1968, *The Pedagogic Task and Work Approach of Nurseries* (Schmidt-Kolmer 1968) was published. This book was written by a collective of authors, including doctors, music and sport teachers and nursery workers, under the overall direction of Eva Schmidt-Kolmer.

Irina Weigl and Christine Weber

Based on empirical knowledge and practical experience, the book described an educational programme for nurseries, including educational aims for specific age groups in areas such as self-help and independence, physical education, play activity, language, understanding the environment, musical education and other creative activities. Although never officially ratified, in the 15 years after its publication the book had a major influence in re-directing nurseries from a medical orientation, which was previously dominant, to an educational and developmental orientation.

By the 1980s, it was necessary to develop a programme which reflected new concepts and research findings. The educational programme proposed in 1968 had become increasingly outdated, and comprehensive analysis of the pedagogical work in nurseries confirmed the need for new guidelines, particularly for language, play and creative activities. In 1988 this new programme, described earlier, was introduced. The research which provided the foundations for this new programme is discussed in Chapter 4.

(For further details on the development of the day care system, see Weigl and Niebsch 1983; Schmidt-Kolmer 1987; Weigl 1987.)

Conclusion

Since the end of the war, there has been a major expansion of the day care system, which is provided and regulated in some detail by the state and based on group care for children. By 1990 there will be nursery provision for over 90 per cent of children, with a place for every child whose mother wants it to attend – though the recent extension of paid leave means that most children do not begin at nursery until they are at least 12 months old. In difficult post-war conditions, priority in nurseries was at first given to physical care and hygiene, but subsequently the system has evolved, placing increasing emphasis on meeting the full range of children's needs through an explicitly educational orientation. The system reflects the GDR's concern to offer employment opportunities to women and the view that, in collaboration with the family, group care can enhance children's experience and development. Nurseries are now seen as the first stage of the education system, and this role is recognised in law.

References

Küchler, B. (1979) *Zur gesellschaftlichen Rolle der Kinderkrippen in der DDR*, thesis for the Humboldt-Universität zu Berlin.
Schmidt-Kolmer, E. (ed.) (1968) *Pädagogische Aufgaben und Arbeitsweise der Krippen*, Berlin: VEB Verlag Volk und Gesundheit.

— (1987) 'Entwicklung der Krippen in der DDR aus historischer Sicht', *Kinderkrippen – Informationen und Empfehlungen zur Erziehung und Betreuung in Krippen und Heiman. Heft 1 und Heimen 1 8–12.*

— (ed.) (1989) *Krippenpädagogik*, Berlin: VEB Verlag Volk und Gesundheit.

Weigl, I. (1987) 'Crèches en R.D.A.', in M. Deleau (ed.) *L'éducation des jeunes enfants: quelques expériences étrangères récentes*, Rennes: Presses Univ. de Rennes.

Weigl, I. and Niebsch, G. (1983) 'Les crèches en République Démocratique Allemande', *Connaissance de la RDA* 17.

Chapter four

Research in nurseries in the German Democratic Republic

Irina Weigl and Christine Weber

Research in this area is characterised by its relevance to practice. It is aimed at the improvement of education and care of children. Also it is interdisciplinary; pedagogical, psychological, medical, social-hygienic as well as nutritional questions are investigated. We present here research related to a new educational programme in nurseries. As mentioned in Chapter 3, discussion material for an educational programme was made available to nursery educators in 1968 (Schmidt-Kolmer 1968). This discussion paper originated from practical experience rather than from a clearly outlined pedagogical theoretical position. The primary benefit of this material was to redirect the work in nurseries from nearly exclusive medical care to pedagogical aims and to provide the basis for a unified approach for nursery educators.

In 1973 a division was formed at the Institute for the Hygiene of the Child and Adolescent, Berlin, to conduct investigations into previously neglected theoretical questions and practical problems. These investigations were intended to lay the foundation for the planning of the 'Programme for Educational Work in Nurseries' (1985).

The development of a programme for educational work in nurseries

The investigations which formed the basis for the new programme (Niebsch 1980) can be subdivided into four approaches:

1 Mainly interdisciplinary experimental investigations which resulted in new theoretical and practice-relevant conclusions that lay the scientific foundation for the new programme of educational work in nurseries. These were large-scale studies regarding language acquisition (Weigl 1976, 1977a, 1977b, 1980a, 1980b, 1981a, 1981b, 1982, 1985, 1986a, 1986b, 1987a), the development of creative skills (Regel 1982), the development of musical skills (Bachmann 1980), play skills (Weber 1983), and

planning educational work (Program für die Erziehungsarbeit in Kinderkrippen 1985).

2 The analysis of research findings from investigations in other disciplines, e.g. medical and hygiene investigations (Niebsch, Grosch *et al.* 1980, which mainly contributed to a section on 'Organisation of daily life'.

3 The re-analysis and re-working of previous research results on the subjects 'Movement education' (Hoffman 1986) and 'Organisation of daily life' (Kempf 1985; Besse 1986).

4 Educational and psychological principles were integrated in the planning of the topic 'Sensory education with instructional materials, building blocks and other objects' as well as in the subject area 'Introduction to the social environment and nature' (Program für die Erziehungsarbeit in Kinderkrippen 1985).

The development of the programme of educational work for nurseries involved the following stages:

1 A comprehensive analysis of pedagogical practice in 14 nurseries (314 children) in 1974 and 1975.

2 Numerous investigations and studies were carried out regarding the deficiencies and problems of current practice. The programme was based on the results of these investigations.

3 The first outline of the programme was worked out in 1979 and given a trial run in 1980. The trail confirmed and further specified the aims, content and methods for the different areas of education.

4 The draft of the programme was revised in 1981 and 1982 based on the evaluation of the first trial period. A second trial period and new evaluation of the draft programme was carried out in five nurseries.

5 The second trial was evaluated and the programme revised in close co-operation with specialists from the Department of Public Education, of the Academy of Pedagogical Science and those at the Humboldt University; at the same time a number of practitioners were consulted. After consultation with these experts a final revision was written.

6 The programme was confirmed by the Minister of Health in 1985. It was decided to implement the 'Programme for Educational Work in Nurseries' in all nurseries in the GDR (Küchler 1985).

The stepwise introduction of the new Programme started in 1985. At that time the Programme was introduced in 22 nurseries. After evaluation of this introductory period the new Programme was introduced to 500 nurseries in the GDR in 1986. The Programme has been used in all nurseries since 1987/1988. An evaluation of the effectiveness of the pedagogical programme is intended to be carried out from 1989. It will inform future research.

Structure of the programme for education in nurseries

Whether children in nurseries feel really happy and secure, are able to develop their personal strengths, individuality, independence, emotions and creativity, is largely dependent on pedagogic practice and whether their needs are satisfied. The principles underlying the new Programme are in the Appendix (pp. 70-1). Within the Programme educational goals are defined for different ages; 6–12 months, 13–24 months (Weber 1985).

Explanation of specific sections of the programme

Introduction

To illustrate the far-reaching aims of education in nurseries a series of overlapping main tasks are illustrated: the maintenance and promotion of health and physical development in children; the development of object-related play and other activities, the development of sensory, perceptual and learning skills; the promotion of language acquisition; the development of positive relationships between educators and children and between peers; moral and aesthetic education. These key areas are integrated into all sections of the programme.

Child development

The development of children during the first, second and third year of life is dealt with in this section. The nursery educator thus has psychological and pedagogic guidelines for her work.

Organisation of daily life

This section is concerned with the health of children. Tasks involve health promotion through the organisation of nap times, meal times, outside activities, organisation of daily routines, of healthy habits, health and environmental control in the nursery.

Great attention is directed to settling the child into the nursery after admission. In this adaptation phase, individual care is provided, depending on how quickly the child settles in. The child needs sensitive, empathic support by staff to prevent problems in this settling-in phase. The specific aims of the nursery educator are:

1 Special attention should be given to facilitate a smooth settling-in by the child (Guhl 1987, Seidel and Grosch 1987). Parents should be informed about the nature of group childcare and parents

should take on the responsibility of adapting the daily routines of the child to the daily rhythms in the nursery before admission.
2 The nursery educator should obtain information about the child's habits, behaviours and individual needs, which should be taken into account during the settling in period.
3 Parents should be informed that the legally required vaccinations should be carried out before admission to the nursery.
4 The possibility of a step-by-step introduction for the child should be discussed by the director and the parents. The mother or father remains with the child in the nursery during this settling-in period.
5 The nursery educator gives special attention to the child during the adaptation period, engaging it in frequent contact and play, and slowly accustoms the child to the other children.
6 The health status and weight of newly admitted children are checked frequently.

Furthermore a series of tasks related to the organisation of a happy, fulfilling life in the group is outlined (Besse 1986, Kempf 1985). The nursery educator should provide opportunities to satisfy the needs of children for social contact, new experiences and increasingly in-dependent activities. This should be enhanced by a happy and conflict-free atmosphere in the nursery. This section of the programme provides a framework for the other educational tasks outlined in the section 'Play' and in the different subject areas.

Finally, detailed recommendations regarding the development of children's skills are outlined. These concern independence in eating, physical care, hygiene, dressing and the execution of instructions (e.g. clearing away trays, watering plants, preparing the table, etc.).

Play

This section deals with play promotion in the first three years (Weber 1986). Different subsections address specific features of play for different ages and make recommendations for the development of play activity in the first, second and third year of life. The function of the nursery educator is to develop children's play into independent and age-appropriate creative activities and to enhance the level of play.

Subject areas

Six different subject areas are differentiated for 2- and 3-year-olds:

1 *Sensory education while dealing with instructional material, building blocks and other objects.* The aim of sensory education is to enable the child to perceive, compare and differentiate on characteristics such as shape, colour, size, etc. Manipulation and

59

play with concrete objects is intended to promote perceptual and memory skills.

2 *Language education* (Weigl 1980a, 1986c). The major aim is the development of active understanding and the nursery educator facilitates language acquisition and production by encouraging the natural motivation of the child to communicate with exciting activities and exposing the child to language.

3 *Introduction to the social environment and nature.* The aim is to facilitate the acquisition of simple concepts and knowledge about objects, plants, animals, changes in nature, adult activities and their relationships. The children learn to observe more carefully and to identify specific characteristics of objects, animals and plants.

4 *Physical education* (Hoffman 1986) supports physical development through encouraging movement patterns: walking, climbing, throwing, pulling and pushing own body (second year), jumping, catching, etc. (third year).

5 *Music education* (Bachmann 1986). The aim is to enable children to listen, recognise and discriminate between different songs and pieces of music. The children move happily to the melodies and sing to them.

6 *Art education* (Regel 1982). Drawing and painting, tearing and sticking, shaping, building and appreciating pictures and sculptures all comprise this subject area and are encouraged.

Each subject area has an identical internal structure:

– A short introduction outlining its significance for personality development of the child and its relationship to the other areas. Aims and tasks of the nursery educator, where major goals for different age groups are stated. The level of activity and achievement of children in the different subject areas is assessed at the end of the second and third year of life to provide new task orientation.

– Another subsection relates to general methods and organisation to be used by nursery educators. It also contains a general strategy for each of the different subject areas.

– A further subsection presents a variety of tasks for integration into the daily routine at opportune moments.

– Another subsection outlines the organisation and content of specific guided activities regarding sensory, language, physical, music and artistic education. These special activities are only introduced after 18 months of age. The subject area 'Introduction to the social environment and nature' is an exception because it has no special activities and should be integrated throughout the daily routine.

Children up to 12 months

The programme for children of less than 12 months has a slightly different and more complex structure. Two subject areas are outlined, musical and physical education, which should be integrated into the daily routine. Also, appropriate educational aims have been integrated in subsections on 'Organisation of daily life', and 'Contact with different types of materials and toys; nursery rhymes and finger play'.

Research relevant to the programme

The programme is based on research in several areas, of which three will be briefly presented here: language development, play and art education. Further details of these studies can be found in the reports cited.

Research on development of language

From experimentation to application

Using insights from previous research, fundamental psychological research into language acquisition in the second year of life was undertaken. Our work, carried out over eleven years, comprised:

1 An empirical, non-interventional, longitudinal and cross-sectional analysis of language development in children attending a creche.
2 Interpretation and evaluation of these analyses were followed by research in three creches for a period of two years (Weigl 1977a, b).
3 Thereupon, a main experiment carried out in six creches (with 35 children) with six creches (46 children) as control group (Weigl 1982).
4 Pedagogical experiments (a) in 7 creches (28 children) and (b) a second experiment with 42 children as the experimental group and 51 as the control group (Weigl, Muhlberg, Guhl 1983).
5 Three experiments with 12 handicapped children.
6 A series of experiments was also carried out that aimed at improving communication throughout the daily activities between educator and children in order to enhance language development (Mitschke and Schostag 1977; Weigl 1980a, 1987a).

The results of these various experiments underlie current practical pedagogical work in creches in the GDR.

Currently, instructions as to method are being worked out for language development work in creches and new manuals for training educators are being prepared (Krippenpädagogik 1990). We shall not describe here the underlying research (see Weigl 1977b, 1980a, 1980b, 1982, 1986a, 1986b, 1987a) but shall proceed to the conclusions that are of particular interest for pedagogical work in creches (Weigl 1986c).

There is no doubt that mastery of a language does not consist in stockpiling a long list of words and sentences or in learning by heart a certain number of utterances. Children extract from the language that they hear a set of lexical units and rules which form the basis from the creative use of language. To be sure, these developments do not occur consciously in the infant. One does not 'teach' the child rules of grammar or other procedures. It uses them without being aware of them. Wilhelm von Humboldt wrote 150 years ago: 'Language has to make unlimited use of a limited number of means.' This identifies the heart of the question: it is not the limited means, that is, words or isolated constructions, that constitute the capacity for language but rather the creative use of these means, the capacity to make unlimited use of them.

The spontaneous processes at the base of successful language acquisition in young children are due to a twofold perception both of language and of action. From the many utterances heard by the child, it chooses the information related to the action and the language that it is capable of assimilating, storing and using (as a function of its stage of development) in order to understand and produce utterances. We have tried to harness these natural processes of language acquisition.

The fundamental principles

The interconnected principles constituting the basis of the process of language acquisition in early infancy that we have derived from our research (Weigl 1982) are as follows:

1 The mechanisms of language acquisition, like all learning
  processes in young children, are closely linked to *practical
  activities* specific to this age and having to do with objects.
  Perception, assimilation and storage of action sequences
  accompanied by corresponding utterances stimulate both the
  infant's cognitive development at the level of practical activity
  and also the processes of language acquisition. In other words, the
  cognitive organisation of perception and of the control of action
  contributes to the acquisition of the linguistic rule system, while
  at the same time the emerging language capacity assists in the

assimilation of action sequences and stimulates the cognitive development of the child.

2 The *perception of language* linked to action is paramount: the processes of language acquisition are based on the twofold perception of language and action and these support both comprehension and production. At the same time the capacity of act intentionally develops, as the infant acquires 'internalised programmes of action'.

3 The infant acquires language in *communicative/co-operative interaction*. Both linguistic and non-linguistic means of communication participate in this process of interaction. Non-linguistic means include, in the first year of life, visual contact, laughter, babble, motor activities. In the second year, they include practical actions with everyday objects or toys. This holds for the third year as well. Our research has shown that non-linguistic means have an extremely important role in language acquisition.

To summarise: the theoretical position adopted postulates that during the second year of life three systems of language acquisition processes are present: the language system, the activity system and the system of social interactions, i.e. communication between adult and child. The social interaction system provides a framework in which speech and action can be perceived by the child and processed. Theory and experimental results have led us to propose a model of the perception, storage and assimilation of linguistic and actional structures in young children.

Language development as a component of creche education

Our analyses of the pedagogy of language development have shown that the absence of a theoretical understanding has repercussions for the methods used by nursery educators, which in turn explains the difficulties and inadequacies of language pedagogy in nurseries. It was noted that pedagogic work tended to be at a purely verbal level and not to be oriented to the relationship between language and object-related activities. Isolated words would be taught, naming objects or pictures. The educators' methods centred on a question and answer game and, consequently, the children's activities were restricted to naming, showing, imitating and repeating. In general terms, one started with the final stage of language acquisition, with verbal production, while completely neglecting the initial phase, namely that of language comprehension.

Another factor contributing to the inadequacies was an underestimation of the potential of the whole range of children's daily activities. Children not only learn during guided activities but rather constantly perceive and assimilate information linked to language and action in the routines of daily life. Our methods for the domain of language development for 2- and 3-year-olds make use of both spheres.

For the first year there is, in effect, no special domain called 'language development'. It is rather an integrative aspect of all pedagogy at this stage and is pursued through different activities. The educator stimulates language development through the day, that is, in tandem with the development of activities of orientation, exploration, prehension and manipulation of objects. The emergence of language comprehension and production is enhanced by direct affective interaction between caregiver and child. The overall goal for the second and third years is to improve competence in understanding verbal utterances linked to concrete actions. Toward the end of the second year, comprehension starts to occur independently of the perception of concrete actions.

General instructions as to method

The programme for education also contains instructions as to method, including the following points:

1 To stimulate comprehension and production the caregiver accompanies her own action with utterances, provides a commentary to the children's actions, and directs children's actions through verbal instructions.
2 Children are encouraged to speak by combining language and action. The educator responds to incomplete utterances with complete grammatically correct sentences, expresses herself clearly, and uses various types of word and sentence (in the second year of life, mainly simple sentences: in the third, the whole range of work and sentences types).
3 Exchanges with children are adjusted to the individual, with specified guided activities for each child.

Developed or complete communicative exchanges consist of three or more units: the impulse, a response, a reaction to the response. These can be extended and result in a real conversation between caregiver and child (see Brown and Bellugi 1964 for a discussion of the concept of expansion). There is no simple relationship between the length of a communicative exchange and its degree of completeness. Most complete communicative exchanges are composed of three or more units. There are, however, also numerous communicative exchanges comprising three or more units in which one finds responses, such as 'good', 'that's it', which cannot be considered complete. Many communicative exchanges of two units are interrupted and therefore incomplete.

Criteria regarding the communication situation

Situations largely determine communicative exchanges. One must always consider context. For activities such as meals, getting dressed and undressed, bodily care, getting children to be able to carry out in practice what is expected of them has priority; communicative processes are subordinate to these goals.

There are certain situations during play in which communicative exchanges can scarcely be expanded, but routine situations can provide opportunities for stimulating language acquisition.

The development of language during guided activities

Guided activities aimed at enhancing language development are introduced at 18 months. On the basis of our research, we have developed some guided activities for 2- or 3-year olds, to be carried out in groups of at most four 2-year-olds or six 3-year-olds. Thus guided activities are based on the child's perception of events and do not aim at the immediate development of specific skills but rather at the long-term mastering of the mother tongue. It is the child's own activity that plays the decisive role. It is reinforced by the affective behaviour of the educator, by her activities with the child and by the use of games, etc. The aim of these guided activities is to enhance the child's language comprehension and production.

Themes

The guided activities are based on a series of play activities. The sequence of these produces a systematic increase in difficulty. The activities are therefore not interchangeable. The choice of activity takes into consideration not only the child's age but also specific goals; that is, activities are linked to the child's experiences.

For 18-month to 2-year-olds the themes provide a number of words and simple grammatical forms. Examples of themes: the dolls and the animals go tobogganing; the dolls and the animals ride on the carousel (or on the see-saw); we are washing the dolls' clothes.

Three guided activities are planned for each theme, and each activity is divided into parts. The first part consists in a systematic presentation, while the second part (transposition) consists in the child playing freely with the objects just presented. The function of the presentation of the three guided activities is to progressively direct perception and assimilation of the language and action. In the first guided activity, the caregiver accompanies actions with utterances which are perceived by the children. For the second guided activity, the theme is not altered but the activity is expanded and varied. In the presentation, the educator makes the children *participate* in the action and comments on what occurs. In the third guided activity, the educator only gives verbal instructions and this time it is up to the children to execute the action.

In the second part (transposition), the child has the opportunity to assimilate the linguistic and action structures and independently use these in individual creative play. The educator takes only a guiding role, giving suggestions when the child is inactive, helping the child where skills need further development, commenting on what the child does.

In the transposition sequence, the child can decide alone what to do, without having a pre-given model to work from. In order to measure the efficacy of this work, we evaluated the children's capacity to act in all the transposition sequences of all the guided activities and recorded the verbal production of the 42 children in the experimental group. We let each member of a control group of 52 children play with the same toys and in similar conditions. The results confirm the significant and considerable advantages of the experimental group with respect both to the capacity to act, and the quantity and quality of verbal production (Weigl, Mühlberg, Guhl 1983).

Enacted scenes using toys

To stimulate language development in 2- to 3-year-olds, scenes are acted out using toys. In these guided activities, it is still language comprehension that is the focus, and the child's verbal activity is only indirectly stimulated. The language of the scenes to be acted out with toys has a more complex character. Different verbs, adjectives, etc. are offered in connection with what is going on 'on stage'. The educator uses direct and indirect discourse while playing the various characters.

We have proposed many themes for these scenes, including 'the large beetroot', 'the animals are hungry', 'the bear's birthday party'. Each theme has a central figure and several secondary ones, the number of which depends on how many children are involved. Each theme has two guided activities; and each of them has, as before, a presentation and a transposition phase. In the presentation of the first guided activity, the educator first plays the scene alone. She tells the story, explains the various elements, and acts out each of the parts. She uses mainly direct and dialogic discourse. In the presentation of the second guided activity, the educator recounts the scene without herself acting it out. Here, she uses indirect discourse. While recounting, she encourages the children to continue the story themselves by asking them questions.

In the second part (transposition) the children can further assimilate and reapply what was presented in the first sequence. The educator and the children play the scene together, whereby the educator plays the central role and each child plays the part of a secondary educator. If a child remains silent, the educator speaks the part and comments on the action.

Summary

The following principles have been derived from the research. They guide practical language pedagogy in nurseries for normal children and the special programme for handicapped children:

1 The adult systematically directs the perception and processing of language and action in the context of communication and co-operation with the child.
2 The success of a child's linguistic development is not to be judged in terms of the quantity of its utterances.
3 Language acquisition is related to activity, it has to do with the activity of the child with respect to concrete objects under the guiding influence of the adult.
4 The emotional, loving attention to each child is a condition for the promotion of language acquisition.
5 The adult uses all the activities of the daily routine as well as guided activities for language enhancing interventions, using a variety of pedagogic techniques.

Research on play

Research studies were carried out between 1977 and 1982 (Weber 1986). Experimental work to verify the effectiveness of instructions given by educators to promote play development were initiated after the analysis of observations in a normal nursery setting. The experiments were carried out on 188 children aged 6–36 months and involved 70 nursery educators. This experimental work resulted in a new approach to the promotion of children's play in the first three years in nurseries, and a corresponding section on play methods in the Programme. The following principles for educational work emerged from these studies.

Play is a voluntary, spontaneous activity of the child who wants to put his fantasies, intentions and wishes into practice. This is both gratifying and satisfying. However, the influence of the adult on the child during play is necessary. It can only be successful if the adult's intervention takes into account the voluntary spontaneous character of the activity and does not restrict the child's activities. Free choice, spontaneity and independence on the part of the child and goal-directed intervention on the part of the adult during play are compatible and characterise the essential 'duality' of play.

Play develops in stages during the first three years of life. It starts with the unspecific manipulation of objects by the young infant and reaches the beginnings of creative play at the end of the third year of life (role play). The development of play requires adult guidance. The withdrawal of adult support for play would be as harmful as permanently prescribing how the child should play. The adult uses indirect ways of influencing play (i) by providing an appropriate environment and toys adapted to the child's age, interests and abilities; (ii) by assisting the child's manipulation of objects and by entering into play with the child; (iii) by supporting and reinforcing the creative initiative of the child and by providing it with the opportunity to observe, try out and explore without being under time pressure. The adult should play with the child, respect his play intentions and show a sympathetic attitude towards the child. This is accomplished by the educator's active reinforcement of play in respecting the individuality of the child's intentions.

Occasionally, an adult directly influences play by being a partner in the play or providing a model. This helps the child to discover new variations of play activities and to learn the social meaning of play sequences (e.g. playing with dolls or toy animals who behave in the role of the mother). The acquisition of play skills also involves active participation in traditional games such as 'Ring, a ring, of Roses', 'quarte', 'dice throwing', all games that have explicit rules.

The educational implication is that appropriate methods should be selected to promote cognitive abilities and ensure that every child has opportunities to express fantasies creatively. The ability to play creatively is a complex process and approaches need to be adapted for different ages. Two different strategies can be distinguished:

6–18 months of age: The focal point is the provision of play materials for independent manipulation and the demonstration of actions and toys in one-to-one interaction. The educator should provide a running commentary to the demonstrated actions. The aim is not to initiate imitations of a demonstrated activity by a child but to provide the motivation for child activities. The child is stimulated by joint activities with the trusted educator, by sympathetic interaction with the educator and through reinforcement by providing encouragement and positive feedback.
19–36 months of age: Play is no longer motivated by demon-strations and commentary. Instead, individual encouragement is given to promote the child's own initiatives. The first step is carefully to observe play in context – younger children often require suggestions from the educator to initiate a play sequence. However, advice and support should not be given immediately as

this may restrict individual initiatives. Choosing an approach is dependent upon knowing the characteristics of each child, including abilities, knowledge and experience. Realistic goals can thus be set and the experience of success assured.

Research regarding the development of artistic abilities

The main fallacy of previous conceptions of art education in the nursery was that specific skills were to be trained and perfected (e.g. the acquisition of techniques for using pencils, the drawing of dots and wave lines or the assembly of building blocks to a particular pattern). It appeared legitimate and plausible that children had to acquire manual ability before they could engage in creative drawing, painting and modelling. This approach was rooted in the principle: 'from the easy to the difficult'. The development of the child's personality as a whole and the promotion of art and sculptural ability as a specific means of representing reality, the need to enrich and enhance relationships with the environment were completely ignored. Creative, individual expression is not dependent on specific technical skills.

Based on a new theoretical conception, Regel (1982) carried out a longitudinal study of 60 nursery children from 18 months of age. The theoretical conception is based on the following ideas:

1 Drawing, painting, glueing, modelling and building as well as conceptual analysis of paintings and sculptures (receptive and productive activities) are considered as creative activities. The characteristics of these activities need to be researched and taught. The educational process thus has to support the acquisition of the element of art, i.e. creative appreciation and production.
2 The creative activities of children should be considered as a special type of play-related learning. The two most important activities for children, play and learning, are symbiotic.
3 Creative activities start in infancy. It is not the aim of creative or art education to accelerate the infants' achievements to a level which can only be attained by older children. Instead the aim is to help infants to recognise and use their own individual creative abilities.
4 The child draws, paints, models and builds appropriate to his own ideas.

Creative activity has to play an appropriate role in the daily routine of children. Productive creation and receptive analysis have to become as important a part in the daily life of children as playing, talking, singing and listening to music.

The following educational implications were drawn from the investigation:

1 The creative ability of children can be enhanced by supporting the child's reception of impressions and experiences and reinforcing his perceptual skills. An important pre-requisite for creative education is attention to forms, colours and other characteristics of objects.
2 The enhancement of creative activity is not restricted to specific guided activities; children need in addition to be motivated throughout the day to paint, to draw, to model and to build. This should be done without interfering with the child's own ideas.
3 Attempts by children to produce an artwork independently should be respected and reinforced.

Furthermore, guidelines are given to educators on how to interpret the child's creative products: they are a representation of what the child has experienced or of what was important, or gave happiness, or caused fear, or other emotions, what has been seen or imagined. It is thus a special representation related to the age of the child. In this process the child also uses other forms of expression: language, imitation, gesture, laughing, movement and so on.

Unfortunately, we often focus too much on what the child cannot do instead of being astounded by how much it has acquired in such a short time. It is surprising how young children are able to express their fantasies and reveal their individuality in creative art.

Appendix

Programme for Educational Work in Nurseries

Pedagogical principles
1 The unity of education, development and health;
2 The guiding role of the nursery educator in the pedagogical process
   – loving care, trust in the child's abilities
   – considerations for age specific needs
   – recognition of individual differences
3 The meaning of play
   – play is an independent activity
   – play is an educational method.

Psychological principles

1 The interaction of development and education;
2 The development of the child's personality as a holistic process;
3 Recognition of the special nature of learning in early childhood:
   – the priority of perception/sensory activities
   – the role of concrete actions and operations
   – communication and interaction between educator and child
     (verbal and non-verbal)
   – the creative and individual character of the children's activities.
4 Education, development and health promotion are integrated into
  daily routines and rhythms, daily sleep periods, outdoor activities.
5 Loving care and consideration for individual differences as well
  as for the creativity of every child is a unifying theme for the
  work of the educator.
6 Play occupies a central role in the daily nursery routine. It is
  considered as a special activity for children but is also used as an
  educational method.
7 The development of the child's personality is influenced by
  educational practices. Education can only be optimised within the
  context of the development of individual children (Weber 1987,
  1988).
8 Different aspects of the child's personality develop separately but
  influence each other. The diversity of influences requires fine
  tuning and integration of different sections of the programme.
9 Knowledge gained from the scientific investigations on learning
  processes are reflected in the programme – the starting point of
  learning in early childhood is the perception of the opportunities
  provided by the environment (Weigl and Raschke 1985; Weigl
  1987b). The role of the adult is not to press for high quality
  achievements in such activities as speaking, painting, etc. by
  children. Instead the focus is to promote and guide active perception, exploration and processing of activities and stimuli
  offered to the child. The child's independent activity, concrete
  actions and interactions between child and adult occupy the
  central role in this process. The effectiveness of the learning
  process depends on providing appropriate stimuli by adults,
  promoting perceptual and information processing abilities and
  considering the creativity and individuality of the child's
  handiwork.

References

'Anweisung über die Erziehung, Betreuung und den Gesundheitsschutz der
  Kinder in den Kinderkrippen', Krippenordnung vom 25. April 1988, in

71

Verflügungen und Mitteilungen des Ministeriums für Gesundheitswesen No. 3.

Bachmann, F. (1980) 'Zur Entwicklung musikalischer Tätigkeiten von Krippenkindern', in E. Schmidt-Kolmer (ed.) *Forschung im Dienste der jungen Generation,* Berlin: Verlag Volk und Gesundheit, 151–90.

— (1986) 'Zum Sachbereich "Musikerziehung" im Program für die Erzienhungsarbeit in Kinderkrippen', *Neue Erziehung im Kindergarten* 7/8: 70–3.

Besse, M. (1986) 'Zur Lebensgestaltung der Kinder in der Kinderkrippe', *Heilberufe* 2, Beilage.

Brown, R. and Bellugi, U. (1964) 'Three processes in the child's acquisition of syntax', in E. Lenneberg (ed.) *New Directions in the Study of Language,* Cambridge: MIT Press, 131–61.

Guhl, C. (1987) 'Erzieherische Maßnahmen zur inhaltlich-organisatorischen Gestaltung des Adaptionsprozesses', *Kinderkrippen. Information und Empfehlungen zur Erziehung und Betreuung in Krippen und Heimen* 1: 40–6.

Hoffman, R. (1986) 'Zum Sachbereich "Bewegungserziehung" im Program für die Erziehungsarbeit in Kinderkrippen', *Neue Erziehung im Kindergarten* 4: 86–7.

Kempf, J. (1985) 'Zum Abschnitt "Gestaltung des Lebens" im Program für die Erziehungsarbeit in den Kinderkrippen', *Neue Erziehung im Kindergarten* 11: 273–5.

— (1987) 'Umsetzung der Inhalte des Programms für die Erziehungsarbeit in den Kinderkrippen und einige methodische Überlegungen', *Kinderkrippen. Information und Empfehlungen zur Erziehung und Betreuung in Krippen und Heimen* 1: 21–31.

Krippenpädagogik (Band I und Band II) (1990) *Autorenkolehtiv,* E. Schmidt-Kolmer (ed.) Berlin: Verlag Volk und Gesundheit.

Küchler, B. (1979) 'Zur gesellschaftlichen Rolle der Kinderkrippen in der DDR', Dissertation, Humboldt-Universität zu Berlin.

— (1985) 'Die inhaltliche Gestaltung der Arbeit in der Kinderkrippe – wichtigste Ziele und Aufgabenstellung in den nächsten Jahren', *Neue Erziehung im Kindergarten* 2/3: 54–6.

Mitschke, A. and Schostag, M. (1977) 'Die Gestaltung der sprechlichen Kommunikation in ausgurählten Abschmitten des Tagesablaufs bei Krippenkindern im 2-Lebensjahr', Diplomarbeit, Humboldt-Universität in Berlin, Sektion Pedagogik.

Niebsch, G. (1980) 'Zur Rolle der Forschung in den verschiedenen Etappen in der Entwicklung der Kinderkrippen in der DDR', in E. Schmidt-Kolmer (ed.) *Forschung im Dienste der jungen Generation,* Berlin: Verlag Volk und Gesundheit, 68–82.

Niebsch, G., Grosch, C., Besse, M., Weber, C. and Seidel, M. (1980) "Gesunderhaltung und Gesundheitsförderung von Krippendern', in E. Schmidt-Kolmer (ed.) *Forschung im Dienste der jungen Generation,* Berlin: Verlag Volk und Gesundheit, 63–7.

Program für die Erziehungsarbeit in Kinderkrippen (1985) *Ministerrat der Deutschen Demokratischen Republik.* Minsterium für Gesundheitswesen

(ed.) Berlin: Verlag Volk und Gesundheit.
Regel, G. (1982) 'Zue neuen Konzeption der bilderischen Erziehung in der Kinderkrippe', *Heilberufe* 2: 447–51.
Schmidt-Kolmer, E. (1968) (ed.) *Pädagogische Aufgaben und Arbeitsweise der Krippen,* Berlin: Verlag Volk und Gesundheit.
— (1987) 'Entwicklung der Krippen in der DDR aus historischer Sicht', *Kinderkrippen. Information und Empfehlung zur Erziehung und Betreuung in Krippen und Heimen* 1: 8–12.
Seidel, M. and Grosch, C. (1987) 'Aspekte des Adaptationsprozesses – Zu ausgewählten Ergebnissen wissenschaftlicher Untersuchungen', *Kinderkrippen. Information und Empfehlung zur Erziehung und Betreuung in Krippen und Heimen* 1: 37–40.
Slobin, D. (1974) 'Kognitive Voraussetgungen der Sprachentwichlung', in H. Lenniger, M. Miller and F. Müller (eds) *Linguistik und Psychologie Bd 2,* Frankfurt: Athenäum Fischer Taschenbuck, 122–65.
Weber, C. (1983) 'Spiel in der Kinderkrippe', *Heilberufe* 4: 147–51.
— (1985) 'Struktur und Inhalt des neuen Programmes für die Erziehungsarbeit in Kinderkrippen', *Neue Erziehung im Kindergarten* 5: 108–11.
— (1986) 'Untersuchungen zum Spiel bei Krippenkindern. Theoretische und praxisrelevante Überlegungen zur Erarbeitung des Abschnitts "Spiel" im Programm für die Erziehungsarbeit in Kinderkrippen', Dissertation, Berlin: Akademie der pädagogischen Wissenschaften.
— (1986) 'Zum Abschnitt "Spiel" im Programm für die Erzienhungsarbeit in Kinderkrippen', *Neue Erziehung im Kindergarten* 1: 18–20.
— (1987) 'Erziehungsstrategian in der Kinderkrippe – Ziel der Erziehung, wesentliche Inhalte und Methoden der pädagogischen Arbeit', *Kinderkrippen. Information und Empfehlung zur Erziehung, und Betreuung in Krippen und Heimen* 1: 15–21.
— (1988) 'Beschäftigung in der Kinderkrippe', *Kinderkrippen. Information und Empfehlung zur Erziehung und Betreuung in Krippen und Heimen* 1: 6–18.
Weigl, I. (1976) 'Zu einigen Grundfragen des Spracherwerbs', *Heilberufe* 6, Beilage.
— (1977a) 'Experimentelle Ergebnisse einer Untersuchung zur Förderung des Spracherwerbs im 2. Lebensjahr', *Heilberufe* 9.
— (1977b) *Zum Spracherwerb bei Krippenkindern,* Berlin: Verlag Volk und Gesundheit.
— (1980a) 'Die Gestaltung der sprachlichen Kommunikation im Tagesablauf bei Krippenkindern im 2-Lebensjahr', *Heilberufe* 2, Beilage.
— (1980b) 'Zusammenhänge zwischen der Entwicklung der Handlungs – und Sprachfähigkeit', in E. Schmidt-Kolmer (ed.) *Forschung im Dienste der jungen Generation,* Berlin: Verlag Volk und Gesundheit.
— (1981a) 'Untersuchungen zum handlungsbezogenen Sprachverstehen im Kleinkindalter', *Osnabrücker Hefte für Sprachtheorie* 20.
— (1981b) 'Investigations into action related language comprehension in early infancy', *Journal of Psycholinguistics* 3: 23.
— (1982) 'Sprache – Handlung – Kommunikation. Untersuchungen zum

Spracherwerb bei Krippenkindern im 2-Lebensjahr', *Habilitationsschrift*, Humboldt-Universität zu Berlin.

— (1985) 'Beziehungen zwischen Sprachperzeption, Handlung und Sprachproduktion im Spracherwerbprozeß', in T. Füssenich and B. Gläß (eds) *Dysgrammatismus*, Heidelberg: Schindele.

— (1986a) 'Sprache – Handlung – Kommunikation. Praxisrelevante Ergebnisse experimenteler Unteruschungen zum Sprachwerb im Kleindalter', in L. Springer and G. Kaltenbeck (eds) *Aktuelle Beiträge zu kindlichen Sprech- und Sprachstörungen*, München: Tuduv Verlag.

— (1986b) 'Différences interindividuelles dans le conportement verbal chez les jeunes enfants', in Lepot-Froment (ed.) *Les différences interindividuelles*, Université Catholique Louvain.

— (1986c) 'Zum Sachbereich "Spracherziehung" im Program für die Erziehungsarbeit in Kinderkrippen, *Neue Erziehung im Kindergarten*, 11.

— (1987a) 'Perception du langage et interaction sociale chez les jeunes enfants', in M. Deleau (ed.) *Langage et communication à l'âge préscolaire*, Presses Univ. de Rennes.

— (1987c) 'Spracherwerbsforschung bei normalen und gestörten Kleinkindern', in Borbonus und Gathen (eds) *Spracherwerb und Spracherwerbsstörungen. Tagungsbericht der XVII*. Arbeits- und Fortbildungsveranstaltung der DSG Düsseldorf, 431–49.

— (1987d) 'Crèches en R.D.A.', in M. Deleau (ed.) *L'éducation des jeunes enfants. Quelques expériences étrangères récentes*, Presses Univ. de Rennes, 7–71.

Weigl, I. and Niebsch, G. (1983a) 'Les crèches en République Démocratique Allemande', *Paris: Connaisance de la R.D.A.* 17: 21–43.

Weigl, I. and Raschke, J. (1985) 'Zu einigen psychologischen Positionen im Programm für die Erzienhungsarbeit in Kinderkrippen', *Neue Erziehung im Kindergaten* 7/8: 166–8.

Weigl, I., Mühlberg, K. and Guhl, C. (1983) 'Wege zur Optimierung der Kognitiven Entwicklung bei Krippenkindern', *Zeitschrift für Pädiatrie und Grenzgebiete* 1.

Chapter five

Day care for young children in Sweden

Anders Broberg and C. Philip Hwang

With more than 8 million inhabitants, Sweden is the largest of the Nordic countries. For the majority of foreigners, our country is probably best known for its high taxes and well-developed social service system. The care taken of our citizens' social welfare, and the responsibility for this care assumed by society, applies in particular to childcare. Sweden has extensive, and still growing, day care services. But these cannot be described in isolation, without discussing other policies for children and families. Day care services are part of a larger system which comprises a number of measures aimed at improving conditions for children and parents.

Employment entitlements for parents

Sweden has developed an extensive system of employment entitlements for parents with young children, the main ones being provided by the Paid Parental Leave Act. Fathers are given the right to two weeks leave in connection with their child's birth and paid at 90 per cent of normal earnings. This permits fathers to take care of other children in the family while mothers are in the maternity ward and enables all family members to spend a week together 'adjusting' to the newest family member. Most Swedish fathers (83 per cent) utilise this right (Riksförsäkringsverket 1986). The Act further entitles either of the parents to be off work after childbirth for up to 9 months full-time or 18 months part-time, again with compensation equivalent to 90 per cent of normal earnings; one of the parents can be off work for an additional 3 months full-time or 6 months half-time or 12 months quarter-time, but at a lower, flat-rate level of compensation. This describes the situation at the end of 1988; further improvements in the length of this leave and in benefit payments to parents taking leave are being introduced between 1989–91, and are discussed below.

Parents are entitled to divide this post-natal leave between themselves as they see fit. Recent statistics show that 22 per cent of fathers had taken at least some of this leave during their child's first year, the average leave taken being one and a half months (Riksförsäkringsverket 1986). One consequence of this part of the Paid Parental Leave Act is that practically all Swedish children are at home with one of their parents until they are at least 9 months old; and that during the whole of the first year, relatively few children are placed in day care (Table 5.1).

Table 5.1 Proportion of children aged 0–3 whose mothers work outside the home, Sweden, 1986

			Child's age (months)			
	Under 9	9–11	12–17	18–23	24–35	36–47
Proportion with mothers working outside the home	8%	23%	60%	65%	65%	75%

Source: Swedish Association of Local Authorities (1987c)

The Act also gives two other employment entitlements, both intended to make it easier to combine parenthood and employment. Parents may take up to ninety days leave per year per child to provide care at home if a child or its normal caregiver are sick; and parents may also have two 'contact' days per child per year to visit the place where their children are cared for, to become better acquainted with the activities carried on and have more contact with the childcare workers. Both types of leave are covered by compensation equivalent to 90 per cent of earnings.

In addition to these rights to paid leave, parents with young children are entitled to unpaid parental leave and reduced working hours. Parents may stay at home until their child is 18 months old (that is for a further 6 months after the end of paid leave) and may take quarter time leave (a 2 hour reduction of daily working hours) until their child reaches 7.

These measures are designed to make it possible for working parents to extend the time they spend at home with their children without running the risk of losing their jobs, and to ensure that children in day care do not have to spend too long outside the home. The 1979 legislation governing the right to a 6 hour working day for parents with small children was motivated by a number of studies from the middle of the 1970s showing that half of all children under the age of 3 in municipal day care services (services provided by local authorities) spent more than 9 hours per day away from home. Children with single parents or with working-class parents spent the greatest amount of time in day care (SOU 1975). The legislation has, to a large degree, had the intended effect; the average number of hours spent in municipal day care has dropped. A 1987 survey showed that fewer than 40 per cent of all the children needing a place in municipal day care required more than 7 hours of care a day (Table 5.2).

Table 5.2 Demand for municipal day care for children under 3, Sweden, 1987

| Type of day care | Number of hours/week child needs out-of-home | | |
	1–19	*20–34*	*35 hours or more*
Nursery	5.6%	50.5%	43.1%
Childminding	19.4%	52.8%	26.7%
Total	10.9%	51.3%	36.8%

Source: Official Statistics of Sweden (1987a)

The current system of day care provision

Municipal day care

Public sector day care is very largely provided by local authorities. There are 274 of these authorities, or municipalities, varying in size from a few thousand to the capital city, Stockholm, with a population of almost one million. Care provided for children below compulsory school age is referred to as 'pre-school', and includes nurseries (*daghem*), mothers' clubs (*öppen förskola*) and kindergartens (*deltidsförskola*). At nurseries, children usually receive full-time care while their parents are employed. They vary considerably in size; the smallest have only 1 or 2 groups, the largest 7 or 8 including one or two for school-age children needing after-school care. The biggest nurseries can have up to 100 children, but this is not common. More typically, nurseries have 3 or 4 groups and around 50 or 60 children.

Some municipalities offer no places in nurseries for children under 3 and others have only a few groups for this young age group. In most municipalities, however, each nursery either has at least one group for children under 3 ('toddler groups') or groups for children under 6 ('extended sibling groups'). In certain cases, primary school children (7- to 9-year-olds) can also be included in 'extended sibling' groups, but during the 1980s there has been a tendency to remove places for school-aged children from nurseries, and instead attach groups for these older children to primary schools.

In mothers' clubs, the municipality provides premises and a pre-school teacher to support parents who are at home with their children.

77

Parents can meet other parents and get advice from the teacher, and their children can meet other children; but parents must stay with their children. At kindergartens, children are cared for in groups on a part-time basis, often 3 hours a day. They provide preparation for school and supplementary social training for children at home or with childminders. All Swedish children are entitled to places in kindergartens from the year of their sixth birthday (Swedish children do not begin school until they are 7), but many municipalities offer children places when they are only 4 or 5 years old.

Most municipalities also support organised childminding schemes (*familjedaghem*). The municipality pays the childminders (*dagmamma*) directly and parents pay the municipality. In 1970, there were 31,000 municipal childminders providing care for 44,000 children. In 1985, approximately the same number of childminders (34,000) provided for 162,000 children. One reason for this change is that an increasing number of childminders in organised schemes are working full-time and they must look after more children to earn adequate salaries. The method of payment has also changed. Previously childminders were paid according to the number of children cared for and the number of hours each child received care; if a child was away, for example because of illness, they were not paid. Now childminders get a fixed monthly salary, but on condition they look after at least four children full-time or provide the equivalent hours of care for children attending part-time; many have to look after 8–10 part-time children to get their salary. One reason so many children attend organised childminding schemes on a part-time basis is that many municipalities only admit children needing full-time care to nurseries, arguing that nursery places are too costly only to be used part-time.

A recent survey of 124 childminders from ten different munici-palities found that their average age was 38 and that they had been employed for just over six years. Three-quarters had their own small children at home and 60 per cent felt the main advantage of their job was being able to stay at home with their own children. On average, they cared for 6.4 children, including their own, and children under 3 spent 30 hours a week in their care (National Board of Health and Welfare 1988).

Local variations in municipal day care

Public support for day care in Sweden is generally high, though it varies widely between municipalities. In 1987, municipal day care was avail-able for 75 per cent or more of pre-school children with employed or studying parents in 35 municipalities, 17 of which were in two large metropolitan areas. Stockholm had the highest level of provision, covering 85 per cent of pre-school children with working or studying parents. Other municipalities with high levels of provision were mainly industrial towns (Broberg and Hwang 1988). Gothenburg, the second largest city, and the surrounding municipalities differed from this general pattern, the number of children with working parents in municipal day care being below the national average (64 per cent vs 68 per cent).

Does the political majority in a municipal council determine the level of day care? In the large metropolitan areas, there is no connection. But elsewhere, there is a high level of municipal day care only in industrial cities with a stable left-wing majority (Table 5.3).

Table 5.3 Municipalities with more than 75 per cent of children with working parents in municipal day care by type of area and political majority

Political majority 1982–88	Type of area		Total
	Metropolitan	Other regions	
Stable left	7	17	24
Stable right	7	1	8
Other	3	0	3

Source: Official Statistics of Sweden (1982, 1985)

Note:'Stable left' = municipality had left-wing majority at 1982 and 1985 elections; 'Stable right' = right-wing majority; 'Other' = majority differed at two elections or small parties held political balance.

Municipalities with the highest levels of municipal day care have emphasised nursery care (Broberg and Hwang 1988). This has been most pronounced in Stockholm – where nurseries provide 86 per cent of all municipal childcare – and its surrounding municipalities. Other municipalities, especially smaller ones, have emphasised organised childminding in their provision of municipal day care.

Private day care

The most common form of private care is childminding. Parents pay childminders directly (usually without the knowledge of the tax authorities) and the municipality does not regulate the quality of care. There are also nurseries run by parent co-operatives, where a number of parents get together to rent premises and employ one or more pre-school teachers, and by various religious or secular organisations; both receive public funds. A very few nurseries are run on a private enterprise basis, and receive no public funds. In the tables in this chapter, all these forms of care are grouped under the heading of 'private care outside the home'.

Some children are cared for in their own homes by nannies, who may live in the child's home, but most of whom only come in during the day; and some children are cared for by relatives, in the child's or relative's home.

Financing day care

The state, municipalities and employers

In the view of the national authorities, day care is a right that, in principle, may be enjoyed by all families with children if they so wish. Consequently, the cost to the individual family of a day care place must not be so high that the family is unable to exercise its right. This has led to a heavy reliance on public funds for financing day care. For the country as a whole, the state and municipalities each contribute just under half the cost of a nursery place. The state contributes just under a third of the cost of places in organised childminding schemes, the municipality just over half (Table 5.4).

Table 5.4 The annual cost of a place in municipal day care and its division between state, municipality and parents, Sweden, 1987

| | Nurseries | | Childminders | |
	Cost (SEK)	% of cost	Cost (SEK)	% of cost
State	29,100	47%	16,500	31%
Municipalities	26,800	43%	29,400	54%
Parents	6,500	10%	8,200	15%

Source: Swedish Association of Local Authorities (1987c)

Municipalities receive central government grants for day care provision via the National Board of Health and Welfare. For nursery care, this is based on a hypothetical 'normal group' of 15 children, the municipality receiving 445,000 kroner (SEK) for each such 'group'. For organised childminding, the State grant is SEK 16,500 per child in full-time care (at least 7 hours a day) and SEK 7,500 per child in part-time care. The state's share of costs is covered by the 'child care charge', a part of the social insurance contribution that all employers have to pay; at present, this 'charge' equals 2.2 per cent of employers' total salary budgets. Municipalities' day care costs are met from municipal taxes levied on companies and individuals, though none of this tax is earmarked for daycare.

Parents' contribution

Parents pay an average of 10–15 per cent of the real cost of day care in the form of direct charges (Table 5.4). A family with an average income of SEK 16,000 per month pays about SEK 1,000 per month (approximately 10 per cent of its disposable income after tax) if it has one child at a nursery; if it has two or more children at a nursery, the total charge is only marginally higher. This average figure, however, conceals large differences between municipalities, both with regard to what parents are charged (Table 5.5) and the way in which the charge is levied. Municipalities are free to decide the level of charges and how charges are determined, as long as they do not make a profit. Income-related and percentage charges are most common. Both methods vary the size of the charge according to a family's income. A small number of municipalities, however, apply a standard charge, where families pay the same regardless of income. The standard charge is most advantageous for high-income families, but for low-income families living in a municipality with a high standard charge, day care can be a major part of their household budget.

Table 5.5 Fees paid for places in municipal nurseries in different municipalities by parents with different incomes, Sweden, 1987

Income level of family	*Parental fee (SEK/month) in municipalities with:*					
	Lowest fee		*Average fee*		*Highest fee*	
	a	*b*	*a*	*b*	*a*	*b*
Low income	0	0	500	640	965	1,300
Average income	500	598	1,035	1,191	1,500	1,833
High income	500	645	1,313	1,482	2,917	3,209

Source: Swedish Association of Local Authorities (1987d)

Note: 'a' = fee if one child in day care; 'b' = fee if 2 children.

Grants to private day care

State grants are also given to nurseries run by parent co-operatives and non-profit organisations. These also receive municipal grants. These vary between municipalities; some give a grant for each place, others give start-up grants plus a rent allowance, while others provide funding for a certain number of employees. The relationship between these nurseries and their local municipality varies in other respects. In some cases, the municipality employs the staff and there is a 'joint queue' system, with parents offered places for their children in either municipal or parent co-operative nurseries, depending on where a vacancy first occurs. In other cases, parent co-operative nurseries are run quite independently.

Other forms of day care receive no public funds and are not regulated by the authorities, on the grounds that services outside the public sector are not the business of the authorities. This is the case for many private services which exist basically because of a shortage of public services.

The aims of public day care

The central government authority for social and health questions is the National Board of Health and Welfare. The Board has national responsibility for all day care services in the public sector. A recent report prepared by the Board – *Pre-school Educational Program* (National Board of Health and Welfare 1987) – and supported by the government, sets forth the different tasks of public day care. (Throughout the report, the term 'pre-school' is used to refer to nurseries and kindergartens, but in its foreword the Board writes that the *Program* 'should be seen as a guide for other childcare for children under the age of seven as regards goals and orientation', which means that childminders in organised schemes are also covered.)

Because they are the responsibility of the Board of Health and Welfare, day care services have always been more connected with and influenced by ideas and values in the health sector than by goals in the formal school sector. There has traditionally been a reluctance to introduce too much school-like activity in nurseries or kindergartens. The *Pre-School Program*, however, presents an educational role as day care's first task.

> All children have an inherent potential to develop, to learn and to
> understand the world around them. Every society strives to develop
> and pass down its culture and its basic values to the next generation
> ... The task of pre-school is, in association with the parents, to
> incorporate the children into society and thereby contribute to the
> continued existence and development of society ... Goal-oriented,
> educational activities of good quality that provide support for the
> total development of the child as well as care and fellowship,
> knowledge and experience are necessary to fulfil this task.
>
> (National Board of Health and Welfare 1987: 12)

This educational role is followed by what most people probably consider to be the primary task of day care, namely the need for safe and secure care for children whose parents are working or studying.

Pre-school should combine the tasks of providing good educational
support for the children's development as well as good care and
supervision ... Society must make it possible for people to combine
parental roles and professional roles so that even parents with small
children can participate on more equal terms in professional life
and community life in general. This necessitates a pre-school
where parents can confidently leave their children.

(National Board of Health and Welfare 1987: 12)

Swedish legislation states that municipal day care has a particular
responsibility for children with special difficulties: 'children who, for
physical, psychological, social, language or other reasons require
special support for their development shall be granted a place in pre-
school ... with priority' (Social Services Act). The *Pre-school Program*
confirms this priority: 'Pre-school is for all children, but is particularly
important for children who require special support for their development' (National Board of Health and Welfare 1987: 12).

Day care is viewed as an asset and opportunity for all children and as
'a complement to the home and the children's social and cultural environment in general'. The *Educational Program* emphasises the need
for close relationships between home and pre-school.

A prerequisite [of parents being able to leave their children with
confidence] is that the contact between the home and the
pre-school is one of trust and that it is possible for parents to feel
that they are involved in and are able to influence the activities of
the pre-school.

(National Board of Health and Welfare 1987)

As well as a clear description of the aims for public sector day care,
the *Pre-school Program* also defines the roles and responsibilities of the
various public bodies with an interest in day care.

Together with the County Administration, the National Board of
Health and Welfare has the supervisory responsibility for
pre-school and other child care ... The tasks of the National Board
of Health and Welfare include drawing up an educational program
for the pre-schools as well as other instructive material for
responsible people in the municipalities and for the staff in the
pre-schools and other child care facilities. The national authorities
are also responsible for some of the pre-school costs, for there
being staff with good basic training and for initiating and
supporting research and development.

> The Social Welfare Board [in each municipality] is responsible
> for expansion and organisation [of day care services] and for
> implementing overall goals and orientation. Riksdagen [Swedish
> Parliament] has decided that municipal guidelines for educational
> activities in pre-school should be drawn up in each municipality ...
> pre-school staff should plan, design and evaluate pre-school
> educational activities on the basis of their knowledge of the goals
> and orientation of these activities, their own group of children and
> the views of parents as well as available resources.

(National Board of Health and Welfare 1987: 9–10)

The *Pre-School Educational Program* reflects a shift in responsibility for day care from national to local level. At the end of the 1960s
and through the 1970s, municipal day care underwent a period of rapid
expansion, characterised by detailed state regulation of planning and
financing. During the 1980s however, a rapid process of deregulation
took place and the municipal authorities' confidence in their ability to
ensure day care adapted to local needs has increased. State regulation
has thus shifted towards general guidelines governing day care activities
in municipalities, combined with support for research and development.

The above quotations all come from Part One of the *Pre-School
Education Program* which deals with 'Goals'. The *Program* also includes other sections on 'Different conditions for child growth and
development', 'Content of pre-school activities', 'Educational methods
in pre-school' and 'Planning of educational activities in pre-school'.
The guidelines are general in character and the *Program* ends with a
section on how municipalities should implement the *Program*, and in
particular 'translating' the general guidelines into specific programs.

Quality in municipal nurseries

In the international debate on different forms of day care and their
effects on child development, quality of care has been attracting increasing attention (Caldwell and Bradley 1984; McCartney *et al.* 1982,
1985; Goelman, in press; Goelman and Pence, in press; Holloway and
Reichart-Ericksson, in press). The techniques used to measure quality
can be divided into two categories. There are methods designed to
measure 'structural' or formal aspects of care, for example the design of
premises; staff training, turnover and ratios; size of child groups; and
regulating controls. Dynamic aspects of quality of care involve assessing the direct interaction between adults and children, for example
what adults and children actually do together, how educational guidelines are implemented, how sensitive staff are to individual needs and

characteristics of children and staff–parent co-operation. Formal aspects of quality are relatively simple to measure and check, whereas the dynamic aspects are not as easy to study. In many cases they require methods and measures used for research in developmental psychology (for example, observations, rating scales and interviews).

In Sweden, formal aspects of the quality of nurseries are regulated by conditions for state grants to municipalities, and by advice and directives issued by the National Board of Health and Welfare.

Design of premises

The pre-school is the everyday environment of both children and adults. Consequently, the furnishings and equipment should be designed for both children and adults ... Noisy and lively activities should be able to take place at the same time as quiet and calm ... rooms should be divided in such a way that they provide acoustic screening ... It is recommended that the pre-school's grounds should measure a total of 80 [sq. m.] per place ... the National Board of Health and Welfare determines the number of places for a pre-school on the basis of a report submitted by the municipal inspector and based on a certain minimum area per children group.

These quotations, from a booklet published by the National Board of Health and Welfare (1978: 73–4), show how far the authorities were prepared to regulate in detail to guarantee that the expansion of day care did not take place at the expense of quality.

Staffing and staff training

Staff working with children under 3 must, in principle, have trained as a children's nurse or as a pre-school teacher. To train as a children's nurse, pupils must complete their 9 years of compulsory education and be at least 16 years old. The course combines theory with practice and provides a basic knowledge of child nursing and development. It lasts two years, so that a children's nurse is at least 18 years old when she begins work.

The course for pre-school teachers lasts two and a half years. It combines theory with practice, but is more theoretical, emphasising pedagogy and developmental psychology. Entrants must be at least 18 years old and have had 11 years of schooling. Many start the course after training as a children's nurse, but this is not a requirement. A newly trained teacher is at least 20–21 years old, often rather older if she has worked first as a children's nurse.

The average monthly salary in March 1987 was SEK 8,381 for children's nurses and SEK 9,225 for pre-school teachers, which can be compared to SEK 11,025 for primary school teachers (Swedish Association of Local Authorities 1987a).

National Board directives require that half the staff in each group must be pre-school teachers and half children's nurses. Due to a shortage of teachers, however, many 'toddler groups' have only one teacher and three nurses. Each centre also has a supervisor who is a qualified pre-school teacher, and a cook and assistants to clean and perform kitchen work.

Group size and staff ratios

The National Board's regulations stipulate that 'toddler groups' should consist of ten to twelve children and four staff. Until only a few years ago this was by far the most common group for children under 3, but recently there has been an increase in 'extended sibling groups' which span the whole pre-school stage. These groups should not contain more than fifteen children and should normally have three staff members; staff ratios can be higher if the group contains many children under the age of 3.

It has been the policy of Swedish authorities, in particular the National Board, to integrate children with special difficulties in ordinary nurseries, and to have people with special training or competence give these children some hours of special help or education, rather than have separate groups for children with different difficulties. Consequently there is at least one child with 'special needs' in many nursery groups. These groups often include additional personnel, 'resource persons', employed specifically to help out with children who have 'special needs'.

The latest report of the Swedish Association of Local Authorities (1987b) shows an average of one adult to 3.7 children (i.e. 4 adults per group of 15 children), including 'resource persons' but excluding supervisors and other personnel.

Responsibility for quality

The *Pre-school Education Program* summarises managerial responsibility for the activities in a municipal nursery:

> The pre-school's management organisation is the [municipality's] Social Welfare Board ... [and] the municipality's different representatives and the pre-school supervisor ... The elected representatives have the final responsibility for the pre-school's scope, quality and development. In this task, they represent the citizens, including the parents ...
>
> It is important that there is a central management for child care – and thus for the pre-school – in which both theoretical knowledge

about and practical experience from the field of child care are combined. The work of the central management should in particular embrace co-ordination as well as long-term planning and the development of activities ... The supervisor holds the managerial responsibility for education at each individual pre-school. This means, among other things, responsibility for work supervision, support and advice to the staff in order to ensure that educational planning and evaluation are carried out and that a development plan is drawn up.

(National Board of Health and Welfare 1987: 3)

New methods for the control of municipal day care

The effects of the central guidelines issued by the National Board have been unmistakable. This was shown clearly when we attempted to use American instruments to assess the quality of day care facilities in Sweden, for example the Early Childhood Environment Rating Scale (Harms and Clifford 1980). Because Swedish nurseries all satisfy the requirements described above, the ones we studied all scored at the top level of the rating scales. Swedish nurseries are thus of high quality measured against formal or structural aspects of day care quality.

As mentioned earlier, the central authorities changed their policy in the 1980s with respect to regulation of municipal activities. When the detailed regulations were abolished, the central authorities developed new methods for evaluating and controlling day care activities. In a recently published report from the Ministry of Finance (1988), an attempt was made to estimate how day care changed between 1971 and 1985. The report contains a striking emphasis on the dynamic aspects of day care quality and suggests ways in which quality would be assessed in the future. It also showed that the deregulation in the 1980s had negative effects in at least two structural aspects of quality. In many municipalities, group size has increased from 15 to 16–18 children, and physical environments have deteriorated because there is generally less space per child in new nurseries than was previously the case. This mainly reflects harsher economic circumstances and Parliament's demand that municipalities expand day care (discussed below).

Quality in organised childminding schemes

The detailed regulation of nursery care contrasts sharply with the almost total lack of central guidelines governing organised childminding schemes. Only lately has the National Board involved itself in trying to regulate and develop this type of care, partly because it is now so common. The Board, though, has become involved at a time when its ability to act firmly at national level is very limited. It is no longer possible to issue directives and regulations similar to those issued in connection with the expansion of centres in the 1970s. This is very noticeable in the Board's booklet which is intended to guide municipal planning of childminding schemes (National Board of Health and Welfare 1988).

Care is usually provided in the childminder's home (though it is also possible for three families to have a municipal employed worker care for their children in the home of one of the families). The quality of the childminder's premises and equipment therefore varies enormously, though they must all meet some minimum requirements and be approved by the municipal authorities. Childminders are also given grants to purchase toys and other equipment. Seventy per cent of the childminders in the recent survey by the National Board had received some form of childcare training. In many municipalities, introductory training (from 50 to 100 hours) is now required. In the long run, the National Board recommends that all childminders should have a training equivalent to a children's nurse.

Earlier directives issued by the National Board (1968, 1977) stated that childminders should care for a maximum of four full-time pre-school children, including their own. But this 'objective' has never become a norm, as in the case of nurseries. In part, this is because grants have never been used to enforce compliance. Current regulations governing the employment of childminders assume a minimum of four full-time children, in addition to any of the childminder's own. As already noted, many childminders care for more children, though mostly on a part-time basis.

Responsibility for the quality of organised childminding

Municipal organised childminding schemes are part of municipalities' daycare activities. They should therefore, in principle, be regulated and controlled in the same way as nurseries, except that a municipally employed childminding assistant has the responsibility and authority held by the supervisor at a nursery. The assistant's main responsibilities are to investigate, assess and choose childminders; place children; provide childminders with advice and support; organise, co-ordinate and develop activities for childminders and children.

It is increasingly common for 4 to 6 childminders to meet regularly with their children in premises used by mother's clubs or at nurseries. These meetings take place once a week or so and enable games and activities to be organised that might be unsuitable in childminders' own homes. Since the children get to know other childminders and 'their' children, it becomes easier to substitute if a childminder falls ill or needs to take time off.

Childcare arrangements for children under 3

Every year, on behalf of the Ministry for Social Affairs, the Swedish Central Bureau of Statistics (SCB) surveys how pre-school children are cared for. In 1987, the survey included a random sample of 105,000 children between the ages of 0 and 6 (Official Statistics of Sweden 1987a). More than 50 per cent of all children under the age of 3 were cared for by their parents, a third were in municipal childcare and the remaining 14 per cent in private care arrangements for example with relatives or childminders (Table 5.6). These statistics include children whose parents are still on parental leave, which distorts the findings somewhat. Many researchers (Andersson 1985; Borjesson 1986; Olsson 1987) have shown that the percentage of children cared for outside the home increases sharply after the child's first birthday, with about 50 per cent of Swedish children in some form of childcare outside the home by 18 months. SCB's statistics for the whole pre-school period (up to 7) show that changes at later ages are relatively modest. About 40 per cent receive care entirely from their parents, rather more (47 per cent) receive municipal day care, while the proportion in private care is the same as the under 3 group (13 per cent) (Table 5.6).

Table 5.6 Proportion of children in different forms of day care, Sweden, 1987

Age of children	At home	Relatives	Paid private care		Municipal care	
			At home	Outside home	Nurseries	Childminders
Under 3	53%	3%	3%	8%	19%	15%
Pre-school (0–6) total	40%	3%	3%	7%	29%	18%
Single parents	18%	3%	1%	5%	51%	23%
Two parents	43%	3%	3%	7%	27%	17%
Parents work 15+ hours/wk	14%	4%	5%	10%	42%	26%

Source: Official Statistics of Sweden (1987a)

These figures refer to all children whether or not their parents work or study. Nearly two-thirds of pre-school children have employed mothers (Table 5.7). The proportion is lower for children under 12 months and higher for older children (Table 5.1). In a study of Gothenburg, Olsson (1987) found that 76 per cent of 2- to 3-year-olds had employed mothers, while 99 per cent had employed fathers. Employed

Anders Broberg and C. Philip Hwang

fathers had longer work hours than employed mothers, many of whom had part-time jobs (Table 5.8). Nearly all employed mothers, and virtually all employed fathers do, however, work over 15 hours a week, and just over two-thirds of children with parents who work over 15 hours a week are in municipal day care, with a majority in nurseries. Some children are cared for only by their parents, leaving 18 per cent in private day care. Childminding is the most common form of private care and relatives, caring for less than 4 per cent of children, the least common (Table 5.6).

Table 5.7 Proportion of mothers with pre-school children who are employed and their hours of work, Sweden, 1987

Not working outside the home	Working outside the home for (hours/week)			
	1–15	*16–25*	*26–34*	*35 or more*
37.7%	5.6%	17.1%	19.3%	20.1%

Source: Official Statistics of Sweden (1987a)

Table 5.8 Proportion of parents with children aged 2–3 who are employed and their hours of work, Gothenburg, 1986

	Not working outside home	Working outside the home for (hours/week)			
		1–20	*21–30*	*31–40*	*40 or more*
Mothers	24%	6%	21%	26%	23%
Fathers	1%	1%	3%	3%	92%

Source: Olsson (1987)

Socio-demographic variations in usage of municipal day care

About 10 per cent of pre-school children live in single parent families. These children are much more likely to receive municipal day care, particularly in nurseries (Table 5.6), because more single parents are employed, and because their children are given priority in admission to nurseries.

By contrast, children with immigrant parents are under-represented in municipal day care. In 1986, 34,000 children under 4 (12 per cent) had immigrant parents (Official Statistics of Sweden 1987b). According to the 1987 SCB childcare survey, 5,000 of the children in municipal day care (9 per cent) had a language other than Swedish (Official Statistics of Sweden 1987a). The most common languages were Finnish, Spanish, Yugoslavian, Polish and Turkish.

90

Fjällhed (1985) compared 'current childcare arrangements' for children aged 9 to 24 months and parents' perceptions of 'ideal child care' in the three largest immigrant groups – Finns, Yugoslavs and Turks – in Gothenburg. 'Current child care' for parents from Finland did not differ from Swedish parents, but a considerably larger proportion identified 'at home with mother or father' as 'ideal'. The other two groups of immigrant parents differed from Swedish parents both for 'current' and 'ideal child care'. More than three-quarters of immigrant parents cared for their children themselves and the same proportion considered this 'ideal' (Table 5.9).

Table 5.9 Current and 'ideal' childcare arrangements for children aged 9–24 months according to birthplace of parents, Gothenburg, 1984

Birthplace of parents	Child care arrangement									
	At home		Relatives		Centre d.c.		Family d.c.		Other	
	a	b	a	b	a	b	a	b	a	b
Sweden	53%	55%	11%	2%	11%	26%	21%	8%	4%	10%
Finland	57%	75%	9%	3%	10%	12%	25%	11%	1%	0%
Yugoslavia	77%	77%	16%	6%	5%	13%	2%	2%	0%	2%
Turkey	73%	79%	20%	7%	7%	14%	0%	0%	0%	0%

Source: Fjallhed (1985).

Note: 'd.c' = day care. Column 'a' = current childcare arrangement; column 'b' = ideal arrangement

Several different surveys show a clear connection between parents' educational and occupational levels and their use of day care. The connections are clearest in the case of the youngest children. The higher the parents' educational and occupational status, the earlier they place their children in day care outside the home. For example, Andersson (1985) found that 50 per cent of 1–2-year-olds and 48 per cent of 2–3-year-olds with working-class parents were cared for in their own homes, whereas for children from middle-class homes the figures were 35 per cent and 29 per cent respectively.

Class differences in use of municipal day care have been explained in various ways. The Swedish Trade Union Confederation (LO) argues that the shortage of places and inflexible opening hours in municipal services make it difficult for working-class parents, many of whom work shifts and inconvenient hours, to use this provision (LO 1987). But a comparison between Stockholm (with well-developed services) and Gothenburg (with less developed services) shows – at least for children between the ages of 3 and 4 – that although the expansion of municipal day care in Stockholm has led to more children from working-class homes going to nurseries (39 per cent in Stockholm compared to 26 per cent in Gothenburg), the class difference remains, with an even greater difference between the two cities for children with middle-class parents; 62 per cent of middle-class children were in nurseries in Stockholm compared to 42 per cent in Gothenburg (Andersson 1985). There are no equivalent data on children under 3, but there is reason to believe that class differences are even larger among this group. A study in Gothenburg shows that many well-educated parents with children between the ages of 9 and 18 months who are not allotted a place in municipal provision make private arrangements; lower-class parents 'choose' to stay at home while waiting for a municipal day care place (Börjesson 1986).

Parents from different social classes also differ in their evaluation of day care arrangements. Working-class parents consider some form of home-based care to be ideal more often than parents from higher social classes (Liljestrom and Dahlstrom 1981; Börjesson 1986; Broberg and Hwang 1987; Olsson 1987). This suggests that the relative unwillingness of working-class parents to place their children in municipal day care has little to do with the availability of the service. More important are class differences in attitude; working-class parents place greater emphasis on the value of parenthood, have a greater desire to be close to their children and mould their development and have more doubts about the quality of collective day care (Liljestrom and Dahlström 1981; Gunnarsson *et al.* 1986).

The past and future development of the system for day care provision

The system of public day care was built up and expanded primarily after 1970 (Table 5.10), with legislation enacted in 1975 and 1977. At the same time parental leave was introduced (1974), while in 1979 legislation was introduced that gave parents of young children the right to a six-hour working day.

Table 5.10 Proportion of pre-school children (0–6 years old) in municipal day care, Sweden, 1960–85

Type of day care	Proportion of children in type of care in:					
	1960	*1965*	*1970*	*1975*	*1980*	*1985*
Nurseries	1.4%	1.5%	4.2%	8.6%	18.4%	27.6%
Childminders	0.5%	1.5%	4.0%	6.5%	12.9%	17.0%

Source: Barnmiljöradet (1987)

The political decisions necessary for the expansion of public day care provision were made possible by the economic boom during the 1960s, when labour shortages became a major threat to further economic growth. Sweden first tried to solve this problem by a massive influx of migrant workers, especially from Finland and southern Europe, and then, when this was not enough, by increasing the proportion of women in the labour force. The other major force behind the political decisions on day care was the demand for women's liberation and equality. LO and the Social Democratic, Liberal and Communist Parties all viewed the expansion of public day care as a major condition for equality between men and women.

Developments in policy have continued through the 1980s. Work on the educational program for municipal day care began under the Liberal/ Conservative government between 1979 and 1982 and was presented in 1987 by the Social Democratic government. In 1985, the Swedish Parliament laid down principles to govern the continued expansion of municipal day care. Parliament's resolution stated that all children have the right to receive municipal day care from the age of 18 months – up to which age parents are legally entitled to take leave of absence from their employment. For children whose parents work or study, the right to day care applies to the hours when such care is required (which places high demands on municipalities to satisfy the demands of shift-workers). Municipalities are obliged to provide either nursery or organised childminding care, and young children (under 3) who are offered a place in a childminder's home must also be offered a place in a mother's club. Finally, Parliament laid down that demand for municipal day care must be met by 1991.

The 1985 resolution also stated that parental leave, paid at 90 per cent of earnings, should be extended to 18 months, as soon as economic circumstances permitted. The Social Democratic government, re-elected in September 1988, is committed to implementing this extension. Parental leave paid at 90 per cent of earnings was extended to 12 months in July 1989 (in other words, converting the 3 months currently paid at a low flat rate to payment at the 90 per cent level).

Some issues concerning the day care system

Nursery care or organised childminding

Recently there has been a substantial debate on whether municipal expansion of day care should concentrate solely on the establishment of nurseries or should involve both nurseries and organised childminding schemes. This debate has been evident in a conflict between the central supervisory authority, the National Board of Health and Welfare, which has recommended that emphasis be placed on nurseries, and individual municipalities, which in many cases have emphasised the expansion of childminding.

In the government study which fostered the expansion of day care in the 1970s, the Commission on Family Support emphasised that childminding could complement nurseries during the period of expansion, when there were still insufficient places in nurseries (SOU 1972). With nursery expansion, the national authorities expected that demand for childminding would gradually diminish. In a later report, however, the Family Support Commission concluded that though 'day care centers are the backbone of child care, family day care homes [childminding] can be a good complement' (SOU 1981). The Commission suggested that childminding could best serve children living in thinly populated areas, children sensitive to infections, children who needed a single caregiver and/or a small group of children or children from immigrant families who needed to receive care from a person who could speak their own language. In the report it was also noted for the first time that 'even if most parents prefer day care centers, there are some who prefer family day care homes'.

This very cautious re-orientation has continued in recent years: that organised childminding can be a satisfactory alternative form of day care is emphasised more heavily today than previously. An example of this is *Municipal family day care homes*, published by the National Board of Health and Welfare (1988) as a complement to the *Pre-school Education Program*. This suggests a number of ways of developing childminding facilities, based on the possible advantages of this form of care including its connection with the children's neighbourhood and the participation of the childminder and her family in the neighbourhood environment; the perception of the childminder providing a home environment with everyday chores in which children and adults participate; the special opportunities for care and attention that exist in childminding; and the closeness to parents and the possibility for natural contacts between parents and childminders. One reason why municipal childminders are taken more seriously today is because they are so numerous. In spite of a very heavy expansion of nursery care, a large number of children, particularly those under 3, continue to be placed in organised childminding schemes (Table 5.6).

The professionalisation of child care

As already noted, the Swedish Trade Union Confederation has tried to explain class differences in usage of municipal childcare on grounds of inadequate availability. As a consequence, LO advocates the expansion of services, more flexible opening and closing times and the provision of 'centre night care', that is nurseries where children with parents working shifts can stay late evenings and at night. Independent experts, even those traditionally close to the labour movement, have shown that the explanation is more complex. Somewhat dramatically, two well-known sociologists summarise the problem in the following way.

What do you do with all the poorly educated, badly informed, socially conservative, traditionally female, old-fashioned Mums, cleaning ladies and working-class women who are ignorant of their own good? They want to be with their kids, have relatives look after them or solve the whole thing privately in some way! And all the while, middle-class women are taking the few available places at day care centres.

(Liljeström and Dahlström 1981: 312)

These researchers agree with Svensson (1981) that Swedish child-care has been too professionalised into what they call a 'service model', and that this has led to a weakening of childcare's roots in everyday society with its informal resources. In the view of Liljeström and Dahlström, working-class women are especially afraid of this type of development because they have learnt, by necessity, to care for and depend on informal social networks:

Many working-class households have developed a co-operation model of mutual help and exchange of services. This model is based on lengthy knowledge of the people involved and knowledge about what relationships consist of, a cultural competence inserted into a real life context of time and space. Its fellowship is to a large extent based on kinship – and that is its limitation.

(Liljeström and Dahlström 1981: 314)

The social segregation, and consequently the risk that nurseries in working-class areas will acquire bad reputations, attract more inexperienced staff, have higher staff turnover, etc., all contribute, say these researchers, to the scepticism of many working-class parents when considering whether or not to place their children in a nursery. They advocate a 'participant model' in which parents' competence and skills can be utilised and where the dividing line between 'public' and 'private' childcare becomes increasingly faint.

Nurseries run by parent co-operatives and other non-profit organisations are examples of this model. Use of these types of nurseries has recently been studied by Unenge (1988), who concludes that so far they are used even more than municipal nurseries, by middle- and upper-class parents.

Supply or demand subsidy

During the period 1973–1985 a family policy emphasising a large-scale expansion of municipal day care has been supported by a Parliamentary majority consisting mainly of Social Democrats, Liberals and Communists. The political parties supporting the expansion of public day care have, in general, agreed that day care can be beneficial for all children, including children under the age of 3, and that women's right to equality with men requires that day care be expanded. The strategy followed has been supply subsidy, using public funds to develop municipal services.

Two of the main non-Socialist parties (the Conservatives and the Centre) have voted against the expansion of municipal day care, expressing concern that the parents' role in bringing up their children has been weakened as a result of a one-sided concentration on public provision of day care. These parties also consider the present system to be economically unjust, since society supports day care only for those who have places in municipal provision, whereas parents who have not been given, or do not want, places in municipal provision for their children receive no financial support. Finally, the two parties are critical that the present funding system excludes private day care (with the exception of nurseries run by parent co-operatives and non-profit organisations). In its party platform, the Conservative Party writes:

> Parents have – and should have – the primary responsibility for the care and upbringing of their children. This presupposes that the parents themselves can choose between many different alternatives on more or less equal terms. In order to increase the freedom of choice and reduce the difference in the financial support given to municipal child care and to other child care, conditions must be improved not only for alternative day care centres but also for parents who care for their own children and those who arrange for care themselves. If the financial support given to municipal day care were cut back substantially, the parents who so wanted would be able to take care of their children themselves during the important early years of their childhood that pass so fast or be able to utilise individual child-care alternatives, adapted to their individual needs and requirements.

> (Conservative Party 1986/7: 146–7)

The Conservative Party also emphasises the injustice that results from differences in usage of municipal day care.

Only half as many large families as single-child families utilise municipal child care. Union-member families also utilise municipal child care far less than professional families, a gap that is becoming wider. The large metropolitan areas receive substantially larger grants in relation to the number of children than do the more thinly populated municipalities. But we all have to pay via local taxes and the so-called child care charge.

(Conservative Party 1986/7)

In the 1988 election, the Conservative and Liberal Parties presented a joint proposal for a child care allowance of SEK 15,000 a year for each child under 7 years of age, to be largely financed by a sharp reduction in state grants for municipal day care – a switch from supply subsidy to demand subsidy. Parents with children in municipal services would thus have to use this allowance to pay increased charges, while parents not using municipal services would gain financially. The parties argued that this proposal would reduce pressure for the expansion of day care, making it easier to comply with the Parliament resolution that municipal day care must be available on request to any child over 18 months by 1991. It was calculated that there would be a particularly large drop in demand for municipal day care for children under 3. Finally, the Conservatives and Liberals wanted to change the system to make it possible to give state grants to all private nurseries, even those not run by parent co-operatives or non-profit organisations.

The Social Democrat Party went to the polls with a commitment to extend paid parental leave and to continue expanding municipal day care to achieve the 1991 target. As already noted, this programme is now being implemented by the Social Democrat government.

Conclusion

Through legislation, the national authorities have assumed responsibility for both facilitating work and study by parents with young children and giving children whose parents work or study the right 'to grow up under reasonable conditions'. The Paid Parental Leave Act is designed to ensure that children and parents have a reasonably long period of closeness under financially secure conditions, and makes it easier for working parents to look after their children when they are ill and to have contact with their children's childcare settings. The national authorities have also fixed a date (1991) by which municipal day care must be sufficient to meet demand; and in the educational program published in 1987 have laid down the aims of Swedish pre-school services. Thus all the different parts of day care have their legal foundations and the sanctions of society. At least on paper, Sweden must be said to have a well-developed day care system.

There has been a very intense political discussion about the future shape of childcare: the previous political majority, consisting of Social Democrats, Liberals and Communists, has disintegrated, with the Liberals making proposals jointly with the Conservative Party. Yet, despite these political differences, there exists a broad political consensus as to the basic goals of family policy, namely that society must assume responsibility for making it economically possible for parents to stay at home with their children until they are at least 18 months old. There is also agreement that society must ensure that all children over 18 months who need care outside the home can obtain care of good quality.

References

Andersson, B.-E. (1985) *Familjerna och barnomsorgen (Families and childcare)*, Report No. 5, Stockholm Institute of Education, Stockholm: Department of Educational Research.

Barnmiljörådet (1987) *Barnfakta, siffror fran barns vardag (Facts about children, statistics on children's everyday life)*, Stockholm: Allmänna förlaget.

Broberg, A. and Hwang, C.-P. (1987) *Barnomsorg i Göteburg: En longitudinell studie (Child care in Gothenburg: a longitudinal study)*, Göteborg: Göteborg University, Department of Psychology.

— (1988) *Barntillsynen i Sverige: En beskrivning av det svenska familjestodet for yngre forskolebarn, med betoning på utvecklingen inom barn-omsorgen (Childcare in Sweden: a description of Swedish family policy regarding pre-schoolers with emphasis on the expansion of public day care)*, unpublished report from Göteborg University, Department of Psychology.

Borjesson, B. (1986) *Småbarnsföräldrars idealiska barnomsorg (Ideal childcare according to parents of young children)*, Göteborg: Göteborg University, Department of Psychology.

Caldwell, B.M. and Bradley, R.H. (1984) *Home Observation for Measurement of the Environment*, Little Rock: College of Education, University of Arkansas.

Conservative Party (1986/7) *Moderat partimotion till riksdagen 1986/87: So 610. Familjepolitiken (Conservative party platform 1986/7: So 610. Family policy)*, Stockholm: Riksdagstrycket.

Fjallhed, A. (1985) *Invandrarföräldrars barnomsorg – Finländare, Jugoslaver och Turkar i Göteborg (Childcare in immigrant families – Finnish, Yugoslavian and Turkish families living in Göteborg)*, unpublished report from Göteborg University, Department of Psychology.

Goelman, H. (in press) 'A study of the relationships between structure and process variables in home and day care settings on children's language development', in A. Pence (ed.) *The Practice of Ecological Research: From Concepts to Methodology*, New York: Wiley.

Goelman, H. and Pence, A.R. (in press) 'Some aspects of the relationships between family structure and child language development in three types of day care', in D.L. Peters and S. Kontos (eds) *Advances in Applied Developmental Psychology, vol. 2 Continuity and Discontinuity of Experience in Childcare*. Norwood, NJ: Ablex.

Gunnarsson, L., Lassbo, G. and Ljungvall, R. (1986) *I valet och kvalet (The hard choice)*, Göteborg: Göteborgs Socialforvaltning.

Harms, T. and Clifford, R.M. (1980) *Early Childhood Environment Rating Scale*, New York: Teachers College Press.

Holloway, S.D. and Reichart-Eriksson, M. (in press) 'The relationship of day care quality to children's free play behaviour and social problem solving skills' *Early Childhood Research Quarterly*.

Liljeström, R. and Dahlström, E. (1981) *Arbetarkvinnor i hem- arbets- och samhallsliv (Working-class women at home, at work and in social life)*. Stockholm: Tiden.

LO (1987) *Den ojämlika baromsorgen (Unequal day care)*, Stockholm: Landsorganisationen i Sverige.

McCartney, K., Scarr, S., Phillips, D. and Grajek, S. (1985) 'Day care as intervention: comparison of varying quality programs', *Journal of Applied Developmental Psychology* 6: 247–60.

McCartney, K., Scarr, S., Phillips, D., Grajek, S. and Schwartz, J.C. (1982) 'Environmental differences among day care centers and their effects on children's development', in E.F. Zigler and E.W. Gordon (eds), *Day Care: Scientific and Social Policy Issues*, Boston: Auburn House.

Ministry of Finance (1988) *Kvalitetsutvecklingen inom den kommunala barnomsorgen (Time-related development of quality within municipal day care)*, Stockholm: Allmänna förlaget.

National Board of Health and Welfare (1968) *Allmänna råd från Socialstyrelsen 1968 (General advice from the National Board of Health and Welfare 1968)*, Stockholm: Allmänna förlaget.

— (1977) *Kommunal familjedaghems-verksamhet (Municipal family day care)*, Stockholm: Allmänna förlaget.

— (1978) *Om forskolan (About pre-school)*, Stockholm: Allmänna förlaget.

— (1987) *Pedagogiskt program för förskolan (Pre-school Educational Program)*, Stockholm: Allmänna förlaget.

— (1988) *Kommunala familjedaghem (Municipal family day care homes)*, Stockholm: Allmänna förlaget.

Oakley, A. (1979) *Becoming a Mother*, London: Martin Robertson.

Official Statistics of Sweden (1982) *Allmänna valen 1982, del 2 Kommunalvalet (The general elections 1982, part 2 – local elections)*, Stockholm: National Central Bureau of Statistics.

— (1985) *Allmänna valen 1985, del 2 Kommunalvalet (The general elections 1985, part 2 – local elections)*, Stockholm: National Centre Bureau of Statistics.

Anders Broberg and C. Philip Hwang

— (1987) *Statistik over statsanställda (Statistics regarding state employees)*, Stockholm: National Central Bureau of Statistics.

— (1987a) *Barnomsorgsundersökningen 1987: Förskolebarn (0–6 å) (The day care survey 1987: Pre-schoolers (0–6 years of age))*, Stockholm: National Central Bureau of Statistics.

— (1987b) *Sveriges folkmängd. Del 3 (Sweden's population, Part 3)*, Stockholm: National Central Bureau of Statistics.

Olsson, E. (1987) *Små barns barntillsyn: utvecklingspsykologiska aspekter samt en beskrivning av 'faktisk' och 'ideal' barntillsyn hos en grupp Göteborgsbarn (The daily life of young children: aspects from developmental psychology and a description of 'actual' and 'ideal' child care among a group of children in Göteborg)*, unpublished report from Göteborg University, Department of Psychology.

Regeringens proposition (1984/85) *Förskola för alla barn (Pre-school for all children)*, Stockholm: Regeringskansliet.

Riksförsökringsverket (1986) *Föraldraforsökringen 1985 (Parental insurance 1985)*, Stockholm: Riksförsökringsverket.

Rubin, L.B. (1976) *Worlds of Pain*, New York: Basic Books.

SFS (1987) *Forordning om statsbidrag till kommunerna för barnomsorg (The edict on state grants for day care to the municipalities)*, Stockholm: Allmänna förlaget.

SOU (1967) *Samhällets barntillsyn – barnstugor och familjedaghem (Swedish Official Report: public day care – day care centres and family day care)*, Stockholm: Liber.

— (1972) *Forskolan. Del 2 – Betänkande från barnstugeutredningen (Swedish Official Report: pre-school Part 2 – report from the investigation on day care centres)*, Stockholm: Allmänna förlaget.

— (1975) *Forkortad arbetstid for småbarnsforaldrar (Swedish Official Report: reduced number of working hours for parents of young children)*, Stockholm: Allmänna förlaget.

— (1977) *Socialtjänst och socialförsäkringstillägg (Swedish Official Report: social services and social insurance)*, Stockholm: Allmänna förlaget.

— (1978) *Föräldraförsäkring – Betankande av familjestödsutredningen (Swedish Official Report: parental insurance – report from the investigation on family support)*, Stockholm: Allmänna förlaget.

— (1981) *Bra daghem for små barn – Betankande av familjestodsutredningen (Swedish Official Report: high quality centre day care for young children – report from the investigation on family support)*, Stockholm: Allmänna förlaget.

— (1982) *Förvärusbete och föräldraskap, åtgärds förslag från Jämställd-hetskommitten (Swedish Official Report: work outside the home and parenthood – suggestions from the Committee on Sexual Equality)*, Stockholm: Allmänna förlaget.

— (1982) *Enklare föräldraförsäkring (Easier parental insurance)*, Stockholm: Allmänna förlaget.

Svenning, C. and Svenning, M. (1979) *Daghemmen, jämlikheten och klassamhället (Day care centres, sexual equality and the class society)*, Lund: Liber.

Svensson, R. (1981) *Offentlig socialisation. Det nya fritidshemmet i i teori och praktik (Socialisation in public life; day care for school-aged children in theory and practice)*, Stockholm: Liber.

Swedish Association of Local Authorities (1987a) *Parternas gemensarmma löne-statistik (Joint statistics on wages)*, Stockholm: Svenska Kommunförbundet.

— (1987b) *Driftskostnadskalkyl för barnomsorgen (Calculation of the running costs for public day care)*, Stockholm: Svenska Kommunförbundet.

— (1987c) *Svensk barnomsorg: en drygrip? (Public day care in Sweden: a costly treasure?)*, Stockholm: Svenska Kommunförbundet.

— (1987d) *Det handlar inte bara om kommunalskatt: Hushållsekonomiska effekter av skillnader i avgifter, skatter och bidrag for barn-familjer och pensionärer (There is more to it than local taxation: effects on households of differences in fees, taxation and subsidies for families with children and for pensioners)*, Stockholm: Svenska Kommunförbundet.

Unenge, G. (1988) *Föräldrass medverkan och inflytande (Parental participation and influence)*, Pedagogisk Rapport, Nr. 23, Jönköping: University of Jonkoping.

Chapter six

Swedish childcare research

C. Philip Hwang, Anders Broberg and Michael E. Lamb

In contrast to countries like the UK and the USA, Sweden has general regulations concerned with staff density and training, group size, daily routines and the design of the child's environment. This does not, of course, mean that all nurseries are identical. Indeed, there are large variations in group composition, atmosphere and staff experience and working methods. These variations, however, stay within certain specified limits. If we compare nurseries and homes, it could fairly be claimed that in Sweden, the variations between different home environments are much larger than the variations between different nursery environments (Gunnarsson, Andersson and Cochran 1987). The purpose of this chapter is twofold. First, we summarise the results of Swedish childcare research. The homogeneity in childcare environments makes Sweden a comparatively easy country in which to carry out such research. The number of studies performed is also relatively large. In this review we shall only describe research involving the comparisons of different forms of childcare. Thus we do not review evaluations of curricula or syllabi, etc. Second, we present results from the Gothenburg Childcare Project, an ongoing longitudinal study of 140 children, initially aged between 11–24 months. This report deals with the first three years of the study.

A review of previous research

One of the first systematic Swedish childcare studies was carried out by Stukát in the mid-1960s. However, this study does not discuss the effects of enrolment in nurseries, but rather the influence of nursery schools on children's development. At that time, nursery schools provided the most common form of childcare in Sweden. The parents of all children starting school provided information concerning children who had applied for places in nursery schools or had actually attended nursery school. From these two groups, a number of children were selected in order to form a nursery school group and a home group. The two groups were matched with respect to the children's age, number of siblings, father's profession and where they lived. One hundred and thirty-nine matched pairs were chosen and these children were rated during their first year at school, their mothers were interviewed, and their teachers filled out a questionnaire. The result showed few differences (and large similarities) between the two groups. In the case of social and emotional development, the only somewhat unsurprising difference was that nursery school children tended to manage better by themselves. The differences were not large, however. In the case of intellectual development nursery school attendance appeared to have some favourable effects. Nursery school children tended to have better elementary knowledge and skills (e.g. oral command of language, sense of locality and vocabulary), but did not, however, perform better on school readiness tests or reading, spelling and arithmetic tests. Nor were their teachers ratings of their school performance appreciably better.

Svenning and Svenning (1979) used similar methods in their study of the effects of pre-school experience on school-age children. With the help of questionnaires sent to parents, the children were divided into six groups, depending on the type of childcare given them during their pre-school years. These groups were: nursery, family day care, family day care and nursery school, home care, home and nursery school, and a group with mixed childcare histories. The children were compared with respect to parental attitudes, achievement tests and grades. There were small differences between children with different childcare histories, but larger differences between children with different social backgrounds.

An example of one type of research that concentrates on the effects of early separation from parents is a study by Hårsman (1984). She studied the adjustment process in twenty-six infants who had been placed in nurseries between 6 and 12 months of age (the study was carried out at the beginning of the 1970s when the parental insurance scheme was not as well-developed as it is today). Matching was utilised in order to ensure that the children cared for in the home were as similar as possible as the children in centre day care with respect to age and social background. During a 5–6 month period, repeated observations were made of the children, and Hårsman reported that the children in nurseries initially showed signs of depression. After about two months, however, these signs of depression began to disappear and after five months there was no difference between the groups. Using the Griffiths developmental test (Griffiths 1954), Hårsman also found differences on the personal-social sub-scale favouring children cared for at home. Children in day care were more clinging than children cared for at home. One interpretation of these results is that the enrolment of children in nurseries at an early age exposes them to stress and makes excessive demands on their ability to adapt. The results do not, however, say anything about possible long-term effects. Hårsman also found large individual differences in the nursery children's ability to adapt. Some children recovered fairly quickly while others had still not done so at the end of the study.

A shortcoming of Swedish childcare studies is that few have follow-up times of more than two years. One of the first longitudinal studies was carried out by Söderlund (1975) who studied a group 7–9-month-olds in Stockholm who had yet to experience any form of childcare outside the home. From these children, a group was formed whose members continued to be cared for in the home. This group was compared with a group of children who received care from childminders and a group of children who were placed in nurseries. The children were assessed with the Griffiths scale before they were placed in organised childcare and again when they were 18 to 24 months old. Söderlund reported that children in nursery achieved higher scores on the motor development scale, but not the other sub-scales, than did children with childminders or at home.

In a follow-up study five years later, Rudebrant and Thörn (1979) found that almost half of the children had transferred to a different form of childcare. Four groups of twelve children were then selected. Three of the groups comprised children with stable childcare histories: i.e. children cared for in only the home, children continuously in nursery, and children continuously enrolled with childminders. The fourth group consisted of children with experience of different forms of childcare. On the Griffiths development scale, the children who experienced a variety of forms of care had the lowest score, but since the groups were small, one must be cautious when interpreting the results. In addition, the differences between the groups were extremely small.

One of the most comprehensive Swedish longitudinal studies was carried out by Cochran and Gunnarsson (Cochran 1977; Gunnarsson 1978; Larner 1982; Cochran and Gunnarsson 1985). This study is also of interest because the researchers used methods that made it possible to compare their results with the results of studies conducted outside Sweden. The research focused on sixty children who had been in nursery since one year of age. Their development at five years of age was compared with that of sixty children who had either been cared for in the home or in family day care. Yet another follow-up study was carried out when the children were 9 to 10 years old.

At the age of one, no differences were observed between the children in different forms of care. Nor were there any group differences in the emotional closeness of the mothers and children. The results obtained from the later follow-up studies also showed very small differences between the groups, which were much smaller than the differences within the groups, of which gender differences were the most pronounced. Girls cared for in homes were more 'obedient' while the girls in nurseries was more likely to manipulate adults in order to get their own way, and in this respect, they were similar to the boys cared for in homes. The boys in nurseries were by far the most peer-oriented group, and they had very little contact with adults. One shortcoming of this study is that no distinction is made between children cared for in homes by their parents and those cared for by childminders; they are regarded as a single group. Another shortcoming is that children in nursery were only studied in the nursery environment and the children cared for in the home were only studied in the home environment.

Finally, Andersson and his colleagues (1986) carried out a longitudinal study of 119 children spanning the entire pre-school period. The study, which was influenced theoretically by Bronfenbrenner's (1979) ecological orientation, does not focus particularly on childcare environments as such; rather, it regards these environments among many significant ecological factors influencing the conditions under which children grow up. When the children were approaching their eighth birthday, their teachers were asked to assess their cognitive and social competence and the children were given verbal and non-verbal aptitude tests. Andersson reported that children who were placed in childcare before one year of age, whether in nursery or with childminders, had developed more favourably in verbal ability, and they were rated as having more verbal facility, and also as more persistent, independent, and confident and less anxious than children cared for at home, or children placed in day care after one year of age.

In sum, it is difficult to provide a conclusive summary of Swedish childcare research. Several of the studies are limited as regards research design, samples studied and research methodology. In only one of the studies described above, for example, were measurements taken both before and after the children had been placed in childcare. Apart from Andersson (1986), few researchers have attempted to take into account other factors that might affect the child (social background, traumatic events in the child's earlier life, etc.). Finally, measurements of the effects are often limited and comparisons difficult with studies in other countries.

The Gothenburg Childcare Project

The aim of this project was to deal with the limitations described earlier as far as possible. More specifically, the purpose of the project was to assess the effects of out-of-home care, in the context of other important life and family circumstances, on several aspects of social, personality and intellectual development. Among the potential influences considered were the nature and quality of in-home and out-of-home care, perceived social support, socio-economic status, and the child's temperament.

The sample consisted of 140 first born children (70 girls) from Gothenburg (Sweden), with no previous experience of out-of-home care. They ranged in age from 11 to 24 months (mean = 15.9 months; sd = 2.9 months) at the time of initial contact. The names of two-parent families were obtained from waiting lists for day care facilities. Parents were then individually contacted by the research staff and invited to participate in the research: 75 per cent of those contacted agreed to participate. The families came from a range of middle-class backgrounds. The representativeness of the children in our sample was determined by comparing their characteristics with those of a representative sample consisting of 10 per cent of all 10- to 24-month-old children in Gothenburg (Broberg and Hwang 1987). With respect to maternal and paternal occupational status, parental ages, the families with children in our home-care and day-care groups did not differ from families with these care arrangements in the larger sample. However, the children in our childminding group had parents who had significantly higher occupational status than childminded children in the city. The reasons for this are not clear.

Methods

Although all of the subjects were drawn from waiting lists for nurseries, the shortage of places meant that the majority could not be accommodated. Some remained in the full-time care of their parents; others were able to obtain childminders. Subjects were thus divided into three groups; nursery (n = 53), childminder care (n = 33), and home care (n = 54). In each case, the parents had placed their children on the waiting list for nurseries, the most popular form of care in Sweden. Children from single-parent families, those with siblings in day care, and those from families facing economic hardship are given priority by the public authorities assigning children to the few available openings. Single-parent families and non-primiparous families were excluded from this study, and a few of the names we obtained were of people in economic distress, so the key factor determining whether the parents obtained the desired assignment was geographic. Did a vacancy occur in their neighbourhood for a child of the appropriate age and sex? In some cases a vacancy became available first with a childminder, and many parents accepted this alternative in preference to waiting for a new placement. When no vacancies occurred, the parents had to provide care at home.

After agreeing to participate in the study, all families were visited in their homes. During this visit, parents were interviewed about their education and occupations, their social networks, father involvement and child temperament. The child's initial response to the visiting adult was also scored and the HOME inventory (Caldwell 1970) was completed. On a second visit, the child was observed interacting at home for 30 minutes with a familiar peer (selected by the parents) of roughly the same age. Those children in one of the alternative care groups began out-of-home care within two weeks of the two home visits. Six weeks later their childcare facilities were visited by a member of research staff who rated the quality of care using Belsky and Walker's (1980) checklist.

Both one and two years after the first interview the families were visited again. During one visit, stranger sociability was again assessed, parents were interviewed about childcare arrangements, and the mothers completed a Q-sort description of their child measuring field independence, ego resilience, and ego control (the California child Q-sort or CCQ), and the quality of home care was sampled using Belsky and Walker's checklist and the HOME inventory. During a second visit, the child was again observed interacting for 30 minutes with a familiar peer, and again quality of home care was sampled using Belsky and Walker's checklist and the HOME inventory. On a subsequent visit to the childcare facility, the quality of care was sampled and a teacher who knew the child well, described her/his personality using the CCQ. Psychologists administered the Griffiths developmental scales, usually in the children's home. Further information is available in the original research reports (Lamb *et al.* 1988, 1989; Broberg *et al.* 1989). Of the 140 children remaining in the study, 115 maintained the original care arrangement until they were 3–4 years old, while 84 maintained the same arrangement throughout. Most children who changed arrangements either changed from family day care to nursery or, because a sibling was born, some children changed from family day care or nursery to home care. There were no significant differences between children and families who changed arrangements and others.

Measures

Social class Hollingshead (1975) scores – weighted sums of the education and occupation scores for each parent – were computed.
The quality of home care was tapped using four measures in each phase: HOME inventory, Belsky and Walker's (1980) checklist (both positive events and negative events scores), and a measure of father involvement. The 45 items of the HOME inventory measure the stimulation available in the home environment. The Belsky and Walker checklist includes 13 positive and 7 negative events, and the observer notes which occur during a 3-minute period. These were averaged over 3 to 4 periods

for analysis, as described in Belsky and Walker (1980).

Paternal involvement was estimated from the full-day diary recalls provided by the two parents, who were asked to recall the previous day and the previous non-working day from midnight to midnight.

Social support During the initial interview, mothers and fathers were asked independently about contacts with and support received from maternal and paternal grandparents, other relatives, friends, and neighbours. Three different measures were then computed for each parent: perceived support from maternal grandparents, from paternal grandparents and from friends and neighbours.

Quality of alternative care settings The quality of care provided in the alternative care setting was also assessed using the Belsky and Walker checklist. The alternative care settings were assessed three times; 3, 12 and 24 months after enrolment.

Child temperament was assessed using Rothbart's (1981) Infant Behaviour Questionnaire (IBQ). Following Frodi, Lamb, Hwang, Frodi, Forsström and Corry (1982), we computed a score of perceived difficulty for analyses.

Sociability was, in the initial phase, assessed upon the interviewer's arrival at the child's home as described by Stevenson and Lamb (1979).

Child personality The child's score for field independence, ego resilience and ego control were computed by correlating the ratings assigned by the mothers or care providers on the 100-item CCQ.

Peer skills The children were observed interacting at home with familiar peers in each phase. The 30-minute peer interaction sessions were divided into consecutive 15-second observation units, followed by 15-second breaks for data entry. For each observation unit, the observer recorded the incidence of any of 23 discrete behaviours or states and also rated the quality of the peer play using Howes' (1980) 6-point rating scale. Three peer interaction scores were derived: positive peer-related behaviours (the sum of the incidences of initiate play, imitate, vocalise, touch, proffer, accept and laugh); negative peer-directed behaviours (the composite total for reject bid, turn away, take away toy, take toy from, have toy taken from, throw, defensive struggle, offensive struggle, strike/hit and cry) and a measure of reciprocal play.

Intellectual development We used scale C of the Griffiths developmental scales. Further details are provided by Griffiths (1970) and Alin-Åkerman and Nordberg (1980). All scores are converted into developmental quotients to adjust for age.

Reliability All observations (peer interaction, sociability, quality of care indexes) were conducted by one of three individuals who trained together using videotapes and pilot subjects until achieving high reliability. For the peer interaction and HOME inventory codes, the criterion was set at 80 per cent exact agreement; for sociability and the Belsky and Walker items, the criterion was 90 per cent. It was impossible to keep observers blind with respect to the group status of the children, but they were not aware of the explanatory model guiding the research, nor of the expectation that group differences would not be significant.

Data analysis strategy

The determinants of individual differences in child characteristics and competencies one year after some of the subjects were enrolled in out-of-home care was assessed using the technique of 'soft modelling' or partial least squares (PLS). This tool, developed by Wold (1975) and Jöreskog and Wold (1982), is intended as an alternative to LISREL in the exploration of complex social phenomena that have been measured indirectly. Like LISREL, PLS summarises patterns of correlation among multiple measures of multiple constructs, of which some are 'determinants' and some 'outcomes' of unobservable processes. An elementary description of PLS is provided by Bookstein (1986). In Figure 6.1 the models tested using PLS analyses are depicted, with variables grouped conceptually in terms of their presumed inter-relations. Group status was not expected to be important, but quality of care, and the factors discussed above, were expected to be influential.

Results

Preliminary analyses of variance revealed that children with child-minders were younger, came from families of higher social status, and were rated less ego-controlled at 3–4 years than were children in the other two groups. Analyses of the alternative care measures revealed that the nurseries received higher scores than the childminders on the Belsky and Walker positive and negative indices for both the first and second assessment phases. These differences were predictable in the light of the greater number of children in nurseries and are not important in the context of the within-group analyses emphasised below. On average, nursery children received more hours of alternate care per week than children in the childminder group. Viewed together, these results indicate that type of childcare, as predicted, had little effect on the children in this study. Overall, the results suggest that children in the three groups were more similar than different, and came from similar backgrounds, although the children in the family day care group came from higher social class backgrounds. Having demonstrated that group status was not a major determinant of individual differences among children, we next turned our attention to identifying the factors that were influential. We considered separately social and intellectual competence.

Figure 6.1 The proposed model depicting the 'determinants' and 'outcomes' included in the analyses

DETERMINANTS

CHILD AGE

CHILD GENDER

INFANT DIFFICULTY

HOME BACKGROUND
Father's Hollingshead I
Mother's Hollingshead I
Belsky and Walker Positive I, II, III
Belsky and Walker Negative I, II, III

HOME – Total, I, II, III

SUPPORT I:
Maternal Grandparents (father)
Maternal Grandparents (mother)
Paternal Grandparents (mother)
Paternal Grandparents (father)
Friends/Neighbours (mother)
Friends/Neighbours (father)

FATHER INVOLVEMENT I, II, III

GROUP
Home/Family/Day Care/Centre Care

SOCIABILITY with strange adult, I, II

PEER PLAY: I, II
Howes, Sum 3-5
Pos. Peer Bids
Neg. Peer Bids

**QUALITY OF ALTERNATIVE CARE
I, II, III**
Belsky and Walker Positive
Belsky and Walker Negative
Hours/Week of Alternative Care
Group Size
Child/Caregiver Ratio
Age Range
Age Mixture

OUTCOMES

PEER PLAY-III
Howes, Sum 3-5
Positive peer bids
Negative peer bids

SOCIABILITY with
Strange Adult, III

PERSONALITY: II, III
Field Independence, Mother
 Ego Resiliency, Mother
Ego Undercontrol, Mother
 Field Independence, Care providers
 Ego Resiliency, Careproviders
 Ego Undercontrol, Careproviders

INTELLECTUAL COMPETENCE

Figure 6.2 Study 1 determinants of Phase III personality ratings

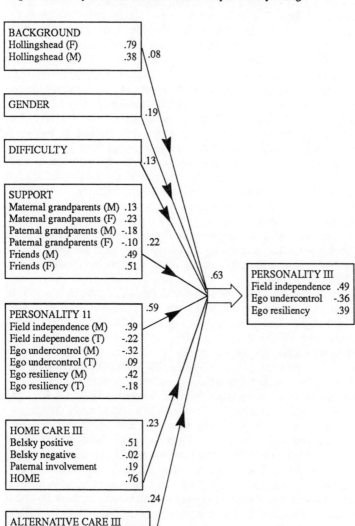

Note: M indicates that the information pertains to mother, F that it pertains to father. T indicates that the information was provided by the teacher or alternative care provider. Group status had no explanatory value and so is not included in the figure.

Social competence

PLS analyses identified a fairly strong model in which several of the determinants identified in Figure 6.1 were significantly related to the personality outcome variables assessed at 3–4 years. Figure 6.2 summarises the predictive model examining the determinants of personality ratings at 3–4 years for the eighty-four children with consistent care histories. It shows that the latent variables support, quality of home care at 3–4 years, and quality of alternative care at 3–4 years all helped explain equivalent proportions of the variance in the personality ratings, with the personality at age 2–3 being, by far, the most predictive. More mature ratings on the personality Q-sort were obtained at 3–4 years when the children had received more mature ratings from the mothers at 2–3 years, when parents reported higher levels of support (especially from friends and neighbours), when the home was more stimulating and fathers were more involved, and when the quality of alternative care was poorer. When the earlier personality ratings were excluded from the model, the net R fell from 0.63 to 0.46 but the relative importance of the other latent variables was unchanged. Again, this probably reflects the fact that the earlier personality characteristics were themselves predicted by variations in family background, support and quality of care (see Lamb *et al.* 1988).

When the model was recomputed with the larger sample (n = 115) of children who maintained the same care arrangements through at least the first two years, the predictive importance of the quality of alternative care and support latent variables fell to 0.16 and 0.15 respectively, whereas the coefficient for personality at 2–3 years rose to 0.67. The net R for the model rose to 0.68. Coefficients within the alternative care latent variable changed dramatically, such that positive Belsky scores and hours per week were positively and substantially (R's = 0.62 and 0.77 respectively) associated with more mature personality ratings.

PLS analyses showed that the peer play and sociability measures tapped constructs that were quite independent of those tapped by the personality latent variables. The relevant model for the social skills outcomes is depicted in Figure 6.3. The net R for the combined prediction was a respectable 0.64. Inspection of the figure indicates the quality of home care, the quality of out-of-home care, social skills at 2–3 years and gender all contributed significantly to observed social skills at 3–4 years, whereas social class and support had modest associations.

Day care experience was unrelated to social skills. Children who were more sociable and playful with both peers and unfamiliar adults came from homes receiving higher scores on HOME inventory and had less involved fathers. They also spent more time in non-parental care facilities characterised by low scores on both the positive and negative

Figure 6.3 Study 1 determinants of Phase III social skills

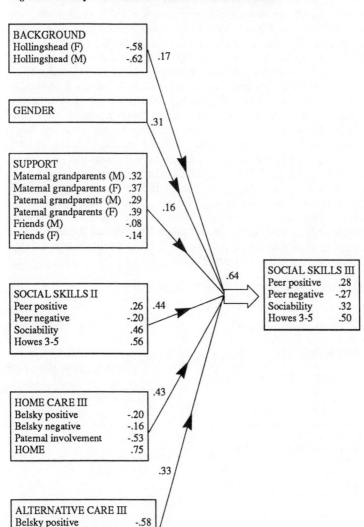

Note: M indicates that mother was the respondent, F that father was. Difficulty had no explanatory value and so it is not included in this figure.

scales of the Belsky and Walker checklist. Girls were more sociable than boys. The prediction by gender, quality of home care and quality of alternative care remained substantial (net R = 0.57) even when prior social skills were not included in the model. As Figure 6.3 shows, previous social skills scores were the best predictor of individual differences in social skills at 3–4 years. This indicates that the auto-correlation between successive measures of social skills is substantial, but that knowledge of prior social skills does not much enhance the degree of prediction achieved using the other predictor variables alone. Presumably this is because scores on the earlier measures of child social skills are themselves determined by variables in this group of determinants – including gender, quality of home care and quality of alternative care (see Lamb *et al.* 1988). When the model was computed again using the sample (n = 115) of children who had remained in the same group through the first two years, the coefficients were very similar (R = 0.63), although the relative importance of the hours per week variable within quality of alternative care latent variable decreased from a coefficient of 0.38 to 0.10, the gender latent variable had a coefficient of only 0.16, while that for support rose to 0.21. In neither model did type of care have any impact on social skills.

Figure 6.4 Best predictors of Phase III Griffiths scores

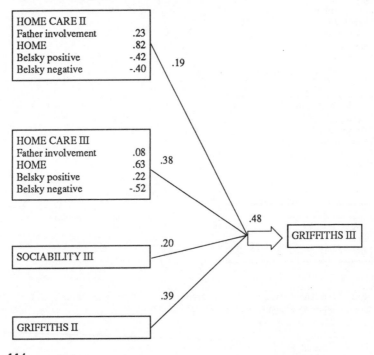

Intellectual competence

In Figure 6.4 we show determinants of the Griffiths scores at 3–4 years. The best predictors of intellectual performance were the contemporaneous and earlier measures of the quality of home care and the contemporaneous rating of the child's sociability. Although the initial quality of home care scores were significantly correlated with scores on the Griffiths assessment at 3–4 years, their inclusion added little, so, for clarity, these measures are not included in Figure 6.4. Inclusion of the contemporaneous measures of out-of-home care, family background, perceived support and initial individual characteristics raised the net R marginally (a maximum of 0.05), but none of these variables contributed substantially to the prediction of Griffiths scores and thus are not included.

Besides previous level of Griffiths scores, the best predictors of developmental status at both ages were the quality of home care and (to a lesser extent) the sociability of the child. It is also worth noting that socio-economic background did not make a significant contribution, and that the correlations between the three quality-of-home-care variables and the family background variable were generally modest. This indicates that quality of care is not simply a proxy index of socio-economic status.

Summary and discussion

Enrolment in alternative care following exclusive parental care at home for an average of 18 months did not significantly affect either observed social skills or personality, which is consistent with a number of studies, in and out of Sweden, indicating that out-of-home care beginning in the second year of life does not have a consistent effect on social competence (Cochran 1977; Gunnarsson 1978; Clarke-Stewart and Fein 1983; Cochran and Gunnarsson 1985; Scarr and Dunn 1985). Although some researchers have reported that out-of-home care experiences positively influence the degree of involvement with peers (Finkelstein *et al.* 1978; Harper and Huie 1985; Schindler *et al.* 1987), a finding that we were unable to replicate in this sample of Swedish pre-schoolers.

We expected that quality of care would be much more predictive than type of care, and this was indeed the case. The results show that the quality of care received both at home and in alternative care settings was influential, as were reported social support, prior competence and gender. In the analyses reported here, the quality of home care had a significant impact both on social skills and reported personality traits. However, this was the case with regard to the quality of home care at 3–4 years. The most consistently informative variable was the score on

Caldwell's HOME inventory; coefficients for Belsky and Walker checklist scores tended to be both more modest and inconsistent.

Vandell, Henderson and Wilson (1987), in a study in the USA, found that the quality of care experienced by twenty 4-year-olds was related to ratings of empathy, social competence and social acceptance four years later. In a study of 3-, 4-, and 5-year-old American children, Kontos (1987) reported that the quality of alternative care had little impact, whereas family background characteristics had larger impact on measures of intellectual and language development. Similarly, in earlier analyses involving assessments at 28 months on our data from the complete sample, Lamb *et al.* (1988) reported that the quality of alternative care, as assessed by non-structural measures, had no significant impact on social competence. By contrast, the analyses reported here revealed associations between quality of alternative care and personality. Personality maturity was facilitated by greater numbers of hours in out-of-home care, by lower scores on the Belsky positive index, and by higher scores on the Belsky negative index. This raises questions about the validity, at least in Sweden, of the Belsky and Walker checklists as measures of quality of care.

Social support had a modest association with child outcomes (especially when personality maturity was the outcome measure), but it was not possible to specify the type of support that was most influential. The generally positive influence of available social support is consistent with research which has demonstrated that high levels of available support enhance the quality of parental behaviour (e.g. Crockenberg 1981) and our results indicate that this may in turn have a desirable impact on children's personality maturity.

Concerning intellectual development, we confirmed the association with quality of home care consistently found in the USA (e.g. Caldwell and Bradley 1984). Our findings thus demonstrate once again the validity of Caldwell's scales, including a composite score comprising 25 of the 55 items on the pre-school version of the HOME inventory. The correlations between contemporaneous measures of home care and intellectual performance obtained in our study were just under 0.40 compared with coefficients of around 0.55 obtained in Caldwell's prior research with heterogeneous samples in the USA. On this account, therefore, our results are consistent with, although weaker than, results previously obtained. Knowledge of the quality of home care provided the best basis for prediction of intellectual competence in children averaging 28 and 40 months of age. In the case of 40-month-olds, knowledge of earlier cognitive competence provided nearly as good information, but knowledge of both sorts of information did not significantly increase the degree to which intellectual performance could be predicted. Presumably the measurable impact of quality of home care would have been even more substantial had there been greater variability in home care, as we found less variability than Caldwell and Bradley (1984). Despite this, however, the HOME inventory was the most useful source of data on the quality of home care.

Our results underscored the formative impact of the quality of home care and indicated that neither the type nor the quality of out-of-home care were important for intellectual outcomes. These findings appear at variance with results reported by both McCartney and her colleagues (1982) and Goelman and Pence (1987), in Bermuda and Canada respectively, who found a sizable association between the quality of out-of-home care and intellectual/linguistic development in children. The divergence between their findings and ours may disappear when we re-examine the quality of alternative care. It is also possible that threshold effects are involved, such that the quality of alternative care is influential only when it falls below a threshold. As was described in the previous chapter, alternative care facilities are generally of high quality in Sweden. It is conceivable that most of these facilities in the study provide at least adequate (supra-threshold) quality for the children.

In sum, our findings are consistent with those of other recent Swedish research by Cochran and Gunnarsson and Andersson and confirmed previous findings that enrolment in out-of-home care during the second year of life does not have clearcut effects on diverse aspects of children's development. Whether or not such experiences are influential – either positively or negatively – may in part depend on the quality of care received, and regardless of the quality of alternative care, the quality of care received from parents at home remains most influential. Other factors proved influential in one or more of the analyses reported here, but it was clear that the quality-of-care variables were the most important. It was also clear, unfortunately, that the quality of alternative care is a slippery and multifaceted construct that requires careful measurement and interpretation to be understood properly. Our ongoing research aims to improve the assessment of the quality of home and alternative care.

References

Alin-Åkerman, B. and Nordberg, L. (1980) *Griffiths utvecklingsskalor I och II*, Stockholm: Psykologiförlaget.
Andersson, B.E. (1986) *Home Care or External Care*, Report No. 2 from the Stockholm Institute of Education.
Belsky, J. and Walker, A. (1980) 'Infant-toddler center spot observation system', unpublished manuscript, Department of Individual and Family Studies, Pennsylvania State University, University Park, PA 16802.
Bookstein, F.L. (1986) 'The elements of latent variable models: A cautionary

lecture', in M.E. Lamb, A.L. Brown and B. Rogoff (eds) *Advances in Developmental Psychology*, vol. 4 (pp. 203–30), Hillsdale, NJ: Erlbaum.

Broberg, A. & Hwang, C.-P. (1987) *Barnomsorg i Göteborg: en longitudinell studie*, Rapport No. 5/1987, Göteborg: Department of Psychology, University of Göteborg.

Broberg, A., Hwang, C.-P., Lamb, M.E. and Ketterlinus, R. (1989) 'Child care effects on socioemotional and intellectual competence in Swedish preschoolers', in J.S. Lande, S. Scarr and N. Gunzenhauser (eds) *Caring for Children: Challenge to America*, Hillsdale, NJ: Erlbaum.

Bronfenbrenner, U. (1979) *The Ecology of Human Development*, Cambridge, MA: Harvard University Press.

Caldwell, B.M. (1970) 'Instruction manual: HOME inventory for infants', unpublished manuscript (obtained from the author, Department of Early Childhood Education, University of Arkansas, Little Rock).

Caldwell, B.M. and Bradley, R.H. (1984) *Home Observation for Measurement of the Environment* (Rev. edn), Little Rock, Ark: College of Education, University of Arkansas.

Clarke-Stewart, K.A. and Fein, G.C. (1983) 'Early childhood programs', in M.M. Haith and J.J. Campos (eds) *Infancy and Developmental Psychobiology* (pp. 917–99), vol. II in P.H. Mussen (gen. ed.) *Handbook of Child Psychology*, New York: Wiley.

Cochran, M.M. (1977) 'A comparison of group day and family child-rearing patterns in Sweden', *Child Development* 48: 702–7.

Cochran, M. and Gunnarsson, L. (1985) 'A follow-up study of group day care and family-based childrearing patterns', *Journal of Marriage and the Family* 47: 297–309.

Crockenberg, S.B. (1981) 'Infant irritability, mother responsiveness, and social support influences on the security of infant-mother attachment', *Child Development* 52: 857–65.

Finkelstein, N.W., Dent, C., Gallagher, K. and Ramey, C.T. (1978) 'Social behaviour of infants and toddlers in a day care environment', *Developmental Psychology* 14: 257–62.

Frodi, A.M., Lamb, M.E., Hwang, C.P., Frodi, M., Forström, B. and Corry, T. (1982) 'Stability and change in parental attitudes following an infant's birth into traditional and nontraditional Swedish families', *Scandinavian Journal of Psychology* 23: 53–62.

Goelman, H. and Pence, A.R. (1987) 'Some aspects of the relationships between family structure and child language development in three types of day care', in D.L. Peters and S. Kontos (eds) *Advances in Applied Developmental Psychology*, Vol. 2. *Continuity and Discontinuity of Experience in Child Care*, Norwood, NJ: Ablex.

Griffiths, R. (1954) *The Abilities of Babies*, London; University of London Press.

— (1970) *The Abilities of Young Children*, London: University of London Press.

Gunnarsson, L. (1978) *Children in Day Care and Family Care in Sweden – A Follow-up*, Research Bulletin No. 21, Department of Educational Research, University of Gothenburg.

Swedish childcare research

Gunnarsson, L., Andersson, B.E. and Cochran, M. (1987) 'Barnomsorg utanför hemmet-forskning kring utvecklingseffekter', in H. Dahlgren, L. Gunnarsson and G. Kärrby (eds) *Barnets väg genom förskola, skola och in i vuxenlivet*, Lund; Studentlitteratur.

Harper, L.V. and Huie, K.S. (1985) 'The effects of prior group experience, age, and familiarity on the quality and organization of preschoolers' social relationships', *Child Development* 56: 704–17.

Hollingshead, A.B. (1975) *The Four Factor Index of Social Position*, manuscript available from the Department of Sociology, Yale University, New Haven, Ct 06520.

Howes, C. (1980) 'Peer play scale as an index of complexity of peer interaction', *Developmental Psychology* 16: 371–2.

Hårsman, I. (1984) 'The emotional and social adjustment of infants to Day Care Centers', paper presented at the International Conference on Infant Studies, April 5–8 New York.

Jöreskog, K.G. and Wold, H. (eds) (1982) *Systems Under Indirect Observation: Causality, Structure, Prediction* (vols. 1 and 2), Amsterdam: North Holland.

Kontos, S.J. (1987, April) 'Day care quality, family background, and children's development', paper presented to the Society for Research in Child Development, Baltimore, Md.

Lamb, M.E., Hwang, C.-P., Bookstein, F.L., Broberg, A., Hult, G. and Frodi, M. (1988) 'The development of social competence in Swedish preschoolers', *Developmental Psychology* 24: 58–70.

Lamb, M.E., Hwang, C.-P., Broberg, A. and Bookstein, F.L. (1988) 'The effects of out-of-home care on the development of social competence in Sweden: a longitudinal study', *Early Childhood Research Quarterly* 3: 379–402.

Larner, M. (1982) 'Effects of day care on social development', Cornell University, unpublished manuscript.

McCartney, K. (1984) 'Effects of quality of day care environment on children's language development', *Developmental Psychology* 20: 1265–77.

Rothbart, M. (1981) 'Measurement of temperament in infancy', *Child Development*, 52: 569–78.

Rudebrandt, S. and Thörn, S. (1979) *Barn på daghem, familjedaghem och hemma – en uppföljningsstudie*, Rapport 6, Institutionen för Pedagogik, Högskolan för lärarutbildning i Stockholm.

Scarr, S. and Dunn, J. (1985) *Mother Care/Other Care*, New York: Basic Books.

Schindler, P.J., Moely, B.E. and Frank, A.L. (1987) 'Time in day care and social participation of young children', *Developmental Psychology* 23: 255–61.

Söderlund, A. (1975) *Spädbarn på daghem, familjedaghem och hemma. Spädbarns utveckling i tre tillsynsformer-en jämförelse*, Rapport 14, Institutionen för Pedagogik, Höskolan för lärarutbildning i Stockholm.

Stevenson, M.B. and Lamb, M.E. (1979) 'Effects of infant sociability and the caretaking environment on infant cognitive performance', *Child*

Development 50: 340–9.

Stukat, K.-G. (1966) *Leskolans inverkan på barns utveckling*, Stockholm: Almqvist & Wiksell.

Svenning, C. and Svenning, M. (1979) *Daghemmen, Jämlikheten och Klassamhället*, Lund: Liber Läromedel.

Thompson, R.A. and Lamb, M.E. (1983) 'Security of attachment and stranger sociability in infancy', *Developmental Psychology* 19: 184–91.

Vandell, D.L., Henderson, U.K. and Wilson, K.W. (1987, April) 'A follow-up study of children in excellent, moderate and poor quality day care', paper presented to the Society for Research in Child Development, Baltimore, Md.

Wold, H. (1975) 'Path models with latent variables: the NIPALS approach', in H.M. Blalock, F.M. Borodkin, R. Boudon and V. Capecchi (eds) *Quantitative Sociology: International Perspectives on Mathematical and Statistical Modeling* (pp. 307–57), New York: Academic Press.

Chapter seven

Day care for young children in the United Kingdom

Peter Moss

The day care situation in the United Kingdom has been remarkably stable since the end of the Second World War brought a return of women to the home from wartime jobs and a closure of many nurseries. Since then, most young children have been cared for at home by their mothers. Most employed mothers have had part-time jobs with care provided mainly by fathers and relatives; for the rest, private childminders have been the main form of care. Successive governments have avoided involvement in the provision of day care for employed parents, limiting public provision to children or families with special 'welfare' needs.

Very recently however signs of change have appeared. An impending labour shortage in the 1990s has created a sudden interest in the employment potential of women with young children. A substantial increase in maternal employment rates seems likely. Day care has become an issue, with the prospect of a large-scale increase in the numbers of young children requiring day care in the 1990s.

Employment entitlements for parents

By European standards, the UK offers a long period of statutory maternity leave – 11 weeks before birth and 29 weeks after. Most women who resume employment after maternity leave, however, do so before the end of the leave period, on average between 4 and 5 months after giving birth (Daniel 1980; Moss and Brannen 1987), partly because less than half of the leave period is covered by any benefit payments, and then mostly at a low, flat-rate rather than on an earnings-related basis. To qualify for leave, women who work more than 16 hours a week must have been with the same employer for at least two years, while those employed for between 8 and 16 hours a week need to have had continuous employment for five years with the same employer. Because of this, and other restrictions, many women, particularly those in lower-skill manual jobs, do not qualify for statutory leave (Daniel 1980).

There are no other statutory employment entitlements for parents, such as parental leave or leave for family reasons.

The current system of day care provision

Publicly-funded day care

Public sector involvement in day care provision is limited. There is no system of demand subsidy, through cash grants, vouchers or tax relief. Indeed, until a change in the 1990 Budget, the UK was unique in taxing employees using nurseries which were subsidised by their employers, the employer subsidy being regarded as a taxable benefit.

Support for services from public funds is through supply subsidy. Publicly-funded services mainly consist of nurseries provided by local authorities; in 1987 (when the UK had a population of 2.2 million children under 3) there were 33,370 places in 794 nurseries. These nurseries take children up to school starting age at 5, but many do not admit babies; a 1983 survey of nurseries in England found that only 20 per cent of children were under 2, 31 per cent were 2–3 and 49 per cent were 3 or 4 (Van der Eyken 1984). Nurseries normally open 10 hours a day; a third or more of children, however, attend part-time, and this proportion has risen substantially in recent years (Van der Eyken 1984).

In addition, a small number of children – 7,200 aged between 0 and 4 in 1988 in England – are placed in private nurseries or with 'childminders' (women who work in their own homes caring for children) by local authorities, who pay their fees; and there are a few places – 1,660 in 1988 in England – at childminders who are sponsored and retained, in effect employed, by local authorities. Finally, a small number of private nurseries also receive some public funds from local authorities or other sources. There is no information about the number of children under 3 who benefit from these subsidies, but as a proportion of all children under 3, it is insignificant.

Together, these various publicly-funded services provide around one full-time place for every hundred children under 3.

Private day care

Most day care for children under 3 is private, with no public funding involved. There is evidence, discussed below, that relatives and particularly maternal grandmothers, remain by far the most commonly used form of care. The next most common form is childminding. In 1985–6, there were some 79,000 childminders approved and registered with local authorities (as they are required to be by law), with 173,478 places or nearly five places for every hundred children under 5; some of these places are used on a part-time basis and some are occupied by school-age children needing after-school care. It has been estimated that most, probably as many as 80 per cent, of childminders are 'registered' (Moss 1987), though this still leaves a substantial proportion who are 'unregistered'.

Childminders provide care in their own homes. In addition, some children are cared for in their own homes by 'nannies', who usually have some relevant training and are employed solely for childcare work; by 'mother's helps', who are usually expected to do some housework; or by '*au pairs*'. There is no information on how many children are cared for this way, though it has been estimated that these caregivers may care for some 30,000 children under 5 (Cohen 1988).

Private nurseries may be provided by individuals for profit, by non-profit organisations, by employers or by local parent or community groups (though this last group usually depend on some support from public funds). In 1988, there were 1,252 private nurseries in the UK, with 33,590 places, or just under one place for every hundred children under 5. Although there is no information on the numbers of children who attend these nurseries, or their ages, the great majority of places are for children aged 2 to 5; the higher staff ratios and other demands of caring for children under 2 have deterred most private nurseries from providing for this age group.

The final component in non-parental day care consists of services mainly intended for children aged 3 and 4, but which admit some younger children. Nursery education is provided by local authorities, mostly on a part-time basis. In 1988, 27,300 under-3s, or just over 1 per cent of the total, were in nursery education in England. Playgroups are mostly independently run, by parent or other non-profit groups or by individuals, and children attend on average for 2 or 3 half-day sessions a week. Some playgroups – less than a third – receive public funds, but the average grant is small (£144 a year in 1987) (PPA 1987). In 1986, 6 per cent of children under 3 went to playgroup (OPCS 1989). Nearly all the under-3s in nursery education and playgroups are over 2 – most indeed are over $2^1/_2$ – and use these services on a part-time basis, at most $2^1/_2$ hours a day. These two services are not discussed further in this chapter.

Local variations in child care

Publicly-funded and private day care are not evenly distributed; there are substantial local and regional variations. Wales and Northern Ireland, for instance, have little or no local authority nursery provision, while there is little provision in private nurseries in Scotland. Combining both types of nursery, England has proportionately more than twice as much provision as Wales, and more than six times as much provision as Northern Ireland. The situation for places in registered childminders is rather different, Ireland and England having similar levels, and twice as much as Wales and Scotland (Cohen 1988).

The variations are even more marked between local authorities. For example, in 1988, out of the ninety-nine local authorities in England with responsibility for day care services, eleven provided no nurseries at all; at the other extreme, nine authorities had forty or more places per 1,000 children under 5 in this type of provision. Highest levels of nursery provision – both local authority and private – were in Inner London. Non-metropolitan counties, which cover most of England outside the main conurbations, had the lowest levels of local authority nursery provision; while lowest levels for private nurseries were more evenly divided between counties, Outer London authorities and authorities in conurbations outside London.

Local differences are less marked for childminders, though still substantial. There are fewer than thirty places at registered childminders per 1,000 children under 5 in ten authorities, while thirteen authorities have more than seventy-five places per 1,000 children. Highest levels for childminding are again found in London, though high rates of provision are more common in suburban Outer London rather than Inner London (Department of Health 1989).

Interpreting these variations is difficult. The figure for childminders only includes those that are registered and the proportion registered probably varies between local authorities. The figures relate to services which take children up to 5 years of age; provision for children under 3 might produce a somewhat different pattern. Some of the variation reflects differences in need and demand; in general, highest provision is in urban areas where more women are in the labour force. Finally, there is a political element: left-wing councils, which predominate in Inner London and other conurbations, in general spend more on services, including day care.

The differing roles of publicly-funded and private day care

Responsibility for publicly-funded day care lies with 'welfare agencies' – the Department of Health in England (which also covers personal social services), the health and social services sections of the Welsh, Scottish and Northern Ireland Offices, and Social Services Departments in local authorities. Education authorities have little involvement with services for children under 3. The main exception is the large Strathclyde Regional Council in Scotland, where all 'pre-5' services, including those for children under 3, are now the education department's responsibility; a few English local authorities are now adopting the same course. Nationally, a few 2-year-olds receive nursery education and the 1980 Education Act allowed local education authorities to provide teachers to work in day nurseries. However, only 7 out of 90 nurseries in a 1983 survey had any full-time teachers on their staff, and 83 per cent had no teaching support of any kind (Van der Eyken 1984). A recent Parliamentary Committee on educational provision for children under 5 concluded that 'it is clear that at present day nurseries do not provide for education in the way we consider necessary' (Education, Arts and Science Committee 1989: para. 7.21).

Public funding of day care is for very specific and limited purposes. Local authority nurseries are provided, or fees in private services are paid, where children are considered to be in need because of some developmental problem or because of the social or economic circumstances of their families. Public day care therefore is only available where children or parents are deemed to be not coping or children are thought to be at risk: children will not be considered for a place in publicly-funded care because their parents are employed, unless the parent concerned is a lone mother or father. In recent years even children of employed lone parents have been less likely to get a place, as Social Services Departments have increasingly used publicly-funded services for children thought to be 'at risk', especially of physical or sexual abuse – 'the outcome has been that local authority day nurseries now operate far more as a specialised social service resource for "at risk" families ... and far less as a day care resource for the general community' (Van der Eyken 1984).

An associated trend has been the rapid development, both by local authorities and non-profit organisations, of 'family centres'. Many of these centres have evolved out of nurseries, and no longer offer full-time day care. Although they vary considerably in the services they provide for children and parents and in their working methods, most serve socially and economically deprived areas and focus on preventive work with families under stress and, in some cases, on community work in their local neighbourhoods (De'Ath 1988).

Because of the specific and limited role of publicly-funded services, working parents with children under 3 must rely almost entirely on either the private market (childminders, nurseries, nannies) or their social network (relatives). The main purpose of nearly all this care is, therefore, to provide for children while their parents are at work.

Regulation, supervision and quality

Local authorities have a legal duty to regulate some types of private day care. All private nurseries, except those on Crown property such as hospitals, and all childminders looking after a child under 5 for more than 2 hours a week for pay must be registered with their local authority. The local authority may impose certain requirements as a condition of registration, such as the maximum number of children to be cared for, but these conditions are left to the discretion of each local authority, as is the degree of supervision once registered. Central government provides broad guidance to local authorities in conducting their regulatory role. This advice covers such aspects as accommodation and numbers of children and staff. It is recommended, for example, that nurseries need to allow more space, higher staff ratios and various toilet and washing facilities if they have children under 2; and that a childminder 'will normally be able to cope with not more than 3 children under 5' (Ministry of Health 1968).

As well as regulation, the public sector has a more positive role, to promote quality, through various kinds of support to childminders and other private services and through funding research. Local authorities employ workers to regulate and support services. The priority and resources allocated to this work vary considerably between authorities, with central government providing no guidelines or standards on the level of resources required to perform these functions adequately. In general, though, both priority and resources are low.

Most local authorities have advisory workers for their own nurseries, but in most cases they have insufficient time to work on a regular and effective basis. In 1983, only 28 per cent of nurseries reported that they saw Social Services advisors 'regularly' (Van der Eyken 1984). Generally, nurseries are left to operate as relatively autonomous institutions.

Support for childminders has increased in recent years, for instance through the provision of training, 'drop-in' centres, equipment and toys and home visits. Despite these improvements, the level of supervision and support in many areas remains low. The National Childminder's Association (NCMA) recommends a minimum of one support visit every three months but in a 1987 survey of local authority workers, only 17 per cent said they visited that frequently; most (59 per cent) said they visited every six months (NCMA 1988). Another NCMA survey, this time of members, found that 41 per cent of these childminders had received at least three visits from a local authority worker in the last year, but 21 per cent had none, while nearly half the childminders in another study, described in Chapter 8, had not been visited in the preceding six months (Martin and Mooney 1987).

In the same study, only a quarter of the childminders had started a training course, 15 per cent currently used a toy library and just one went to a childminders' group. In a fourth study, of four areas deliberately chosen because relatively extensive support services were provided, the proportion of childminders who had attended a training course varied from 16 per cent in one area to 84 per cent in another and the proportion who regularly used a childminders' group ranged from 23 per cent to 76 per cent (Ferri and Birchall 1986). The 1987 NCMA survey of local authorities concludes that:

> In terms of the services which are currently being provided [to childminders], we were encouraged by the range but disappointed by the low numbers, particularly of a practical nature [e.g, training, drop-ins, toy libraries and equipment loans] ... [which] were only on offer from a minority of authorities.

(NCMA 1988)

Supervision and support appears to be less among the relatively few private nurseries that take very young children. In the study described more fully in Chapter 8, researchers visited 32 of the 33 private nurseries in the London area which admitted children under 12 months of age. Most of these nurseries were attached to workplaces, often hospitals, and 9 were not registered with their local authority. Only 12 reported regular visits either from Social Services Departments or from any other public health or welfare agency. This increased the isolation of these nurseries, most of which were 'one off' institutions run by organisations responsible for no other day care services.

The role of the public sector in supervision, quality control and improvements is particularly important since the private sector invests virtually no resources in these tasks itself. This is not surprising given that the private sector consists mostly of individual caregivers, providing a service in their own home or the child's, plus a small number of independent and isolated nurseries. Surprising or not, the ability and willingness of the private sector to undertake an active role in supervision and quality is an important factor where the private sector has such a dominant position in service provision.

Day care workers

The workforce providing day care for under 3s is overwhelmingly female. Beyond that, little is known for certain about them. Most relatives who provide care are grandparents, and likely to be 50 or over. By contrast, many workers in day nurseries and providing care in children's own homes are young, in their 20s (Cohen 1988). Many childminders have their own young children, of pre-school and primary school age, and their average age is mid-to-late 30s (Moss 1987). As to ethnicity, there is no information except for a survey of local authority nurseries, which found the proportion of ethnic minority staff to be far lower than the proportion of ethnic minority children attending (Van der Eyken 1984).

The pay and conditions for day care workers are poor. Many relatives receive no pay at all; among other groups of workers, pay is below the average for women in non-manual occupations and far below that for men in non-manual occupations. The worst pay and conditions are among women providing care either in their own home or the child's home. Most childminders, for instance, work over 40 hours a week, for a gross income (that is before deducting their substantial costs) of well under half average pay for women in non-manual jobs. Few get paid holidays or other benefits, such as membership of a pension scheme (Moss 1987; Cohen 1988).

Training is generally limited or non-existent. In local authority nurseries, senior staff increasingly have social work or other higher qualifications. Most workers in these and private day nurseries have a Nursery Nurse Examination Board (NNEB) qualification, a two-year course for which there is no entrance qualification; most students start at 16 and qualify by 18. This background does not equip workers in local authority nurseries to perform the increasingly narrow and specialised 'social work' tasks being placed on them, a problem acknowledged by the government in the late 1970s:

> The priorities observed in allocating day nursery places have led to special problems in looking after the children and also to much work having to be centred on the parents whose difficulties with childrearing may be compounded by low income, inadequate housing and lack of community support. The NNEB Certificate, while giving trainees an excellent basic knowledge of normal child development, does not fully prepare them for work with parents and children with multiple problems.

> (DHSS/DES 1978)

Many nannies also have an NNEB qualification; indeed, it has been estimated that 40 per cent of NNEB students become nannies once qualified. By contrast, most mothers' helps and *au pairs* have no training (Cohen 1988). The same is true of childminders, although an increasing number of local authorities now offer short courses (Moss 1987).

Childcare arrangements for children under 3

As this introduction suggests, there is a very limited amount of day care provision for children under 3 in the United Kingdom. Most children in this age group are cared for only by their parents, predominantly by their mothers, apart from being left occasionally with a relative, friend or other babysitter. The main source of data on use of day care is the General Household Survey (GHS), a national survey conducted annually by the government. In 1986, the most recent year for which GHS data is available, nearly 15 per cent of children under 3 received some form of regular non-parental care (Table 7.1). However, more than 40 per cent of this group were 2-year-olds at playgroup or nursery education.

Table 7.1 Proportion of children under 3 using various day care services, UK, 1986

| Type of childcare | Age of children (months) | | | |
	0–11	12–23	24–35	Total 0–35
	%	%	%	%
Nursery school	0	0	3	1
Playgroup	1	2	16	6
Nursery	1	2	5	3
Childminder	3	5	5	5
* Relative, not household	3	5	9	6
* Member of household	2	1	2	5

Source: OPCS 1986 and (for 1979) re-analysis of 1979 GHS base tape

Note: * these two types of care are not included in the 1986 GHS; figures given here are taken from 1979 GHS.

The 1986 GHS excludes two important types of day care – relatives and nannies. The 1979 GHS, the last before 1986 to ask about day care, found that 12 per cent of children under 3 received regular (i.e. at least weekly) care either from a relative or a 'live-in' nanny (Table 7.1). Since there was little change in usage of other types of day care between 1979 and 1986, it seems probable that these two types of care continued to provide for between 10–15 per cent of children.

For working parents with a child under 3, relatives provide the main form of non-parental childcare, followed by childminders (including friends and neighbours who provide care). Nannies and nurseries come far behind. Parents themselves provide a significant proportion of care, either caring for their children while they are working or, more commonly, by having working hours that do not overlap. Many mothers have part-time jobs at times when they know their partners will be at home; for example, 44 per cent of part-time employed women with pre-school children work either in the evening or at night compared to under 15 per cent of other women in part-time jobs (Martin and Roberts 1984) (Table 7.2).

Peter Moss

Table 7.2 Childcare arrangements while mothers at work for children under 5 UK, 1979 (Study 1), 1980 (Study 2)

Childcare arrangements	STUDY 1 (Children aged 8 months)		STUDY 2 (Children aged 0–4 years)	
	A	B	A	B
	%	%	%	%
With mother	13	18	7	17
Father	11	43	12	39
Relative	39	23	47	29
Childminder	23	9	29	13
Nursery	3	2	15	9
Nanny/*au pair*	3	1	5	1
Other	7	3	–	–

Source: STUDY 1 – Daniel 1980; STUDY 2 – Martin and Roberts 1984

Note: A – mother employed full-time; B – mother employed part-time.
Percentages do not add to 100 for Study 2 because some women made more than one arrangement.

Because of the admission criteria applied, children in local authority nurseries are least likely to have employed parents and most likely to come from lower social class and materially poor backgrounds. A disproportionately high number of ethnic minority children attend, especially children of Afro-Caribbean origin (Van der Eyken 1984). By contrast, the expense of nannies and private nurseries, and the fact that workplace nurseries are often provided for workforces with a relatively high proportion of women in higher skilled jobs (for instance, in hospitals), means that most children cared for by these services come from higher social class and materially advantaged backgrounds; usage will be low among ethnic minority families. This suggests that such nursery provisions as there is will be most used by children from either end of the social class spectrum. This is confirmed by the 1986 GHS. Eight per cent of children aged under 5 with a father in a professional or managerial job went to a nursery as did 7 per cent of children with their father in a semi-skilled or unskilled manual job, compared to 5 per cent of children with fathers in intermediate jobs.

Childminders appear to be used more by higher than lower social class parents. Relatives however are most often used by lower social class parents (Bone 1977; OPCS 1981; Moss 1986, 1987; OPCS 1989).

Factors affecting the development of day care provision

Ideology

Day care provision for children under 3 in the UK occurs in the context of a particular ideology about parenthood and childcare which has been dominant for many years. The main components of this ideology have been that children should be in the full-time care of their mothers until at least the age of 3; that separation from the mother before this age is likely to be harmful to the child; that mothers with children under this age should not be employed; and that the main role of fathers is to provide financially for their families. This ideology has not been entirely static; some developments have occurred over the years. Fathers are now expected to be present at the birth of their children and to 'help out' with them at home. The proportion of women who agree with the statement that a married woman with children under school age ought to stay at home has decreased over the last twenty years – from 78 per cent in 1965 to 62 per cent in 1980 and 45 per cent in 1987 (Brook, Jowell and Witherspoon 1989).

Such changes are important, but their significance should not be over-stated. Men may be doing more to care for their children, but even in dual-earner families women continue to do the greater part of this work and most still feel that they have responsiblity for the care and upbringing of children (Brannen and Moss 1988). Up to the early 1980s, a majority of women continued to believe that mothers of young children should not work at all, and even by the late 1980s, nearly half still held to this view. Moreover, a majority of the remainder (15 per cent in 1965, 25 per cent in 1980 and 29 per cent in 1987) still took the implicitly negative view that 'a married women with children under school age should only work if she needs the money'. By 1987, only a quarter held that 'it was up to her whether to go out to work or not' and there was still no support for the proposition that women with young children 'ought to work'.

This survey data covers the full age range of pre-school children. Opposition may remain greater to women with children under 3 going out to work, particularly if they work full-time. Some support for this view, and evidence of continuing strong support for a gender-based division of work, comes from the 1987 British Social Attitudes Survey, where respondents were asked to choose which of six work arrangements they thought was best for a family with a child under 5. Most (76 per cent) opted for the mother being at home, with virtually all the rest preferring the mother in part-time employment, while 93 per cent preferred an arrangement where the father worked full-time. Only 3 per cent opted for both parents working similar hours (Ashford 1988).

Another influential aspect of ideology concerns the private nature of children and their care, a view put in its most extreme form by right-wing 'free-marketeers' who 'regard the decision to have a child as the same as any other spending decision in these days of contraception...It is the same as deciding to buy a CD player or a car...it is an entirely personal matter' (David Willetts, Director of Studies at the Centre for Policy Studies, quoted in the *Guardian*, 14.7.88). While many would not state the position in quite such materialistic terms, there remains widespread support for the view that having children and caring for them are essentially private issues and that childcare should be left to 'parents' (in effect, nearly always mothers (Brannen and Moss 1988)), unless a child should be 'at risk' from his or her parents or unless the parents are inadequate and unable to cope.

Policies

This dominant ideology has influenced the policies of successive post-war governments. During the Second World War, the urgent need to attract women into the labour force led to a rapid increase in nursery provision. Once the War ended though, the process began of running down this provision; the number of places in local authority nurseries is now less than half the 1945 level. This run-down was associated with a redefinition of the purpose of publicly-funded services, which excluded most working parents and assumed that these services should only be provided where a child or its parents had some problem. The post-war direction was set in a government circular to local authorities, issued as soon as the fighting had stopped.

> The Ministers concerned accept the view of medical and other authority that, in the interest of health and development of the child no less than for the benefit of the mother, the proper place for a child under 2 is at home with his mother. They are also of the opinion that, under normal peacetime conditions, the right policy to pursue would be positively to discourage mothers of children under 2 from going out to work; to make provision for children between 2 and 5 by way of nursery schools and classes; and to regard day nurseries as supplements to meet the special needs of children whose mothers are constrained by individual circumstances to go out to work or whose home circumstances are in themselves unsatisfactory from the health point of view or whose mothers are incapable for some good reason of undertaking the full care of their children.
>
> (Ministry of Health 1945)

This circular laid down a policy which, in essentials, has not changed. Indeed, the role of public services for children under 3 has been more tightly prescribed over time. Two-year-olds have never been provided for in nursery education on any significant scale – and there was no significant increase in nursery education for older children until the 1970s. A 1968 circular reaffirmed that 'wherever possible the younger pre-school child should be at home with the mother ... because early and prolonged separation from the mother is detrimental to the child' (Ministry of Health 1968).

This 1968 circular further defined who should have priority for publicly-funded day care. Priority groups included 'lone parents who have no option but to go out to work'; children needing 'temporary day care on account of the mother's illness'; children 'whose mothers are unable to look after them adequately because they are incapable of giving young children the care they need'; children for whom 'day care might prevent the breakdown of the mother or the break-up of the family', and so on. Overall, provision was limited to children or parents who 'need help'. The notion of day care as a generally available service, open to any family needing or wanting it, was never even considered. Since this circular, priority has become even more narrowly defined with, as already noted, fewer children of lone working mothers receiving services as more emphasis is placed on 'at risk' children.

While the view that day care is an essentially private issue may have implicitly influenced earlier policy statements, it has become more explicit in the 1980s under the Thatcher administration. The position was spelt out in Parliament by a junior minister in the Department of Health with responsibility for day care services – 'day care will continue to be primarily a matter for private arrangement between parents and private and voluntary resources, except where there are special needs' (John Patten, *Hansard* 18.2.85, Col. 397). More recently, the Department of Health began a memorandum prepared for a Parliamentary Select Committee by restating the government view 'that in the first instance it is the responsibility of the parents to make arrangements, including financial arrangements, for the day-care of pre-school children' (Education, Arts and Science Committee 1989).

Policy on day care in the 1980s has also been influenced by the supply-side economic policies of the Thatcher administration, in particular keeping statutory requirements on employers to a minimum. This has underlain the government's erosion of maternity leave entitlements since 1979, and its opposition to the adoption of a draft Directive on Parental Leave put forward by the European Commission in 1983. The one exception to this policy of non-intervention in the relationship between employment and parenthood has been a consistent policy interest by successive governments in the improvement of child-minding. In a circular in 1978 (DHSS/DES 1978), local authorities were 'invited' to review their support and advice services, including in-service training, for childminding. Limited sums of money have also been given to support innovatory projects.

Childminding has received official support for several reasons, in-cluding its 'low cost' and its flexibility which 'has advantages for the working parent in that it may be more readily be arranged to suit hours of work'. It is also supported because it is regarded as the type of care closest to the 'ideal', that is the child cared for by its mother, and because it is believed by some officials that children under 3 are too young to benefit from group care. The 1978 circular observes that a good childminder can provide care 'that is the nearest substitute to [the child's] own home' and is 'more in tune with his limited capacity for social contacts than the communal experience of a day nursery'.

A final feature of the policy of successive governments has been to avoid setting any national standards or targets for day care. On the issue of how much publicly-funded provision is made, 'the level of childcare provision is a matter for local authorities to consider in the light of circumstances prevailing within their area' (John Patten, Department of Health Minister, *Hansard* 13.12.83, Col. 43). Similarly, while some guidance is offered to local authorities about standards, no standards have been set for supervision and support of services.

The labour market

Since the War, very few women in the UK have remained in the labour force throughout their childbearing years. The great majority have con-tinued to leave the labour force for a period of years when they have their first child (Martin and Roberts 1984; Joshi 1987). At any one time, less than 30 per cent of women with a child under 5 have been em-ployed.

A distinguishing feature of the UK labour market is the large number of part-time jobs. Women with children are heavily concentrated in these jobs, with the heaviest concentration among women with young children. In 1985, for instance, 29 per cent of women with a child under 5 were employed, 20 per cent had part-time jobs and three-quarters of these part-timers actually worked less than 20 hours a week (Moss 1988).

Until very recently, therefore, there has neither been a major push by women with children under 3 into the labour market, nor a major pull to bring them in due to labour shortages. There has been some movement into employment, with more women returning to work between births, but much of this has been into very part-time jobs, which have enabled women to 'fit in' employment around domestic commitments and to use a variety of informal child care arrangements, including fathers and relatives. In this situation, there has been little effective pressure on government or employers to intervene to support child care provision.

Some consequences for children

Type of care

For a variety of reasons, there are few nursery places for children under 3, and especially for children who are not social work referrals. Day care very largely occurs in domestic, non-group settings, with nannies or childminders or relatives. Care by relatives is most common; the experience of care in this setting is likely to differ not only compared to group care but also compared to care by a childminder or nanny. The child cared for by a relative, which in most cases means its grandmother, will know the caregiver in advance; the child's parent and caregiver will have a quite different relationship compared to a parent and minder or nanny; and the caregiver will generally be older and less likely to have other children to care for. In a recent study of children under 3, described in Chapter 8, the average age of relatives providing care for children aged 18 months was 51, and 70 per cent cared for no other children under 5 years of age. Childminders had an average age of 37, and only 23 per cent had no other under-5s to care for.

The narrow role of local authority nurseries, increasingly used as a social work resource, means they provide environments characterised by high concentrations of children with developmental and behavioural problems. In a study of four nurseries run by one authority, 35 per cent of children had significant behaviour problems, compared to 11 per cent of children in nursery education and 3 per cent of children at playgroups. Nearly half the children had delayed speech development (McGuire and Richman 1986).

Until very recently, few private nurseries have taken young children, especially the youngest age group under 18–24 months. Those that do face cost pressures, since providing good quality care for very young children is particularly expensive. Without very substantial subsidies from some other source, for instance employers, private nurseries must either concentrate on older children or economise – on accommodation and equipment, staff levels, staff pay and conditions, cover for absent staff, etc. Examples of all these were found in the private nurseries in the London area admitting children under 12 months of age, in the study described in Chapter 8; for instance, at the age of 18 months, children in the study who attended these nurseries were experiencing staff/child ratios varying from 1:2.4 to 1:8.5.

Instability of care

There is evidence that childminding is more unstable than nursery care, in the sense that children are more likely to be moved from childminders than from nurseries (Moss and Brannen 1987): this evidence applies to the UK, but it may be that childminding, based as it is on one individual providing care, is inherently more unstable, defined in this way. A system that has a preponderance of childminders compared to nurseries will therefore accentuate this type of instability.

The system is, however, more generally unstable, partly a consequence of the poor pay and conditions of most day care workers, described above. There is evidence to confirm high turnover among childminders, with women moving out of the work when their children get older or when employment opportunities with better pay and conditions become available (Moss 1987). But turnover is also thought to be high among other day care workers, including nursery workers, nannies and mothers' helps (Van der Eyken 1984; Cohen 1988).

Standards of care

Day care for children under 3 depends heavily on market forces. In such a situation, it might be expected that there would be some relationship between standards of care and parental resources, both material and otherwise. There is little information on quality and no system to monitor overall quality and who gets better or worse quality. The one attempt to assess which children get better or worse care at childminders did find some evidence to support the expectation of how market forces would operate. A quality of care rating found that children whose mothers were born outside the British Isles came off worst; while on an overall assessment, including standards of housing and equipment as well as quality of care, children of mothers born abroad and children whose mothers were in lower occupational groups received a poorer service (Mayall and Petrie 1983).

More generally, given the low priority and resources for issues of quality in both the public and private sector; the poor pay and conditions of many childcare workers; the high demands placed on public sector services by the admission criteria in operation; the diffuse nature of the private sector, its reliance on parental fees and the variability and general under-resourcing of the regulatory system; and the complexity of providing high quality environments and experiences for very young children – it would be surprising if services of consistently high quality had developed. Indeed, it would be surprising if a substantial proportion were not seriously inadequate. The absence of information on quality means that there is no way of testing whether this rather pessimistic assumption is, in practice, correct.

Current developments in day care

This chapter has been written at the beginning of a period of rapid change; in the late 1980s and early 1990s, day care for children under 3 is likely to alter more than in the previous forty years. The main reason is an increasing demand for labour, especially in the service sector, as the economy has expanded after the deep recession of the early 1980s. This has coincided with a fall in the number of young people leaving school, the result of the decrease in birth rate which began in the mid-1960s; between 1985 and 1995, the number of 15–19-year-olds will decrease by 26 per cent. As a consequence, women are taking most of the new jobs. Of the 1.6 million jobs created between June 1983 and March 1988, 1.3 million (740,000 part-time and 550,000 full-time) went to women, and women are projected to take up to 80 per cent of the 900,000 new jobs expected to be on offer between 1988 and 1995. Many of these women will come from the group who currently have the lowest employment rate, those with pre-school children, with a consequent rapid increase in their employment rate.

In a matter of a few months during 1988 and 1989 'growing awareness of the decline of school leavers – and the subsequent need for employers to attract mature female workers – has forced child care provision to the forefront of political and corporate debate' (Smith 1989). The government's response has been to give permission to its own departments to set up workplace nurseries; and to warn employers of the consequence of demographic change and of their need to take steps to attract women workers – 'employers in this country must realise that the only way to defuse the demographic timebomb ticking away underneath them is by taking the initiative themselves to support family life and to support mothers who want to work' (John Patten, Home Office Minister with responsibility for co-ordinating government policies for women, quoted in the *Independent*, 12.1.89). A Ministerial Group on Women's Issues has also considered day care and announced a number of new initiatives (Home Office Press Release, 11.4.89).

What the government will not do, and in this remains consistent with previous policy, is to take a leadership or strategic role, for example developing a day care policy with objectives and targets, planning services, providing public funds for services or to subsidise parents' day care costs (for example, through tax relief), or intervening actively and substantially to ensure the development of high quality in services. The approach is typified in the initiatives proposed by the Ministerial Group on Women's Issues – encouragement of a 'voluntary accreditation scheme [to] provide information about the availability of childcare facilities and guarantee the quality of provision'; guidance to local education authorities and school governors 'encouraging the use of school premises for after school and holiday playschemes'; support for the voluntary sector through 'the pump-priming of projects and the encouragement of partnerships between employers and the voluntary sector'; and encouragement to employers 'to use the tax reliefs available to provide childcare facilities'.

The one initiative involving legislation – an amendment of the law 'to improve the registration and enforcement arrangements for day nurseries, childminders and playgroups' – does provide some potential for strengthening the regulation of private services to ensure minimum standards. Coming into force in 1991, the new Children's Act, for example, requires (rather than, as before, only permitting) local authorities to make conditions when registering private services, and lays down a minimum requirement for inspecting services (at least once a year). Despite these changes, the impact of the new legislation will depend to a large degree on how individual local authorities decide to use the law, for example what conditions they choose to make and whether or not they exceed the legal minimum for inspection visits; a lot of scope will remain for local variations. While the Ministerial Group emphasised that 'choice and high standards are the key to the provision of childcare', the Group's initiatives do not seriously address how these objectives might be achieved *throughout* the day care system.

Government has defined its role in the development of day care for employed parents as marginal, involving the continuance of some degree of regulation together with encouragement and guidance to others to make provision. In particular, it looks to employers and the private market to provide the necessary services and to introduce other measures – such as altering working patterns – that will assist working mothers (and it is important to note that the whole discussion in the UK is concerned with mothers, and getting them into the labour force; the implications for men's role in childcare and other 'domestic' areas have received virtually no discussion).

Some employers are beginning to respond. Increasing numbers are altering working patterns to suit women with children, either informally or formally through, for example, increasing the range of jobs that can be done on a part-time basis and the introduction of career-break schemes, some of which offer the possibility of resuming employment on a part-time basis. There has also been a surge of interest in employer support for day care. This support may take various forms – some method of subsidy for day care costs, including a voucher scheme planned by a staff discounts agency best known for its luncheon voucher scheme; sponsoring places in nurseries; and providing nursery care either alone or in partnership with other employers and, in some cases, local authorities. The most ambitious example has been the announcement by a major bank that it plans to set up 300 workplace nurseries.

The other trend has been a growth in private services. Newspaper reports and other anecdotal evidence suggest increasing use of nannies and mothers' helps. The number of registered childminders in England has increased by 28 per cent between 1985 and 1988 (this follows a 74 per cent increase between 1977 and 1985, but much of this earlier increase was probably accounted for by local authority efforts to register 'unregistered' childminders, rather than a real increase in child-minding). The clearest evidence comes from a 44 per cent increase in private nurseries in England between 1985 and 1988, by comparison with a 4 per cent growth between 1977 and 1985. The pace of increase may well be speeding up even more. According to a newspaper report, 'the EOC [Equal Opportunities Commission] says it has received dozens of calls recently from people with childminding experience who are thinking of setting up businesses to run nurseries'. The report concludes that 'in the 1990s, it seems, childcare is going to be big business' (Smith 1989).

Conclusions

Most children the UK receive full-time parental care up to the age of 3. For those who do not, most are cared for in a partially regulated and fragmented private sector, by relatives, childminders, private nurseries and nannies. The rest are found in a relatively small publicly-funded sector, which has increasingly become a social work resource, used for children and families with a variety of serious problems and disadvantages. Successive governments have rejected extending the role of the public sector, insisting that care for children with working parents must remain a private issue for parents and employers.

A growing labour shortage during the late 1980s and early 1990s will lead to a major increase in employment rates among women with young children and in the number of children receiving day care. In the face of this, the Thatcher administration has chosen to maintain a policy of minimal intervention, relying on day care being delivered by employers and the private market. It has defined the issue purely in terms of the labour force, and viewed day care as a commodity whose main function is to increase the supply of labour. Broader issues – of child welfare, equality of access to good quality services for women and children, how day care services relate to other services for children and families and the relationship between parenthood and employment – have been ignored.

The result will be a very substantial growth in workplace and private for-profit nursery care. Most children under 3 however will continue to be cared for in non-group settings – with relatives, childminders and nannies – though the proportion will fall and the distribution between these types of provision may alter with time.

Reference

Ashford, S. (1988) 'Family matters', in Jowell, R., Witherspoon, S. and Brook, L. (eds) *British Social Attitudes: The 1987 Report*, Aldershot: Gower.

Bone, M. (1977) *Preschool Children and the Need for Day Care*, London: HMSO.

Brannen, J. and Moss, P. (1988) *New Mothers at Work*, London: Unwin Hyman.

Brook, L., Jowell, R. and Witherspoon, S. (1989) 'Recent trends in social attitudes', in T. Griffin (ed.) *Social Trends 19* HMSO: London.

Cohen, B. (1988) *Caring for Children: Services and Policies for Childcare and Equal Opportunities in the United Kingdom*, London: European Commission.

Daniel, W. (1980) *Maternity Rights*, London: Policy Studies Institute.

De'Ath, E. (1988) *The Family Centre Approach*, London: The Children's Society.

DHSS/DES (1978) *Circular Letter: Co-ordination of Services for Children under 5*.

Department of Health (1989) *Children's Day Care Facilities at 31 March 1988 England*, London: Department of Health.

Education, Arts and Science Committee (1989) *Educational Provision for Under Fives*, London: HMSO.

Ferri, E. and Birchall, D. (1986) *A Study of Support and Training for Childminders*, Report to the DHSS, National Children's Bureau.

Joshi, H. (1987) 'The cost of caring', in J. Millar and C. Glendinning (eds) *Women and Poverty*, Brighton: Wheatsheaf.

Martin, J. and Roberts, C. (1984) *Women and Employment: A Lifetime Perspective*, London: HMSO.

Martin, S. and Mooney, A. (1987) 'Do childminders get the help they need?' *Social Work Today* 18: 25.

Mayall, B. and Petrie, P. (1983) *Childminding and Day Nurseries: What kind of Care?*, London: Heinemann.

McGuire, J. and Richman, N. (1986) 'The prevalence of behaviour problems in three types of preschool groups', *Journal of Child Psychology and Psychiatry* 27: 455: 72.

Ministry of Health (1945) *Circular 221/45*.

—— (1968) *Day Care Facilities for Children under Five: Circular 37/68*.

Moss, P. (1986) *Child Care in the Early Months: how child care arrangements are made for babies*, London: Thomas Coram Research Unit.

—— (1987) *A Review of Childminding Research*, London: Thomas Coram Research Unit.

—— (1988) *Child Care and Equality of Opportunity*, Brussels: European Commission.

Moss, P. and Brannen, J. (1987) 'Discontinuity in day care arrangements for very young children', *Early Child Development and Care* 29: 435–49.

NCMA (1988) *A Survey of Local Authority Childminding Services*, London: NCMA.

OPCS (1981) *General Household Survey 1979*, London: HMSO.

—— (1989) *General Household Survey 1986*, London: HMSO.

PPA (1987) *PPA Facts and Figures 1986*, London: PPA.

Smith, M. (1989) 'Employers concentrate on children', *Financial Times*, 23.2.89.

Van der Eyken, W. (1984) *Day Nurseries in Action: A National Study of Local Authority Day Nurseries in England, 1975–1983*, Report to the Department of Health, Department of Child Health Research Unit, Bristol University.

Chapter eight

Research on day care for young children in the United Kingdom

Edward C. Melhuish

The main forms of day care for children under 3 years of age in Britain are relatives, childminders and nurseries. Relatives are the most commonly used form of day care but have never been studied. Childminders are the next most common and have been the most frequently researched form of day care. There are two forms of nursery in the UK: that provided by Social Services Departments and almost exclusively used for children who are regarded as 'at risk' or having some special need, and private sector nurseries. Social Services nurseries are generally not available to dual-earner households, who may use private nurseries which consist of workplace nurseries, community nurseries and some private enterprise nurseries. Such nurseries are available only to a small number of employed women who are predominantly in higher status occupations.

Review of research

The literature on day care in Britain is limited. This chapter will deal with that research reported in the last twenty years which has considered the possible influence of day care upon children. First the issue of day care versus home care will be considered. Second, comparisons between types of care will be covered and, third, studies involving within type of care comparisons will be discussed. After this overview a recent research project on day care will be discussed in greater depth.

Day care versus home comparisons

One of the earliest comparisons of day care versus home care was by Moore (1975), reporting data on children who had experienced day care in the 1950s. From a longitudinal study of a community sample of children, two groups were selected for comparison. The exclusive mothering group of 57 children had not had non-parental care during the first five years apart from occasional babysitting. The day care (diffuse mothering) group of 48 children had all experienced at least one year of full-time (greater than 25 hours/week) non-parental care before age 5. For some children this care would have started before age 3 and others later. The types of care included nursery schools, day nurseries, child-minders and relatives. Hence the day care studied was very diverse both in terms of type of care and children's age.

Moore reported differences between the groups at 6 and 7 years, and also in adolescence, primarily among boys, there being only a few differences of borderline significance for girls. For boys of age 7 the 'exclusive mothering' group achieved better reading scores. There were differences in personality, with mothers reporting greater fastidiousness and conformity in the 'exclusive mothering' group and greater aggressive non-conformity in the day care group. Psychologists' ratings also showed more excitability, aggression and less timidity in the day care group. The differences seemed to persist into early adolescence when differences in interests appeared, with the day care group having interests more often in athletic and social activities and the 'exclusive mothering' group showing greater internalisation of parental interests and standards. Moore reports more insecurity and fears at 6 for those children who had had a greater number of placements in day care, suggesting the importance of stability of care. The major problem of interpretation of this study is that the great diversity of type and timing of day care for the sample makes extrapolation to other samples problematic. In addition, as Moore acknowledges, the groups selected *post hoc* on broad criteria of day care use were likely to differ in other characteristics which are also likely to affect child variables.

Subsequent research involving home versus day care has focused on childminders and has been heavily influenced by the pioneering work of Mayall and Petrie (1977). They studied 39 children, aged 2–3 years, attending registered childminders in Inner London, and for 27 of these compared adult-infant interaction during 20 minutes of an interview with the childminder and with the mother. Mothers were found to be more responsive than childminders to the children. The children were also found to be below age norms on a standard assessment of language development. However no comparison group of children were tested for language development; these scores may have been typical for children from families such as those included in this study. Another finding was that ethnic minority children received worse quality childminder care.

Raven (1979, 1981) reported a study of two groups of 3–5-year-olds. One group was with childminders and a demographically similar group were cared for at home only. Scores on measures of language development and social adjustment revealed no differences between the two groups of children. However, the scores of both groups were below age norms and if only the childminded group were considered, then similar conclusions to those of Mayall and Petrie (1977) would be drawn, illustrating the danger of using developmental data without appropriate comparison groups.

Bryant *et al.* (1980) did a similar study to Mayall and Petrie (1977) working with childminders in Oxfordshire. They recorded the approaches by the child and affectionate acts toward the child, during 20 minutes of an interview with both mother and childminder. They also recorded the number of positive and negative remarks about the child during the interview and rated expressed warmth towards the child. Overall they conclude that a child's activities at a childminder's do not differ markedly from those of most children at home, and there were no differences observed for approaches by the child toward childminder or mother. However a larger proportion of children were described as detached and inactive during the interviews with the childminder than with the mother. The researchers drew attention to difficulties in the home situation of a substantial number of children in this study and such factors may well be influential in producing the results found. Children who were not with minders were not studied by these methods and so a comparison group was not available. A quarter of the childminders were rated as cold and unresponsive, and the authors conclude that while most childminders are warm people they often fail to develop a close relationship with the child. Generally this study presents evidence illuminating the diversity of childminding including some apparently poor quality care.

The most recently completed study of childminders is that reported by Davie (1986). Sixty-nine registered childminders in three areas of Staffordshire were studied, and interviews took place with most of the parents. For fourteen children, aged 2½ to 3½ years, detailed observations were made at the childminder's and at home. Davie reports minding as being of generally good quality with the majority of children receiving warm responsive care, with a good range of stimulation. The observations revealed children to be more inhibited at the childminder's than at home, producing fewer questions and demands, and not being so 'naughty'.

Comparisons between types of care

Using similar methodology to their previous study of childminders, Mayall and Petrie (1983) compared childminders and public sector nurseries for the under-2s. For a sample of children cared for by a childminder, childminder and mother were interviewed, during which interaction between adult and child were observed for 20 minutes (as in the 1977 study). Similar results were found indicating that childminders could not be regarded as substitute mothers as the relationship differed.

Childminders were more likely to talk of the relationship with the child in terms of child management. The observations revealed the children interacted less with their childminder than with their mother, including less bodily contact, and childminders were less controlling than the mothers. Forty children were also studied at fifteen local authority nurseries, with nursery staff interviewed about the children and their experiences. It emerged that there were different patterns of daily experience provided at childminders and nurseries. Nursery children played more out-of-doors, had more training in toileting and feeding and had more routine rests, while childminding children had more outings.

Studies concentrating on one type of care

Studies of the variation within type of care have largely concentrated on nurseries. An exception is one study which deals with childminders, Shinman (1981) conducted an interview study of all registered childminders in an area of Inner London; 10 per cent of the childminders were rated as being of distinctly poor quality and only 25–30 per cent were rated as providing a distinctly happy environment for children. Shinman also noted that childminders with their own children under 5 were more likely to play with children in their care, and these childminders overall tended to be more 'child-centred' and to have friendly relations with the parents. Overall the study emphasises the great diversity amongst childminders.

Studies of nurseries in Britain are few and limited in scope. Garland and White (1980) studied nine nurseries in London; three public sector and six private sector. The research consisted of a series of descriptive case studies of the functioning of the nurseries at the level of overall organisation and at the level of childcare, with little quantitative data. Organisational factors such as the ideology of adult-child relationships influence childcare practices. While all nurseries had staff who worked long hours for poor pay and with generally short job tenure, there were also some marked differences between public and private sector. Private sector nurseries had staff with lower levels of training and qualifications and also a markedly worse staff-child ratio.

Other studies of nurseries have focused on public sector nurseries. Bain and Barnett (1980) studied twelve children at one Social Service Department nursery in London. The majority of the children had problematic home backgrounds, but Bain and Barnett concluded that the nursery experience added to children's developmental difficulties and that these became apparent at school. Such pessimism may or may not be warranted but without adequate comparison groups such conclusions could be misleading and inadequately justified. The study did reveal issues of concern including the high number of caretakers for the children, the high level of aggression in the nursery and the youth and inexperience of the staff.

Another study in London by McGuire and Richman (1988) draws attention to the linkages between management style, group structure and child behaviour in six Social Services nurseries. The study relied on interview with nursery staff and systematic observations of children in the nurseries. McGuire and Richman describe a dimension of management style, which they term 'ethos', which varies from an autocratic, rigid adult-centred approach to a more democratic, flexible, child-centred approach. The more autocratic management styles were associated with larger group size. Where the head of the nursery was more openly involved with staff and children, there was greater parental consultation and more adult initiated interaction with children.

Research on day care in Britain has consisted of small-scale, local studies, spread over a substantial period. This makes generalisation and comparison problematic. Research on this topic in Britain has had low priority from funding agencies reflecting the low priority for day care in a society where such issues are largely viewed as private rather than public concerns.

The Thomas Coram Research Unit (TCRU) study

Design and sample

This study was designed to investigate the impact of employment and childcare decisions on women and children in dual-earner households having their first child. 255 women and their first-born children were recruited from 4 sources:

1 *Health Visitors* in four Health Districts, who produced 83 referrals.
2 *Large public and private sector employers* of women in London, who were asked to refer names of women currently on or about to take maternity leave. Forty-seven employers referred at least one employee, and altogether this source produced 1,051 referrals.
3 *Seven hospitals* with large maternity units allowed a research team member to visit their post-natal wards weekly, to contact all women who had just had a first child. This produced 2,874 referrals.
4 *Nurseries* The research team contacted all thirty-three nurseries in Greater London which, at that time, took children under one year of age from two-parent households with both parents employed. Twenty-one were workplace attached (mostly for health education sector employees), nine were provided by community

or voluntary groups and three were privately run. All but one
agreed to co-operate and produced 98 referrals.

The sample contained four sub-groups. Three sub-groups consisted
of women who intended to return to full-time employment after
maternity leave and use a relative, childminder or nursery for day care.
The fourth sub-group consisted of women who would not return to
employment after maternity leave. In order to make the sample
relatively homogeneous for other variables, the sample was selected
according to several additional criteria: both parents were living together and having their first child; the mother was born in the British
Isles and had been working full time up to the pregnancy; and for those
women who would return to employment, they would do so on a
full-time basis (30+ hours/week) and before the child was 9 months of
age.

From the original 4,106 women screened, 295 women were asked to
take part in the study, and of these 255 were interviewed at the first
contact, an initial response rate of 83 per cent. Subsequent attrition was
low and 243 women and children were seen throughout the study. It was
intended to have equal numbers of women in higher status and lower
status occupations. However this proved impossible due to the
differential rates of return to employment for different occupational
groups (Table 8.1).

Table 8.1 Maternal occupational status before child's birth

	Home	Relative	Childminder	Nursery	Total
Higher status (professional, managerial)	29	14	57	30	130
Lower status (sales, clerical, manual)	41	42	31	6	120
Total	70	56	88	36	250

Note: There were five cases who used other forms of day care.

Few higher status women used relatives for day care. There was little
nursery provision for children under 2 years of age available to dual-
earner families. Such private nurseries as existed were largely used by
women in higher status occupations, in particular women in health and
education services, where there were more workplace nurseries.

The first contact

This occurred at 4–5 months after the birth and was used to collect information before the return to employment and non-parental care had an effect. At this contact information was collected by:

1 an interview with the mother;
2 the Revised Infant Temperament Questionnaire (Carey and McDevitt 1978);
3 a diary of the child's week;
4 the Bayley Scales of Infant Development (Bayley 1969);
5 an observation of mother-infant interaction in the home.

Information collected from these sources was used to address the question of whether the children in the study sub-groups differed in their development or experiences before day care started. The data from the initial contact showed that there were no significant differences in developmental status or temperament. The diary data revealed that where the mother would return to employment there was a greater use of babysitters, even before the return to employment. The observations revealed that there were no significant differences overall in patterns of mother-infant interactions. However there was an intriguing gender-by-returner interaction effect. Where the mother would not return to employment there was more mother-child interaction when the child was a boy than when it was a girl: this did not occur amongst other women. This suggests that women who did not return to employment differentiated between boys and girls more than women who returned to employment, and may match a greater equivalence of gender roles between mother and father in dual-earner households.

When the child was 18 months old

At 18 months of age, Melhuish (1988a) considered how the children's experiences in the home, relative, childminder and nursery sub-groups compared. Knowing the answer is useful in judging how well various types of childcare meet the developmental needs of children and may be useful in explaining any differences in child behaviour or development which might emerge. When the children were 18 months old and were put in day care for more than 20 hours per week, the parents were asked for permission to approach the caregiver. The visits to the caregiver consisted of an interview and two separate one-hour observations of the child in the day care setting. Observations at home were also done for children who had not been in day care. The observations were scheduled to occur during 'free-play' periods where the child was active, and to avoid scheduled routines such as mealtimes. The observational data were used to compare children's behaviour and interactions in the four childcare environments.

There were some behaviours which did not differ between childcare settings. These behaviours were holding, individual play, crying and gestures. However there were many behaviours which varied markedly. For attention (to and from the child), and verbal and non-verbal vocalisations (to and from the child), there was a distinct trend – the greatest occurrence was in the home, followed by relative then childminder with least occurrence in nurseries. Responsiveness followed a very similar pattern except that home and relative were equivalent. Activities involving the simultaneous participation of two or more people showed a reverse pattern being greatest in nurseries and least in the home. Affection both to and from the study child was lower in nurseries than in other environments. Aggression was greater in nurseries, although as almost all aggression was between children this was a consequence of the greater number of children in nurseries. Melhuish *et al.* (in press a) has details of results and analyses.

Cognitive and language development

Melhuish *et al.* (1986) investigated the relationship between day care experience up to 18 months and cognitive, language and socio-emotional development. Cognitive development was measured with the Bayley Scales mental development index, and the mothers' records of the children's utterances were used to compute the number of single words and word combinations produced by the children. The means for cognitive and language measures of the four groups are shown in Table 8.2.

Table 8.2 Means of cognitive and language measures at 18 months of age

	Home	*Relative*	*Childminder*	*Nursery*
Bayley MDI (cognitive)	114	107	114	117
Number of single words	85	45	72	38
Number of word combinations	9	12	7	1

The groups differed in socio-economic status, which is likely to affect development. Taking this into account, did the children who experienced different types of care differ in their progress in cognitive development? This question involved consideration of change in cognitive development from the first contact at 4–5 months to 18 months of age. In order to analyse the data for change in cognitive development the form of regression analysis described by Plewis (1985) was used. This allowed comparison of care groups after allowing for cognitive development at 5 months and the effects of the socio-economic variables of parental occupation, income and mother's education. The results indicated that only mother's education was associated with progress in cognitive development, type of care having no independent effect.

Measures of language development, derived from maternal records of language production, were the number of single words and number of word combinations used by the child. The validity of this data was tested by having an independent assessment of language development using the Reynell Language Development Scales (Reynell 1969) for twenty-three children. The high correlation (0.86) between rankings based on the maternal record data and the Reynell scores was strong evidence that these measures were valid indicators of language development. The differences between day care groups were tested using a log-linear regression to allow for differences in maternal education.

There was no significant effect of care group for single words produced – but a significantly smaller proportion of the nursery group had high numbers of word combinations. The nursery group did not show a deficient level of language development, in terms of being outside the ability range considered normal; they were however less likely to have language records indicative of advanced language development. The results are particularly striking when the socio-economic advantages of the nursery group over the other groups are considered. The nursery group parents had higher status jobs, more qualifications and higher salaries, and more advantaged groups would be expected to show better language development, yet in this study the nursery group did worse than the other groups. Melhuish *et al.* (in press b) contains further details of results and analyses.

It could be argued that where women are full-time employed they have less opportunity for noting the words used by their child. However, at 18 months of age, the language used by the child is such that a parent with only evening and weekend experience of being with a child can keep an accurate record. Also this point would apply equally to all the employed women, yet it is only for the nursery group that the effect on number of word combinations appeared. The hours of non-parental care for the childminder group were higher than for the nursery group, so differences in time with mother cannot account for differences in language scores between the care groups.

Socio-emotional development

When the children were 18 months old, data on socio-emotional development derived from three different measures, two based on observer reports, and the third based on the mother's report.

1 The stranger approach/separation/reunion sequence.
2 Seven ratings from the Infant Behaviour record (Bayley 1969), which were completed by the observer during home visits. These ratings were responsiveness to persons, mother and observer, co-operativeness, fearfulness, tension and general emotional tone.
3 A socio-emotional development questionnaire, completed by mothers, which obtained data on socio-emotional development from the mother's experience of the child. It was developed because no equivalent method existed appropriate for 18-month-old children. Items focused on the child's actual behaviour rather than parental attitudes, although inevitably any parental report technique will to some extent reflect parental as well as child characteristics. The questionnaire covered eight areas: sociability, emotional expression, self-punishing behaviours, empathy, fear of strangers, separation anxiety, tolerance of departures from daily routine and independence.

There was a significant effect for type of day care on aspects of socio-emotional development. In the stranger approach sequence the children who had experienced nursery care showed less signs of pleasure when approached by a stranger than the children in the other groups, but did not show more displeasure or upset. It was not the case that they appeared more upset by the stranger, rather they seemed less excited and showed less positive signs of emotion. This relative indifference probably reflected the greater experience of a wide range of people that these children had as a consequence of their non-parental care experience. Those children who were temperamentally difficult also showed fewer positive signs to the stranger, presumably reflecting the child's habitual mode of response to new people.

When separated from the mother in the presence of the stranger, least concern was shown by the home sub-group, followed by the relative and childminder sub-groups; the nursery group showed most concern. The differences show a notional continuum from home individual care, through to out-of-home, group care. While such a result may reflect differences in the attachment of the children to their mothers, it should not automatically be taken as doing so. Indeed the behaviour of the children upon reunion was comparable for all groups and behaviour at reunion is generally regarded as the most important aspect of behaviour in the classification of attachment.

These results reflecting the effects of day care experience for the approach/separation/reunion sequence held for both boys and girls and all categories of temperamental difficulty. Temperamental difficulty independently affected the responses during the stranger approach and response upon separation from the mother.

The ratings of the Infant Behaviour Record (completed by the observer) also pointed to different socio-emotional behaviour for the children in the nursery sub-group. They were noted as showing less orientation to people and more negative mood. These findings are consistent with the pattern of results from the approach/separation/ reunion sequence.

The two types of data based upon direct observation revealed significant effects associated with day care experience. The third type, the socio-emotional development questionnaire which is based on the mother's report, revealed none. Such a discrepancy may occur because the items of the questionnaire were not appropriate. Alternatively, mothers' reports may not have been sensitive to the differences between their own children and other children of a similar age. This may be due to lack of experience of a range of similar age children, or the tendency to idealise the behaviour of their own child. However the data from the two types of direct observation data were mutually supportive, and the differences reflecting day care experience were consistent.

When the children were 3 years old

At this contact data were derived from:

1 an interview with the mother;
2 an interview with the main non-parental caregiver;
3 the Behavioural Style Questionnaire (a temperament measure);
4 the British Ability Scales (4 cognitive measures);
5 a Social Behaviour Questionnaire;
6 a diary of the child's week;
7 observations of the child with main day-time caregiver.

Observations of children

The observations of the child with its main day-time caregiver was a major source of information about the characteristics of the child's daily experience, particularly of interactions. Affection in interaction was recorded as the sum of the frequencies of affectionate acts such as kisses, hugs, caresses, smiles and affectionate utterances. Overall there were significant differences between childcare groups, with mothers and relatives showing higher levels of affection toward the study child than childminders who were in turn more affectionate than nursery workers. Affection expressed by the study child did not differ significantly between types of childcare.

Play was considered in terms of individual play, joint play between the study child and another (adult or child) and group play where several people including the study child were involved. Individual and joint play did not show significant effects for type of childcare. Not surprisingly there was a significant childcare effect for group play, with more occurring in nurseries than other types of care.

Aggression was infrequent and occurred almost always between children; there was more aggression in the nursery than the other three types of childcare and also more with childminders than at home.

In looking at all vocal communications addressed to the study child, there are clear differences between the four childcare environments. The paired comparisons reveal that children in the home, relative and childminder groups received significantly more vocal communication than children in the nursery group and that the home group received significantly more than the childminder group. The pattern was also true if language or non-language vocalisations were considered separately. Gestures occurred much less frequently than vocal communications and did not differ significantly between groups.

As at 18 months of age, responsiveness to a child's communications was considered in terms of whether another's communication followed the child's communication. This overall measure of responsiveness showed nurseries were significantly less responsive than the other three childcare settings. Also responsiveness in homes was greater than at childminders.

Cognitive development at 3 years

At 3 years of age the child's development was considered in terms of several aspects of cognitive and socio-emotional development.

The children's cognitive development at 3 years of age was measured by four sub-tests of the British Ability Scales: naming vocabulary, verbal comprehension, recall of digits and visual recognition. These provided sub-test scores which could be combined to give an overall IQ. As there were substantial socio-economic differences between the groups, which would be expected to affect the scores, it is necessary to allow for these socio-economic factors in assessing childcare effects.

A cognitive measure (overall IQ or sub-test score) was therefore subjected to a regression analysis which tested for the effect of the total amount of non-parental care experienced once gender, initial cognitive development, and socio-economic variables had been allowed for. In addition, separate regression analyses were performed on four mutually exclusive groups – children who had had wholly home care, extensive relative care, extensive childminder care, and extensive nursery care – to test for the effects of different types of childcare.

For overall IQ, there were substantial effects for mother's education and father's occupational status, but no independent effects of non-parental care. It is possible that effects on individual sub-tests are masked when the overall IQ scores are considered. Therefore the same analyses described above were carried out for the four sub-tests. In the case of individual sub-test scores, there were effects for mother's education or father's occupational status for all sub-tests, greater education or status being associated with higher scores. For naming vocabulary the nursery and childminder groups scored significantly lower than the other groups. The other sub-tests did not show significant differences between the different types of care. These effects were produced after socio-economic variables had been allowed for, suggesting that the earlier observed difference in language development at 18 months of age is reflected at 3 years of age in the children's differential vocabulary.

Socio-emotional development at age 3

The measures used were derived from the Behavioural Screening Questionnaire, which gave a score for behaviour problems; the Social Behaviour Questionnaire, which gave scores for aggression, verbal sociability, independence, timidity, and positive sociability; and the ratings of social behaviour completed by fieldworkers after home visits. In analysing these data, similar analyses were used as for the cognitive measures to test for the effect of total amount of non-parental care and separately for the effects of type of childcare.

There were no significant effects for behaviour problems. For aggression and independence there were effects of parental education, with both decreasing with greater parental education. Verbal sociability was only related to cognitive development at 18 months. Timidity showed a significant effect for total amount of non-parental care, representing a tendency for children with more non-parental care experience to be less timid. Other variables only approached significance. Positive sociability, which represented the child's propensity to show positive social characteristics such as sharing and empathy with others, was greater for girls, and also amongst the nursery group.

Data from the rating scales completed by fieldworkers showed that sociability to the fieldworker, co-operation, positive mood and talking to the fieldworker all increased with increased day care experience. The effects were stronger when the amount of day care for the period 18 to 36 months was considered, indicating that recent day care experience was most important in affecting social behaviour toward the fieldworkers. Co-operation, positive mood and amount of talking were also related to the previous level of cognitive development.

The results from the ratings are consistent with the lower level of timidity reported by the mothers of children with substantial day care experience. The women often mentioned the increase in sociability that would derive from increased social contact as a possible benefit of day care and these findings bear out those expectations to some extent.

Summary and discussion

Is there an overall effect of day care as compared with home care on cognitive and language development? The results of this study say no. Were there differences in cognitive and language development associated with different types of non-parental care? There were: the nursery group had a lower level of language development at 18 months of age. Differences in language development are likely to bé reflected later in differences in verbal abilities. Hence the inferior results on the naming vocabulary scale suggest that this effect persisted at 3 years of age.

Different aspects of development are likely to be differentially sensitive to environmental influence at different ages and to be most sensitive when at their most rapid rate of development. At 18 months of age, children are at that stage of language development where word combinations are starting to be acquired and there is rapid development (Brown 1973). Hence this aspect of language development might be particularly susceptible to environmental influence at this age. At another age an aspect of development other than language may become susceptible to an environmental influence such as day care experience.

The reason for this effect of type of care can probably be found by considering the data on children's experience in different forms of care. The children's experience in nurseries at 18 and 36 months of age shows several variables that might be expected to affect language development. In particular the communication addressed to children and responsiveness that children's communications received were lower in the nurseries than other childcare environments. These are aspects of interactional experience which might be expected to affect language development. In this regard the findings of this study parallel those of McCartney (1984) on the effects of quality of day care on language development. McCartney found that language development was poorest in nurseries rated lower on quality of care where a central feature of quality was the degree of verbal responsiveness. Also both Carew (1980) and Rubenstein and Howes (1983) found that children enrolled in day care facilities with more responsive caregivers had higher cognitive and language scores.

Was there an overall effect of non-parental care as compared with home care on socio-emotional development? There was. The results indicated that 3-year-olds with greater non-parental care will be less timid and more sociable towards unfamiliar people. Were there differences in socio-emotional development associated with different types of care? The results indicated several differences. At 18 months of age, children's reactions upon separation from the mother became more negative as the type of care and child experienced changed from home individual care to out-of-home group care. The children who had nursery care were less concerned with an unfamiliar person and were rated as showing less orientation to people and more negative mood. At 3 years of age, the picture had changed somewhat in that nursery children, as well as showing less timidity and greater sociability as noted above, also were judged by mothers as showing a greater degree of pro-social behaviour.

Rutter (1981) noted that the relationship between day care and socio-emotional development warranted further study. This viewpoint followed from the confusing pattern of research findings in this area. One aspect of the confusion in this area has been the neglect of the potential importance of the age of the child when entering day care. Vaughn *et al.* (1980) found that day care was associated with insecure infant-mother attachment when the day care started in the first year of life, but not when the day care started after the child's first birthday. Typically, those studies which find no relationship between socio-emotional development and day care involve children who start day care considerably later, often when the children are in their second year.

Infant-mother attachment is usually established in the period 6–12 months of age (Ainsworth *et al.* 1978). Belsky (1988) has argued that the pattern of results from several studies supports the interpretation that day care started in the first year of life is associated with more anxious infant-mother attachment, and that such effects on attachments will have consequences for later socio-emotional development.

The children in the study started day care before 9 months of age. This is largely a consequence of the nature of maternity leave provision in Britain. It could be argued that current provisions often lead to children starting day care at an age which on theoretical grounds would not be advantageous. Infant-mother attachment is being established over the first 12 months of life and hence the children in this study began day care during the period when attachment was being established. It would have been useful if the study could have compared children who started day care after 12 months with those who started before 12 months of age. It is possible that the effects associated with day care experience are related to this age of starting.

The fact that this study involved children who started day care before 9 months means that the study should find the effects of day care on child development that Belsky's (1988) arguments would predict. However, the results both at 18 months of age and 3 years of age are most easily interpreted not as effects of day care but as the effects of type of care in that the effects are strongest for nursery care. The nursery care provided for the children in this study was not of good quality, and hence this effect of type of care may be a function of differences in quality of care between types. In particular the low level of responsiveness and adult-child interaction in nurseries are likely to affect developmental progress. The poor quality of nursery care observed in this study is likely to be a consequence of social context factors in that results of similar studies in countries with better developed and re-sourced systems of nursery care do not find equivalent results (e.g. Hwang, Broberg and Lamb, this volume). There were generally negative results for the nursery group at 18 months of age, and rather more positive results at 3 years of age. Possibly the organisation of nursery care in Britain is better adapted to the developmental needs of 3-year-olds than 18-month-olds.

There are some considerations to be borne in mind in evaluating these results. First, the nurseries were private nurseries, most of which were very isolated with little or no external support. Garland and White (1980) found that private sector nurseries had worse adult/child ratios and staff qualifications than public sector nurseries. Different results might be achieved in nurseries which are better resourced or have better external support.

Factors which are likely to account for the differences observed between childcare settings include group size and adult-child ratio, which vary across the groups in a parallel way to the pattern of results (see Table 8.3). Schaffer and Liddell (1984) found that joint attention and responsiveness were markedly less for children in dyads (1 adult and child) than larger groups (1 adult and 4 children). Group size was found to be a major determinant of staff-child interactions in day care by Ruopp, Travers, Glantz and Coelen (1979). One of the consequences of larger group size and poorer adult/child ratios is that staff become more involved in controlling children than interacting with them (Ruopp *et al.* 1979; Sylva, Roy and Painter 1980).

Table 8.3 Adult/child ratios for childcare settings

	Home	Relative	Childminder	Nursery
Mean adult/child ratio	1.0	1.3	2.5	4.6
Range adult/child ratio	1–2	1–3	1–5	2.4–8.5

Other factors which are also likely to be important in contributing to the differences observed are accommodation, equipment and staffing in terms of training and experience, demands made of staff and morale. Fifty-eight per cent of nurseries complained about inadequacies in their accommodation. Although the majority of nursery staff had some train-ing, they were younger than other caregivers in the study and only a third had their own children whereas almost all relatives and child-minders were mothers. Whilst some nurseries provided good support for staff there were others that were poorly resourced with consequent increase in the demands made on staff, e.g. no cover for absent staff. Stability of care is also likely to be important. Stability can be in terms of placements or in terms of caregivers. From the child's point of view stability of caregivers is probably the most important, and this is likely to be particularly important for children acquiring basic communication skills in that early child communications tend to be idiosyncratic and familiar caregivers will usually decode the idiosyncracies appropriately whereas unfamiliar caregivers are more likely to misunderstand or not to comprehend at all, with consequences for the responsiveness the child receives. In nurseries the greater number of staff and high staff turnover may well produce considerable instability of caregivers for a child.

This range of factors leading to differences in children's experiences of day care or quality of day care are likely to be influenced largely by aspects of the social context, which is not conducive to well-developed childcare provision in Britain as discussed by Moss (this volume).

References

Ainsworth, M.D.S., Blehar, M.L., Waters, E. and Wall, S. (1978) *Patterns of Attachment: A Psychological Study of the Strange Situation*, Hillsdale, NJ: Lawrence Erlbaum Associates.

Bain, A. and Barnett, L. (1980) *The Design of a Day Care System in a Nursery Setting for Children Under Five*, Report to DHSS.

Bayley, N. (1969) *The Bayley Scales of Infant Development*, New York: The Psychological Corporation.

Belsky, J. (1988) 'The "effects" of infant day care reconsidered', *Early Childhood Research Quarterly* 3: 235–72.

Brown, R. (1973) *A First Language*, Cambridge, MA: Harvard University Press.

Bryant, B., Harris, M. and Newton, D. (1980) *Children and Minders*, London: Grant McIntyre.

Carew, J. (1980) 'Experience and the development of intelligence in young children', *Monographs of the Society for Research in Child Development* 45 (6-7, serial no. 187).

Carey, W.B. and McDevitt, S.C. (1978) 'Revision of the infant temperament questionnaire', *Pediatrics* 61: 735–9.

Davie, C. (1986) *An Investigation into Childminding in North Staffordshire*, Report to DHSS.

Garland, C. and White, S. (1980) *Children and Day Nurseries*, London: Grant McIntyre.

Hwang, C.-P., Broberg, A. and Lamb, M. (this volume) 'Swedish day care research', in E.C. Melhuish and P. Moss (eds) *Day Care for Young Children: International Perspectives*, London: Routledge.

McCartney, K. (1984) 'Effect of quality of day care environment on children's language development', *Development Psychology* 20: 244–60.

McGuire, J. and Richman, N. (1988) 'Institutional characteristics and staff behaviour', paper presented at the Annual Conference of the British Psychological Society, Leeds, April 1988.

Mayall, B. and Petrie, P. (1977) *Minder, Mother and Child*, London: University of London Institute of Education.

Mayall, B. and Petrie, P. (1983) *Childminding and Day Nurseries: What Kind of Care?* London: Heinemann.

Melhuish, E.C. (1987) 'Socio-emotional behaviour at 18 months as a function of daycare experience, temperament and gender', *Infant Mental Health Journal* 8: 364–73.

— (1988a) 'Young children's experience of different types of day care', paper presented at the third European Conference on Developmental Psychology, Budapest, Hungary.

— (1988b) 'Etude du comportement socio-affectif a dix-huit mois en fonction du mode de garde', in B. Cramer (ed.) *Psychiatrie du Bébé: Nouvelles Frontières*, Paris: Editions Eshel.

Melhuish, E.C., Mooney, A., Martin, S. and Lloyd, E. (1986) 'The developmental progress of 18-month-old children, related to their day care experience', paper presented to the Association of Child Psychology and Psychiatry, London.

— (in press a) 'Type of day care at 18 months: I Differences in interactional experience', *Journal of Child Psychology and Psychiatry*.

— (in press b) 'Type of day care at 18 months: II Relations with cognitive and language development', *Journal of Child Psychology and Psychiatry*.

Moore, T.W. (1975) 'Exclusive early mothering and its alternatives: the outcome to adolescence', *Scandinavian Journal of Psychology*, 16, 255–72.

Plewis, I. (1985) *Analysing Change: Measurement and Explanation using Longitudinal Data*, Chichester: John Wiley.

Raven, M. (1979) 'A comparison of the language competency and social behaviour of childminded and non-childminded three- and four-year-old children', M.Sc. Dissertation, University of London Institute of Education.

— (1981) 'Review: The effects of childminding: How much do we know?' *Child: Care, Health and Development* 7: 103–11.

Reynell, J. (1969) *Reynell Developmental Language Scales*, Slough: National Foundation for Educational Research.

Rubenstein, J.L. and Howes, C. (1983) 'Socio-emotional development of toddlers in day care: The role of peers and individual differences', in S. Kilmer (ed.) *Advances in Early Education and Day Care*, San Francisco: JAI Press.

Ruopp, R., Travers, J., Glantz, F. and Coelen, C. (1979) *Children at the Center*, Cambridge, MA: Abt Books.

Rutter, M. (1981) 'Socio-emotional consequences of daycare for preschool children', *American Journal of Orthopsychiatry* 51: 4–27.

Schaffer, H.R. and Liddell, C. (1984) 'Adult-child interaction under dyadic and polyadic conditions', *British Journal of Developmental Psychology* 2: 33–42.

Shinman, S. (1981) *A Choice for Every Child? Access and Response to Pre-school Provision*, London: Tavistock.

Sylva, K., Roy, C. and Painter, H. (1980) *Childwatching at Playgroup and Nursery School*, London: Grant McIntyre.

Vaughn, B.E., Gove, F.E. and Egeland, B. (1980) 'The relationship between out-of-home care and the quality of infant-mother attachment in an economically disadvantaged population', *Child Development* 51: 1203–14.

Chapter nine

Day care for young children in the United States

Deborah Phillips

Day care in the USA has been described as a patchwork quilt. This is an apt analogy given the vast diversity of arrangements used by US families, the uneven regulation of day care and the paucity of national data concerning the supply, quality and costs of care. The lack of a coherent day care system in the USA is not an accident of history. It is the heritage of a social system that cherishes individualism and family privacy to the neglect of collective responsibility for children.

Employment entitlements for parents

Many industrialised countries have developed complementary day care and parental leave policies that offer parents some flexibility in deciding when to return to work after the birth of a child. The USA has not done so. No federal statute guarantees pregnant women the right to take temporary leave from employment after birth. Federal law does require that pregnant women be eligible for disability benefits where they are available, but only five states require employers to provide these benefits. Some private businesses provide maternity benefits to their employees but, in many instances, this means an unpaid leave for a couple of months with no guarantee of reinstatement.

Current system of day care provision

Forms of day care

There are four broad categories of day care in the United States: (1) informal care, that is provided by relatives; (2) in-home care, provided by a non-relative in the child's home; (3) family day care, in which one adult cares for several children in her own home; and (4) day care centres, about half of which are now run on a for-profit basis. These arrangements vary along several dimensions including overall use, cost, age range of children served, typical training of the caregiver(s), regulatory status, and funding sources. Very little is known about the distribution of these forms of care across different regions of the country, or of the total space available in each type.

Quality and characteristics of care

Quality varies tremendously within every form of day care. Centres, however, are much more likely to offer care by a trained adult compared to other forms of care (Clarke-Stewart 1987; Howes this volume). Centre-based arrangements are also specifically designed to meet the needs of children, whereas home environments often contain hazards that appear to lead home-based caregivers to be more restrictive toward children (Howes and Rubenstein 1985). Small ratios of adults to children, on the other hand, are more prevalent in non-centre arrangements. An additional, qualitative distinction between home-based and centre-based care in the United States concerns the children's daily activities. Home-based arrangements tend to be less explicitly educational and less structured overall, whereas centres are more likely to plan for learning (Prescott 1973; Clarke-Stewart 1987; Goelman and Pence 1987).

State regulation of day care is the only official means of assuring a minimum level of safety and quality. The federal government plays no role in this area, despite repeated attempts to establish federal day care standards. Moreover, only two of the forms of care described above, family day care homes and day care centres, are regulated to assure that they meet minimal standards of quality. With respect to centre-based care, both private, for-profit and public, non-profit centres must meet state standards in all states except Idaho (this state only regulates centres and family day care homes that receive federal funds, leaving a vast number of arrangements totally unregulated). Typically centres must be inspected on an annual or biannual basis prior to receiving a license to operate. However, a few states exempt church-run centres from regulation and several exempt part-day programmes. These twelve states are strongholds of evangelistic churches which are highly organised to fight attempts to regulate their religiously-oriented day care programmes: they believe that 'It is a sin against God for any ministry of the church to be controlled by the state' (Phillips 1988).

With respect to family day care homes, forty-six of the fifty states require regulation or registration. Regulation of family day care homes generally entails a state inspection, as with centres, although they typically occur much less frequently. Registration of homes requires only that providers put their names on a list maintained by a state agency. In contrast to day care centres, most family day care homes are not regulated despite state requirements, either because they are too small to fall under state regulations (most state laws pertain only to homes with three or more children) or because they choose to operate illegally or 'underground'.

Licensing standards for day care also vary widely across states with respect to their provisions as well as coverage and enforcement. Some states combine stringent regulations with rigorous enforcement. Massachusetts, for example, requires that 'lead teachers' be trained in child development and that one adult be responsible for no more than three infants. On the other hand, Alabama requires only that staff have a high school diploma and permits one adult to care for six infants.

Funding of day care

Federal, state and local governments provide some funds for day care through both direct grant programmes and indirect mechanisms such as tax credits that reimburse individuals. Government support tends to be channelled to centre-based arrangements and to regulated family day care homes, since many public funding programmes contain requirements that they be used in regulated services. Among regulated services, both non-profit and for-profit arrangements receive public funds. In 1977, for example (the most recent year for which national data are available), 25 per cent of for-profit centres and 57 per cent of non-profit centres received funds from at least one federal programme (Coelen, Glantz and Calore 1979). Charitable organisations and foundations also contribute small amounts to day care, generally on a very local level.

Employers are the final source of non-parental funding. Out of the approximately six million businesses nationwide, around 2,500 provide some form of support for day care, about 500 in the form of centres in or near the workplace (Friedman 1985). The more common source of employer support is 'salary reduction' whereby a portion of one's salary is paid in the form of a non-taxable day care benefit. In the large scheme of things, employers are not a major source of day care support in the United States.

Most day care in the United States is funded privately by parent fees. This can be a considerable expense for families. In 1985, the average weekly cost for care for children under age 5 was about $37 (Hofferth 1987; US Bureau of the Census 1987), thus for 52 weeks a year, the average annual cost of care approached $2,000.

Costs, however, vary widely by type of care and the age of the child. Informal care provided by a relative is the least expensive day care option in the United States. Both in-home and centre care can be extremely expensive. The monthly cost of a full-time nanny in Boston, for example, ranges from $260 to $340, centre care ranges from $75 to $150 and family day care ranges from $40 to $160 (Friedman 1985).

The upper end of these ranges represents costs of care for infants. Relative care, on the other hand, is frequently provided without charge.

Supply of day care

Minimal data exist on the supply of different day care arrangements. There is virtually no national information on the supply of unregulated day care, and only a modest amount of information on regulated care. It does appear, however, that the supply of licensed centres has grown steadily over the last ten years. In 1976, the National Day Care Supply Study (Coelen *et al.* 1979) reported 18,307 day care centres with a total capacity of 1.01 million children. In 1986, a survey of each state's licensing office (NAEYC 1986) revealed a total supply of 62,989 day care centres, of which 39,929 were estimated to be in operation with a total capacity of approximately 2.1 million children.

These data suggest that the supply of licensed centres and their capacity have more than doubled in the last decade. This is consistent with the almost 50 per cent growth in use of centre-based care just in the last five years by full-time employed mothers with children under 5 years old. Nevertheless, little is known about changes in the age distribution of children in licensed centres. In 1976, 14 per cent of such centres enrolled children 2 years old and younger (Coelen *et al.* 1979). We do not know if this percentage has changed over the last decade to accommodate the growing demand for infant and toddler care.

The supply of regulated family day care homes has also increased during the last decade, although not at the fast pace of centres. In 1977, the National Day Care Home Study estimated the supply of regulated family day care homes in operation at 73,750 with an enrollment of 304,000 children (Fosburg 1981). By 1986, state licensing offices reported 165,276 family day care homes (NAEYC 1986), of which approximately 105,417 were in operation. On the basis of the 4.0 to 4.3 child average enrollment figure for regulated homes provided by the National Day Care Home Study, in 1986, 434,603 children could have been accommodated in regulated family day care homes. However, to a much greater extent than with centre-based programmes, these figures fail to reflect the actual supply of family day care homes given that the vast majority are unregulated. With respect to the age mix of children in family day care homes, infants represented about 10 per cent of enrolments and toddlers somewhat less than 50 per cent in 1976 (Fosburg 1981). Again, we know little about current patterns of enrollment by age of child.

One of the more unique elements of the day care market in the United States is the presence of for-profit centres. This sector has flourished during the past decade (Hofferth and Phillips 1987). Although no national statistics exist on the day care industry, most experts agree that more than 50 per cent of centres are operated on a for-profit basis. Within the for-profit sector, over 2,000 centres are operated by 'chains', in which a central corporation operates centres around the country using uniform curricula, supplies and even buildings. Kinder-Care Learning Centers, the largest of the chains, now operates 1,200 centres in over forty states. The major share of for-profit centres, however, are operated by single owners and, accordingly, are called 'mom and pop' centres.

Multiple purposes of day care

Day care is highly controversial, in large measure, because debates about day care serve as a metaphor for conflicting values regarding non-maternal care of children, poverty, working mothers and the relation between the family and the government (Phillips and Zigler 1987). This climate of controversy has impeded development of a coherent rationale for investing in efforts to make day care available, affordable and of decent quality. There is no agreement, for example, concerning whether day care is a social intervention or an economic convenience; a service for children, for adults or for families; a comprehensive developmental programme or basic caretaking; a supplement or a substitute for parental care. Equally striking are contradictory portrayals of day care as a hotbed of sexual abuse or an effective intervention for abused children; as a beneficial early intervention programme or as a threat to mother-infant bonding; or as undermining of family values or as a vital family support service.

Day care, in practice, fills multiple roles. Three roles have been especially prominent in social debates. (1) day care as a child welfare service for the care and protection of children, (2) day care as early education, and (3) day care as a support for working parents, particularly in the context of public welfare. Day care also provides jobs primarily for women, a vehicle for parent education and a conduit for the delivery of comprehensive social services to disadvantaged families.

Day care as a child welfare service

The most long-standing purpose of day care in the United States has been to provide temporary, daytime care for children from poor, troubled and abusive families. The earliest services, day nurseries, emerged during the latter half of the nineteenth century in urban areas affected by rapid immigration and industrialisation. Their clientele consisted of destitute children of immigrant families, widowed mothers and other poor groups for whom maternal employment was essential (Fein and Clarke-Stewart 1973; Steinfels 1973). Eligibility for day care was thus premised on family inadequacy: parents without problems presumably did not need day care (Phillips and Zigler 1987). The immediate purpose of the day nurseries was humanitarian. They were established by private, philanthropic groups, and later maintained by social welfare organisations. In the spirit of preserving rather than replacing the family, the day nurseries provided an alternative to permanent institutionalisation in orphanages on the one hand, and to child neglect during maternal working hours on the other. Establishment of the day nurseries was also motivated, however, by fears about the consequences of failing to 'Americanise' poor and immigrant children. These children and their parents were viewed as a threat to society, the answer to which involved socialising children to value cleanliness, obedience and US standards of morality. The desired outcome was assimilation into mainstream American culture. Thus, care for children emphasised socialisation and hygiene, supplemented with parenting classes (Ruderman 1968; Joffe 1977).

The contemporary ancestor of this tradition can be found in the fact that, in most states, responsibility for day care resides in social welfare agencies. The enduring association between day care and child welfare can also be found in public perceptions that day care, particularly that which is publicly-funded, is a service for poor families; this lends it remarkably low status and marginal public funding.

Day care as early education

Early education came to the United States in the 1920s in the form of demonstration nursery schools based largely in universities (Scarr and Weinberg 1986; White and Buka 1987). The nursery schools were designed by developmental psychologists as laboratories for the study of child development. Childrearing became an experimental science, akin to developing hybrid corn. The nursery schools were supported by parent fees and university contributions, and served middle- and upper-class families. This stood in contrast to the low-income clientele of the day nurseries.

In the 1960s, early education moved from university laboratories to low-income neighbourhoods as part of the War on Poverty (Zigler and Valentine 1979; Laosa 1984; White and Buka 1987). What was good for middle-class children became an imperative for poor children in the context of grave concerns about the long-term public ramifications of poverty, poor preparation for school and subsequent low motivation and school performance. Project Head Start was launched in 1964 as a centrepiece of the War on Poverty. It was a multi-purpose programme, designed to equip children with the cognitive, social and physical skills necessary for success in school. The long-term goal was to launch children on a path that would divert them from a life of poverty.

The early education rationale for day care is unique in two ways. First, it raises concerns about the quality of day care environments. Head Start is explicitly designed to compensate for children's disadvantaged home environments, thus asserting the critical need for high-quality, developmental care. Second, the early education theme is largely restricted to children between 3 and 5 years of age. Recently, however, this theme has begun to creep into the rhetoric surrounding justifications for day care for younger children. Infant and toddler day care is portrayed as the initial installment in a long-term investment in productive students and workers (Council for Economic Development 1987), thus creating incentives to provide high-quality programmes for these youngest citizens.

Day care as a support for adult employment

Reduction of poverty has provided the most long-standing rationale for public policies in the area of day care. This rationale is seen in the Head Start model. It is also seen in this third purpose, for which day care is tied to *adult* poverty programmes (Phillips, in press). Specifically, day care is provided as a necessary adjunct to policies that mandate training and employment for adult welfare clients. This role emerged during the 1960s in conjunction with a growing consensus that the major welfare programme for poor families with children, Aid to Families with Dependent Children (AFDC), should promote maternal employment as a bridge to self-sufficiency, rather than support mothers to stay home.

Unlike Head Start, with its preventive focus, day care that is linked to public welfare is cast as a programme for adults and is neither designed nor judged for its effects on children. The goal is economic rather than developmental, namely to reduce government expenditures on welfare by employing low-income mothers. Expanding the supply of day care and reducing its costs, rather than upgrading its quality for children, are the major policy goals (Phillips and Zigler 1987; Phillips, in press).

In sum, the roots of day care in the United States are allied with poverty, welfare and families that were labelled 'inadequate' (Scarr and Weinberg 1986; Phillips and Zigler 1987). Within this tradition, two central disparities have arisen. The first is between high quality care as a service for children and low-cost care as a service for adults. The second is between care as a welfare service and care as early education.

Childcare arrangements for children under 3

Relatives and family day care homes are the most commonly used forms of day care for children under age 3 (Table 9.1). Together they account for 69 per cent of infants (under 1 year) and toddlers (1- and 2-year-olds) receiving day care. They are the least expensive and most informal types of care and are typically convenient to or in the child's home. In-home care by a non-relative is less commonly used and is actually on the decline. Day care centres provide close to 20 per cent of the care for infants and 23 per cent for toddlers. This constitutes dramatic growth since 1965 when between 2 and 6 per cent of children under age 3 were in centre-based care (Table 9.2). Between just 1982 and 1985, the percentage of children under age 1 in centre-based care grew from 8 per cent to 19 per cent (Phillips 1988). This pattern of substantial reliance on informal forms of day care is easily understood given the top priorities indicated by parents when they select day care: cost and convenience. The supply of centre-based care for young children is also extremely tight.

Table 9.1 Day care arrangements for infants and toddlers of employed mothers, US, 1984–5

Type of care	Under 1 year	1 and 2 years
Relative	38%	34%
Sitter, in-home	12%	7%
Family day care home	31%	35%
Day care centre	19%	23%

Source: US Bureau of the Census, 1987

This pattern of use varies somewhat with the employment status of the mother (Table 9.2). As of 1982, relatives provided the major share of day care for infants and toddlers with full- and part-time employed mothers, although they are rather more important for mothers with part-time employment. Their use has declined somewhat since 1965, however, for both groups of mothers. Reliance on family day care homes, in contrast, has grown, accounting for about one-third of arrangements used by both full- and part-time employed mothers. In-home, sitter care has also declined, particularly among full-time employed mothers, while centre care has risen for both groups, but is used substantially more by mothers who work full-time compared to part-time workers.

Families using different forms of care also differ in ethnicity and socio-economic status. Black mothers are more likely than white mothers to rely on day care provided by a relative other than the father and somewhat more likely to use centre care (US Bureau of the Census 1987). They are also less likely to rely on non-relative care in home

168

settings. Similar patterns apply to lower-income mothers compared to higher-income mothers.

Table 9.2 Day care arrangements for children under age 3 of employed mothers, US, 1965–85

Type of care and maternal employment status	1965	1977	1982	1985
Relatives				
Part-time	56%	47%	49%	35%
Full-time	49%	43%	41%	
Sitter, in-home				
Part-time	19%	15%	12%	9%
Full-time	22%	8%	8%	
Family day care home				
Part-time	23%	28%	33%	34%
Full-time	24%	38%	36%	
Day care centre				
Part-time	2%	9%	9%	22%
Full-time	6%	11%	16%	

Sources: Hofferth and Phillips 1987 (1965, 1977, 1982 data); US Bureau of the Census 1987 (1985 data)

Note: 1985 data are not disaggregated by part-time/full-time employment.

Ramifications of the purposes and structure of day care

The lack of any co-ordinating structure for the day care system in the United States, while affirming 'free market' economic beliefs, has had several negative ramifications with respect to issues of equity, planning, the day care workforce and regulation of quality.

Economic stratification

There are two tiers in day care in the United States, one for poor families and a second for non-poor families. These two income groups use different types of programmes and, within types, use different providers. For example, in-home nannies are not found in lower-class homes. With centre-based care, the for-profit sector and particularly the day care chains, such as Kinder-Care, cater to middle-class families. The non-profit sector is somewhat more mixed economically. This is, in part, due to the fact that direct government subsidies to support the day care costs

169

of low-income families have typically been granted to non-profit centres, and, in some cases, to regulated family day care homes. Moreover, day care is a neighbourhood-based service. Parents want day care that is close to home and similar to the culture of the family. Thus, the income segregation of United States' neighbourhoods is reflected in a segregated day care market.

Gaps in service

In the absence of any state-wide or national planning, there are no assurances that the availability of day care corresponds to patterns of need. For example, there is a dearth of information concerning rural care. In urban areas, the challenge is one of matching supply to demand. In a recent study in Los Angeles County, the supply of day care appeared adequate until the county was divided into population areas. Severe shortages of care were then found in the central city which is characterised by high rates of employment among black mothers and in-migration of Latino children whose mothers also work at high rates (Hill-Scott 1988). Few regions, however, have the resources necessary to inventory the supply and demand for childcare. Information regarding how much and what types of care need to be developed, for whom and at what cost is rarely available even at a local level.

Day care workforce

The haphazard nature of day care in the United States, combined with enduring perceptions that day care work is an extension of women's biological mothering role, is also reflected in the workforce of day care providers. Overall, it is estimated that the number of day care workers providing direct service to children lies between 2.8 and 3.4 million (Phillips and Whitebook, in press). The number of workers grew by 13 per cent between 1983 and 1985, with the most dramatic growth occurring among those who work outside of their own homes.

Behind these numbers lies a remarkably diverse labour force. Day care workers range from untrained women who have no education beyond a high school diploma to highly trained professionals who have worked in day care for years. This range of expertise can be found in almost every form of care, including regulated family day care homes and centres. In twenty-eight states, for example, regulations require neither prior experience in day care nor training in child development for family day care providers. No prior education or on-going training are required of centre staff in seven states (Morgan 1987).

Day care workers do have several characteristics in common. They are almost exclusively female. Their wages hover around the poverty level, earning them the dubious distinction of being ranked the second most underpaid workers in the nation (the clergy are first) by the National Committee on Pay Equity. In 1986, when the poverty level was $11,200, the median annual income of day care workers was under $10,000. They receive very few benefits. For example, over 40 per cent of centre-based staff reported that they had no medical insurance in a 1987 survey (Kontos and Stremmel 1988). At most, 20 per cent of day workers report participating in a retirement plan (Phillips and White-book, in press). Day care workers also have among the highest turnover rates of any occupation in the United States. The Department of Labor estimates that 42 per cent of all non-home based day care workers (e.g., those who work in centres) and 59 per cent of all home-based workers need to be replaced each year just to maintain the current supply of providers.

Unregulated care

The majority of day care services are provided outside of the formal market of regulated, visible day care. This distinguishes day care from most other major services in the United States, including medical care, child welfare services and home care for the elderly. Estimates place the share of unregulated family day care homes at 90 per cent of the total supply of family day care (Fosburg 1981). All care in the child's own home is unregulated, and out-of-home arrangements that involve fewer than 3 children are also typically not regulated. This is not equivalent to an 'underground' market, because it is operating legally and in the full knowledge of parents, providers and policymakers. One can only guess about the range of quality in these unregulated arrangements, about their stability and the working conditions of the providers. There are, however, strong voices in support of maintaining this informal market and resisting the encroachment of government regulation.

Government policies affecting day care

The evolution of federal policy

Day care remained the responsibility of the charitable, professional and private sectors until the economic depression of the 1930s led the federal government to assume a direct role. Federal involvement was not sparked primarily by an interest in child welfare, but rather by an interest in providing unemployed teachers, social workers and the like with jobs created through the Works Progress Administration (WPA), the major jobs programme of the Depression era. The so-called 'WPA nurseries' were funded throughout the Depression, but were then abruptly terminated with the other WPA jobs programmes when the economy recovered.

During the Second World War, the federal government again became involved in providing day care. Publicly-funded provision was essential to enable women to work in the war factories whose traditional male labour force had been decimated by the draft. In 1945, $52 million was spent on day care services in war-impacted areas. But, with victory, the Second World War centres lost their federal funds.

Both the WPA nurseries and the Second World War centres deviated from the child welfare model of day care. First, use of day care was considered patriotic: it was necessary to save the country from economic collapse and, then, from wartime defeat. Second, day care funds were channelled through education, rather than welfare, agencies. This distanced these emergency programmes from traditional day care. Third, reliance on day care was portrayed as a temporary expedient, needed only until women could return home to their natural roles as full-time mothers. Thus, the federal government dissociated itself from the heritage of day care, and sent a clear message that its involvement was crisis-driven and temporary.

Several significant developments that challenged this aloof posture of the federal government were set in motion after the Second World War. First, concern about rising levels of poverty was joined by the recognition that single mothers required social services, such as day care, if employment was to become a feasible alternative to public assistance. Federal support for services targeted on poor families, including day care, was expanded accordingly. This brought the federal government squarely in line with day care's traditional role as a service for non-mainstream families. Federal day care was linked to welfare dependency.

The second development was national concern about the adequacy with which our educational system was preparing a technologically-sophisticated labour force, prompted when the Russians launched the Sputnik satellite. The War on Poverty, declared in 1964, was about education, progress and productivity. Project Head Start, created in 1965, was the early childhood component of the War on Poverty. It consists of part-day programmes that provide a comprehensive range of education, health and social services to low-income children and their families to ameliorate the presumed negative consequences of living in a 'culture of poverty'. Here again, federal support for day care was linked to poverty. But, with Head Start, the vehicle was a preventive programme designed to provide compensatory education to children, rather than a welfare programme targeted on poor mothers.

The third development occurred in the unlikely context of a debate about tax equity. Since 1954, the US tax code has contained a provision

that helps families recover money spent on care of dependents. Originally, this provision was designed to support the employment of low-
income women who had to work out of economic necessity. But, as the
demographics of working women shifted to encompass all income
groups, the argument was made that day care expenses are an ordinary
and necessary business expense for working women, and should not be
restricted only to the poor. This argument prevailed and the dependent
care tax credit is now primarily a benefit for non-poor families.

The federal role in day care has evolved into three strands. The first
strand is provision for low-income families in the context of welfare
legislation. The second is support for Head Start which provides
comprehensive care and education for low-income children with the
long-term goal of preventing poverty. The third strand consists of the
substantial support for day care through the tax system. These three
strands remain today, and are joined by the participation of state and
local governments.

The current shape of government day care policy

Federal day care support

Most public support for day care originates from the federal government. Federal support is a conglomeration of selective responses to
selective needs. A variety of programmes has evolved over time, some
of which provide direct services to low-income families (e.g., Head
Start), some of which are tied to welfare benefits, and some of which are
channelled to non-poor families through the dependent care tax credit.
Head Start and the Social Services Block Grant (SSBG) are the largest
of the direct service programmes. About 1,200 Head Start Programs
nationally provide services to 452,000 pre-schoolers aged 3 and 4 years,
about 16 per cent of all eligible children. The SSBG provides federal
funds to states for the full range of social services. Discretion over
specific uses of the SSBG funds is left entirely to the states. Prior to
1981, about 20 per cent of the funds were spent on day care. Since then,
national data on the distribution of SSBG funds have not been collected.

Low-income families on welfare may receive either Head Start or
SSBG subsidies. Low-income mothers who work are also eligible for an
alternative source of day care support. Specifically, employed mothers
on AFDC are eligible for a day care disregard. Under the disregard,
mothers pay providers directly and then deduct the amount paid – up to
a statutory maximum of $160 per month per child – from their monthly
income before their AFDC benefit level is calculated. As a consequence,
they are not penalised for working and spending money on day care. In
twenty-six states and the District of Columbia, mothers can receive

AFDC and thus remain eligible for the disregard if their husband is unemployed; elsewhere, two-parent families are not eligible for AFDC or the disregard. (This information reflects policy in the United States as of 1988. Presently, states are implementing a major new reform law which requires that all states allow mothers with unemployed husbands to remain eligible for AFDC. This new law also increased the childcare disregard to $175 per month for children over age 2 years and $200 per month for children age 2 years and younger.)

The Dependent Care Block Grant is another major source of federal day care support. Non-poor families who pay taxes may claim a credit against their tax liability for a portion (20 per cent to 30 per cent) of their day care expenses up to a total expense of $2,400 for one child and $4,800 for two children.

The federal government also provides food subsidies to centres that serve primarily low-income children and to family day care homes through the Day Care Food Program. This programme requires that all programmes receiving subsidies be regulated by their state. It has served as a major catalyst for family day care homes to join the regulated day care market.

It is readily apparent that day care support is highly stratified by income. Different types of subsidies are offered to families in different income brackets. Head Start, the SSBG, the AFDC disregard and the Day Care Food Program are targeted on low-income families, whereas the tax credit supports the day care expenses of non-poor families who earn enough to have a tax liability. In 1986, for example, 70 per cent of the tax benefits went to families with annual earnings over $25,000.

Since 1980, federal funds for the programmes targeted on the poor have declined dramatically in value. Funds for the SSBG, for example, are now worth 50 per cent of their 1975 funding level and 75 per cent of their 1981 level in inflation-adjusted dollars. In contrast, federal expenditures (via lost taxes) on the tax credit have more than tripled from $1.2 billion in 1981 to an estimated $3.4 billion in 1986 and $4.4 billion in 1990 (Haskins 1988). Thus, there has been a major shift from support that is targeted on poor families to support that goes primarily to non-poor families.

Day care support by individual states

Very few states are characterised by leadership in the area of day care. Instead, state level agencies in the areas of education and social services administer federal programmes, typically add state funds to the pool of day care support and are solely responsible for licensing day care programmes. Maintenance, rather than growth and careful planning, is the norm.

There are no national data on the amounts spent by the fifty states on day care. The only consistent information concerns state responses to federal budget cuts in the SSBG. Some states have increased their day care funds, while others have maintained or decreased funding. For example, 35 states provided less SSBG day care in 1985 than in 1981, 33 states lowered their day care standards and reduced enforcement staff to save costs and 20 made it more difficult for mothers on AFDC who were receiving job training to qualify for day care benefits (Children's Defense Fund 1984, 1987).

The consequence is widening disparities across states in the availability of day care support for low-income families. Some states, such as Massachusetts and California, have expanded their state day care funds and embarked on creative new initiatives (Phillips, in press). Other states, such as Louisianna and Texas, which have weak state economies and relatively less progressive views about services, have reduced their support for day care substantially.

Local day care support

Variation in the adequacy of day care services at the state level is matched by even greater variation at the local level. Again, information is spotty and based largely on local profiles. These profiles, however, encompass cities such as Detroit, which is struggling to sustain quite limited resources, and San Francisco, which has initiated several innovative programmes in recent years.

One of the most significant developments at the local level is the emergence of resource and referral programmes. Built on a federal model to co-ordinate community day care services in the 1970s, these programmes serve as brokers between parents in search of day care and day care programmes that can meet their needs. They have also provided an infrastructure for day care in some portions of the country. In addition to improving access to day care, 'R & R' programmes co-ordinate community services, such as caregiver training, toy lending libraries, needs assessment, advocacy and administration of government programmes, such as the Day Care Food Program. Their funding comes from a blend of government, corporate, foundation and charitable support. Where this support is unavailable, as in many rural areas, R & R services are rarely found. In most large urban areas, R & Rs provide a crucial co-ordinating role in the context of a pluralistic and confusing day care system.

Current day care system: contributing factors

Government day care policies are the end-product of fifty years of piecemeal policymaking. No overarching plan or efforts at co-ordination have guided the accumulation of day care services and benefits. The result is an extremely fragmented, inconsistent array of policies across states and localities. The lack of a co-ordinated policy is, however, not the inadvertent result of inattention. It is a deliberate response to strongly-held values about family privacy and individual choice.

Ideology about families, children and government

The most fundamental values that have influenced day care policy in the United States concern prevailing views of the ideal family. This ideal family is self-reliant, nurturant and economically self-contained. Privacy and domesticity have prevailed over any sense of collective responsibility for children, and the younger the child, the stronger these views. Within the family, it is the mother who is cherished as the nurturer and socialiser of children. The psychological concept of attachment (Bowlby 1969) has infiltrated public perceptions of ideal childrearing, leading to views that *only* mothers can offer children what they need to develop. The sharing of this childrearing function, entailed by day care, is anathema to this value system (Scarr, Phillips and McCartney 1989).

This view of families, mothers and children places a burden on government involvement in a wide variety of family and child issues that simply does not exist to the same degree in other countries. A conspicuous disparity is enforced between government and family functions, such that the two realms are not only separate, but are antagonistic. The childrearing function of the family is rigorously protected from government 'intrusion'. Accordingly, any deviation from the norm of non-intervention requires a very powerful justification. The traditional justification emphasises the need to protect children from adverse circumstances, such as child abuse and neglect. Government can step in as a 'parent' in cases where the child's own parents are inadequate or deviant. This rationale provides a benevolent motive for government intervention, while preserving the norm of the self-sufficient family, protected from interference.

Day care policies lie at the heart of this fundamental dilemma concerning public versus private responsibility for childrearing, posing a serious challenge to this value system. Families who are *not* inadequate need day care. For many families, good quality care is simply beyond their financial means without some form of subsidisation. Moreover, government leadership is needed to address the inequities and inefficiencies that have arisen in the day care market, precisely because it has been left to grow haphazardly without adequate planning and support. But, this government role has been vigorously resisted.

176

No better illustration of this resistance exists than that provided by an attempt in 1971 to pass comprehensive federal day care legislation. The Comprehensive Child Development Act of 1971, based largely on the Head Start model, would have extended federal support for good quality day care to non-poor families. The authors of the legislation, Senator Brademas and Representative Mondale, felt strongly about uncoupling day care and welfare.

Quality comprehensive programs can help all children and should be available in this country – on a voluntary basis – to all children as a matter of right, regardless of their economic, social and family background. Preschool in this country has become a privilege for the very rich and, to the extent that public programs are currently provided, for the very poor.

(Senator Mondale, *Congressional Record*, Sept. 1971, p. S30969)

The $2 billion legislation that contained the Comprehensive Child Development Act was passed by Congress with the support of a broad coalition of labour, church, social welfare and citizen's organisations. But President Nixon vetoed the legislation, in particular, because of its extension of federal funds to support day care for the middle class. The veto message labelled the programmes proposed by the Act as 'family weakening' and as advocating 'communal approaches to childrearing over against the family-centred approach' (*Congressional Record*, 10 Dec. 1971, pp. S21129-30). A bone had been tossed to the few, but vocal, opponents of federal day care. The veto message had a chilling effect on efforts to channel federal resources to quality day care persisting for fifteen years (Phillips and Zigler 1987).

Contemporary demographic trends and political pressures

In the late 1980s, the equation of government day care with intrusion into private family life has been challenged by relentless growth in maternal employment, particularly among middle-class families who constitute an important political constituency. Additionally, more politicians now have working wives, and they too are facing day care problems. As a consequence, over the last five years, day care has made its way onto the policy agenda as an issue that must be addressed.

Two demographic trends are driving the political debate about day care. First, as a result of childbearing among the large baby boom cohort born during the 1950s and early 1960s, the childhood population is again increasing after almost two decades of decline. The number of pre-school children began to rise in 1980, and by 1990 is expected to reach 23 million children under 6 years of age (Hofferth and Phillips

1987). Second, these figures hold important implications for day care because the mothers of these children are now more likely to work than they are to stay home during the day (see Tables 9.3 and 9.4). In 1977, 32 per cent of all mothers with a youngest child 1-year-old or younger and 42 per cent of mothers of 2-year-olds were in the labour force. Ten years later, these figures were 52 per cent and 59 per cent, respectively. Thus, as of 1987, over half of all mothers with children under 1 year of age were in the labour force, passing the critical 'majority' threshold. If current trends in maternal employment continue, by 1995 over two-thirds of pre-school children will have a mother in the work force (Table 9.3) (Hofferth and Phillips 1987) and, based on current employment patterns, close to 70 per cent of these mothers will work full time. Moreover, these trends characterise *all* mothers, regardless of race and marital status. Extensive reliance on day care has become a universal need (Phillips, in press).

Table 9.3 Actual and projected proportion of children under 6 with a mother in the labour force, US, 1970–95

Children	1970	1975	1980	1985	1990	1995
Under 1 year old	*	31%	38%	48%	*	*
Under 6 years old	29%	36%	43%	49%	58%	65%

Source: Hofferth and Phillips 1987: Table 1

Note: * = no information.

From the employers' perspective, these trends are particularly compelling. By 1995, roughly two-thirds of all new labour force entrants will be women (Johnston 1987). Eighty per cent of women in their childbearing years are expected to have children during their work life. The ability of employers to retain an essential part of their labour force is thus increasingly linked to the availability of day care. This contemporary social reality, combined with fears about the adequacy with which young children are being prepared for school and ultimately for the workforce, has brought the corporate sector into advocacy for day care. In 1987 a major report, issued by a prestigious national group of business leaders, called for 'quality day care arrangements for poor working parents' as a national imperative (Council for Economic Development 1987). These are the opinion-shapers of our society, and they are genuinely concerned about the consequences of failing to provide adequate day care: loss of female employees in whom they have invested years of training and job experience, as well as the potential loss of an adequately trained future workforce.

These demographic pressures, which might be expected to produce greater government receptivity to day care coincided with pressures to limit federal spending and a political agenda that favours deregulation and privatisation (Kahn and Kamerman 1987). The Reagan administration sought to reduce not only spending, but also the overall federal presence in day care. As a symbol of this retreat, no agency or individual in the federal executive branch has responsibility for day care. It was hoped that local governments, as well as the business and charitable sectors, would pick up this responsibility. But, this simply did not happen enough to compensate for federal budget cuts and growing demand for day care.

Table 9.4 Labour force participation rates of mothers of infants and toddlers, by marital status, US, 1977–87

Year and family status of mothers	Age of youngest child	
	1 year or younger	2 years
1977		
Total mothers	31.6%	42.3%
Wives	31.4%	40.9%
Women maintaining families	33.1%	52.8%
1982		
Total mothers	43.3%	52.0%
Wives	43.1%	51.3%
Women maintaining families	44.3%	55.9%
1987		
Total mothers	51.9%	58.5%
Wives	52.6%	59.0%
Women maintaining families	47.5%	56.2%

Source: News (August 12, 1987), US Department of Labor, Bureau of Labor Statistics, 'Over half of mothers with children one year old or under in labor force in March, 1987'

As the Reagan administration drew to a close, and demographic pressures continued to increase, a new climate of receptivity to federal day care proposals appeared to be emerging. In response to a public opinion poll conducted in late 1987, 34 per cent of respondents indicated that they would support increased taxes in order to pay for quality day care. Presidential candidates discussed day care in a far more visible way than in any prior presidential campaign. And, the advocacy of business leaders is extremely significant. These factors have converged to lend day care a visibility and urgency that it simply has not had in recent years.

Caregiving environments in the United States

Ecological models remind us that individual day care settings are profoundly affected by the broader social trends and values that have been discussed thus far (Bronfenbrenner 1979, 1986). The plight of caregivers who receive neither social status nor adequate compensation is a direct function of the national reluctance to accept day care as a normal part of children's lives. Among the numerous other examples of how the social context of day care in the United States affects caregiving environments, two are discussed here: parent-provider relationships and continuity of care for children.

Parents and providers

Howes (Chapter 10, this volume) has discussed research that illustrates inequities in the types and quality of arrangements used by low-income, highly stressed families as compared to the arrangements that are used by families whose incomes offer them greater choice in day care options. These research results capture the two-tiered structure of the United States' day care system in which different types of subsidy and a neighbourhood-based day care market produce vast inequities in service based on family income, as well as race (Phillips, 1984). As a consequence of these findings, relations among home and day care environments have emerged as a dominant question in the research literature, reflecting the fact that children in day care are actually negotiating two environments. In ecological models, this is a question about mesosystems, systems that link two environments that contain the child (Bronfenbrenner 1979).

Other factors affect caregiving environments. Among the most pervasive effects of the national ambivalence about shared childrearing is the tension that typically characterises parent-provider relationships. Powell (1980) and Kontos and Wells (1986) have documented the negative perceptions that caregivers can hold toward parents, and the jealousy that parents often harbour towards caregivers. In a society that links healthy development to mother-infant attachment, separating mother and child is cause for guilt on the part of mothers and disparagement of 'mother substitutes', a label not uncommonly assigned to day care staff. The dismally low pay of day care providers compounds these tensions, given that many care for the children of parents who themselves have substantially higher earnings.

Continuity of care

A second factor that is affected by the social context is the degree of continuity experienced by children in day care. As Howes (Chapter 10, this volume) has documented, children fare better in stable caregiving environments characterised by consistency in the adults who care for them. Yet, the low status and compensation accorded to day care providers in the United States has contributed to tremendously high turnover rates in this profession. In a recent study of child care staff (Whitebook, Howes and Phillips 1990), one centre in Phoenix reported that to maintain a staff of ten day care providers, twenty-seven providers were hired over the period of a year. The major reasons given by workers who leave their jobs concern poor pay, benefits and working conditions (Whitebook, Howes, Friedman and Darrah 1982). Ironically, they simultaneously report that they enjoy the daily work with children.

A second manifestation of low continuity of care for children can be found in the daily routines of many day care programmes. Not only do staff turnover frequently, but replacing them with adequately trained adults has become so difficult that programmes are hiring the minimum number of staff allowed by licensing standards and, in essence, living on the edge of compliance. Again, preliminary data from the new study of day care staff (Whitebook, Howes and Phillips 1990) reveal that centres are structuring their classes in 'accordion' style. A few children arrive between 7:00 and 8:00 and are placed in a room with one caregiver. At 8:00 more children arrive, so the group is divided and two caregivers are now required to staff the two groups. By 9:00, most children have arrived, four groups are created, and perhaps as many as six caregivers are now available. At the end of the day, the accordion folds back up, so that by 6:30 only one group and one caregiver are needed. From the child's perspective, it is possible to experience five different groups of peers and at least that many different staff during a single day. In this context, continuity of care is little more than a myth that programmes cannot begin to approximate. Social attitudes about day care are partially responsible for producing precisely the types of environments that can lead to the negative developmental outcomes so feared. Many other examples of this paradoxical situation exist in the United States. The uneven quality of care across states and localities that has arisen in the absence of federal day care standards confronts many children with sub-standard rearing environments. Low funding levels leave many families who need financial support to purchase good quality care with no option but to use low quality, unstable arrangements. It is estimated that about two million children are left alone at home for portions of the day (US Census 1987), in part due to the unavailability of appropriate after-school day care programmes.

Deborah Phillips

Conclusion

The social context of day care in the United States has worked against the development of a cohesive, stable system that meets the needs of most families. Instead, a patchwork of day care has evolved in incremental steps, leaving many holes and uneven coverage. Contemporary pressures, driven largely by demographic changes in the American family, suggest that this context is at a crossroads. Whether the net effect is a better system of day care, or simply another series of incremental, uncoordinated steps, is the topic for a future chapter.

References

Bowlby, J. (1969) *Attachment*, NY: Basic Books.
Bronfenbrenner, U. (1979) *The Ecology of Human Development*, Cambridge, MA: Harvard University Press.
— (1986) 'Ecology of the family as a context for human development: research perspectives', *Developmental Psychology* 22: 723–42.
Children's Defense Fund (1984) *State Child Care Fact Book*, Washington, DC: Children's Defense Fund.
— (1987) *A Children's Defense Budget*, Washington, DC: Children's Defense Fund.
Clarke-Stewart, A. (1987) 'Predicting child development from child care forms and features: the Chicago study', in D. Phillips (ed.), *Quality in Child Care: What Does Research Tell Us?* Washington, DC: National Association for the Education of Young Children.
Coelen, C., Glantz, F. and Calore, D. (1979) *Day Care Centers in the U.S.A. National Profile, 1976–1977*, Boston, MA: Abt Associates.
Council for Economic Development (1987) *Children in Need: Investing in the Future*, NY: CED.
Fein, G. and Clarke-Stewart, A. (1973) *Day Care in Context*, NY: Wiley.
Fosburg, S. (1981) *Family Day Care in the United States: Summary of Findings*, Boston, MA: Abt Associates.
Friedman, D. (1985) 'Corporate financial assistance for childcare', *The Conference Board Research Bulletin*, No. 117, NY: The Conference Board.
Goelman, H. and Pence, A. (1987) 'Effects of child care, family and individual characteristics on children's language development: The Victoria Day Care Research Project', in D. Phillips (ed.), *Quality in Child Care: What Does Research Tell Us?* Washington DC: National Association for the Education of Young Children.
Haskins, R. (1988) 'Summary of federal provisions for child care', unpublished manuscript prepared for the Committee on Ways and Means, US House of Representatives, Washington, DC.
Hill-Scott, K. (1988) 'No room at the inn: the crisis in child care supply', in J. Lande and S. Scarr (eds) *The Future of Child Care in the United States*, Hillsdale, NJ: Erlbaum.
Hofferth, S.L. (1987) 'Child care in the US', statement before the Select

Committee on Children, Youth, and Families, US House of Representatives, Washington, DC, July 1, 1987.

Hofferth, S.L. and Phillips, D.A. (1987) 'Child care in the United States, 1970 to 1995', *Journal of Marriage and the Family* 49: 559–71.

Howes, C. and Rubenstein, J. (1985) 'Determinants of toddlers' experience in daycare: age of entry and quality of setting', *Child Care Quarterly* 14: 140–51.

Joffe, C. (1977) *Friendly Intruders: Childcare Professionals and Family Life*, Berkeley, CA: University of California Press.

Johnston, W.B. (1987) *Workforce 2000: Work and Workers for the 21st century*, Indianapolis, IN: Hudson Institute.

Kahn, A. and Kamerman, S. (1987) *Child Care: Facing the Hard Choices*, Dover, MA: Auburn House.

Kontos, S. and Stremmel, A.J. (1988) 'Caregivers' perceptions of working conditions in a childcare environment', *Early Childhood Research Quarterly* 3: 77–90.

Kontos, S. and Wells, W. (1986) 'Attitudes of caregivers and the day care experiences of families', *Early Childhood Research Quarterly* 1: 47–67.

Laosa, L. (1984) 'Social policies toward children of diverse ethnic, racial, and language groups in the United States', in H.W. Stevenson and A.E. Siegel (eds), *Child Development Research and Social Policy, vol. 1*, Chicago, IL: University of Chicago Press.

Morgan, G. (1987) *The National State of Childcare Regulation, 1986*, Boston, MA: Wheelock College.

NAEYC (1986) *The Childcare Boom* Washington, DC: National Association for the Education of Young Children.

Phillips, D. (1984) 'Day care: promoting collaboration between research and policymaking', *Journal of Applied Developmental Psychology* 5: 91–113.

— (1988) 'The future supply and demand for child care in the United States', in J. Lande and S. Scarr (eds) *The Future of Child Care in the United States*, Hillsdale, NJ: Erlbaum.

— (in press) 'With a little help: child care and children in poverty', in A. Huston (ed.), *Children and Poverty*, Cambridge: Cambridge University Press.

Phillips, D. and Whitebook, M. (in press) 'The child care provider: pivotal player in the child's world', in S. Chehrazi (ed.), *Day Care: Psychological and Developmental Implications*, NY: American Psychiatric Press.

Phillips, D, and Zigler, E. (1987) 'The checkered history of federal child care regulation', in E. Rothkopf (ed.), *Review of Research in Education, vol. 14*, Washington, DC: American Education Research Association.

Powell, D. (1980) 'Toward a sociological perspective of relations between parents and child care programs', in S.J. Kilmer (ed.), *Advances in Early Education and Day Care, vol. 1*. Greenwich, CT: JAI Press.

Prescott, E. (1973) 'A comparison of three types of day care and the nursery school-home care', paper to the Society for Research in Child Development, Philadelphia, PA.

Ruderman, R. (1968) *Child Care and Working Mothers*, NY: Child Welfare League of America.

Scarr, S. and Weinberg, R. (1986) 'The early childhood enterprise: care and education of the young', *American Psychologist* 41: 1140–6.

Scarr, S., Phillips, D. and McCartney, K. (1989) 'Dilemmas of child care in the United States: working mothers and children at risk', *Canadian Psychologist* 30: 126–43.

Steinfels, M. (1973) *Who's Minding the Children? The History and Politics of Day Care in America*, NY: Simon & Schuster.

US Bureau of the Census (1987) *Who's Minding the Kids?* (Series P70, No. 9) Washington, DC: US Department of Commerce.

White, S. and Buka, S.L. (1987) 'Early education: programs, traditions, and policies', in E. Rothkopf (ed.), *Review of Research in Education, vol. 14*, Washington, DC: American Education Research Association.

Whitebook, M., Howes, C. and Phillips, D. (1990) *Who Cares? Child Care Workers and the Quality of Care in America. Final Report of the National Child Care Staffing Study*, Berkeley, CA: Child Care Employee Project.

Whitebook, M., Howes, C., Friedman, J. and Darrah, R. (1982) 'Caring for the caregivers: Burn-out in child care', in L. Katz (ed.), *Current Topics in Early Childhood Education, vol. 4*, NY: Ablex.

Zigler, E. and Valentine, J. (eds) (1979) *Project Head Start. A Legacy of the War on Poverty*, NY: The Free Press.

Chapter ten

Caregiving environments and their consequences for children: the experience in the United States

Carollee Howes

In the United States infants and toddlers attend an extremely hetero-geneous variety of day care arrangements. In form these arrangements range from in-home care provided by a relative or paid sitter through family day care, in which a woman cares for one or several children in her home, to centre care. In-home care ranges from specially trained 'American' nannies to illegal immigrants who do not speak English and do housework as well as childcare. Family day care can be a warm and competent caregiver who serves as a social support to families as well as a teacher of children or it can be a depressed and isolated woman who believes she has no marketable skills so takes in babies. Likewise centre care can provide excellent individualised loving and stimulating care or can be a 'baby warehouse' with too many children and too few care-givers. Despite the diversity of care arrangements we can identify ele-ments of care common to all childcare arrangements. In every childcare arrangement we can describe interactions with adults, attachment relationships with adults and relations between families and childcare. In almost all arrangements we can describe relationships and inter-actions with peers.

Children's experience of childcare comes from their interactions with adults and peers, their relationship with the caregiving adult and the continuity or discontinuity between experiences in day care and at home. These experiences can promote optimal development or could put the child at risk, particularly for poor social-emotional development. Children's particular experiences depend on variations in key features of the childcare environment. These features include the number of children cared for by each adult caregiver (child:adult ratio), the number of children in the child's primary group (group size), the training of the caregiver, developmentally appropriate activities and, indirectly, the status and salary afforded the caregiver in the larger society.

We have generated a substantial body of research to support links between some day care features including child:adult ratio, group size, caregiver training, developmentally appropriate activities and infant and toddler age children's experiences in childcare (Ruopp, Travers, Glantz and Coelen 1979; Howes 1983; Howes and Rubenstein 1985; Howes and Olenick 1986; Howes and Stewart 1987). The provision of developmentally appropriate activities is dependent on caregiver training in child development and early childhood education. We have documented relations between such training and positive child development (Ruopp, Travers, Glantz and Coelen 1979; Howes 1983). We do not, yet, have data to link caregiver status and salaries directly to child outcomes. However, staff turnover is implicated in childcare quality (Howes and Olenick 1986; Howes and Stewart 1987). Furthermore childcare arrangements that pay higher salaries have lower staff turnover (Howes, Whitebook and Pettygrove 1986).

In the following sections of the chapter I review research describing infant and toddler experiences in day care in the United States. I discuss interactions with adults, attachment to adults, interactions with peers and family and childcare continuity. For each section I describe the links between children's experiences in care and aspects of day care quality.

Interactions with adults

Researchers interested in studying child/adult interaction within infant toddler day care have turned to the literature on mother-child interaction for descriptions of optimal caregiver behaviours (e.g. Rubenstein and Howes 1979). One aspect of caregiver behaviour that, in United States mother-child research, is most strongly associated with healthy child functioning is a constellation of behaviours referred to as contingent, sensitive or responsive. In general these constructs are used to characterise caregivers who respond consistently and appropriately to child bids (e.g. for help and attention) and who initiate interactions geared to the capacities, intentions, goals and moods of the child as well as his or her current developmental level.

Parents who are more responsive (relative to parents who are less so) have children who are securely attached to them (Ainsworth, Blehar, Waters and Wall 1978; Belsky, Rovine and Taylor 1984), who perceive themselves as having more control over what happens to them (Skinner 1986), who do more exploring of their environments (Jennings, Harmon, Morgan, Gaiter and Yarrow 1979; Easterbrooks and Goldberg 1984), who perform better on cognitive tasks (Bradley, Caldwell and Elardo 1979; Beckwith and Cohen 1983), and who are more socially competent with peers (Bakeman and Brown 1980).

In the 1970s several researchers used the constructs of sensitive, contingent and responsive to assess adult caregiver and child interaction in infant and toddler day care (Cochran 1977; Rubenstein, Pedersen and Yarrow 1977; Golden, Rosenbluth, Grossi, Policare, Freeman and

Brownlee 1978; Rubenstein and Howes 1979; Carew 1980). The pattern of results from these studies is similar to the mother-child studies. The constructs are appropriate for assessing caregiver-child interactions in childcare of all forms. Moreover children enrolled in day care with more sensitive, responsive and contingent caregivers had higher cognitive and language scores (Carew 1980; Rubenstein and Howes 1983), and were more socially competent (Rubenstein and Howes 1983).

What features in a day care environment for infants and toddlers facilitate sensitive, responsive and contingent adult caregiving? I addressed this question in three studies. In the first study (Howes 1983) I observed 40 toddler-caregiver dyads, 20 in centre care and 20 in family day care homes. I collected information on the conditions of caregiving in the day care settings. These conditions of caregiving included the adult:child ratio, the number of adult caregivers, environments designed for children's activities, the hours of caregiver-child contact, the extent of responsibility for housework, the caregiver's experience as a caregiver and her training in child development. Caregivers in both forms of day care were better able to provide sensitive, responsive and contingent care when there were fewer children and more adults in the setting, when they worked shorter hours, had less responsibility for housework and worked in environments designed to be safe and appropriate for children. Caregivers with more training in child development were more sensitive, responsive and contingent than caregivers with little or no training.

In a second study (Howes and Stewart 1987) I designed a measure of adult play or involvement with children that reflects caregiver sensitivity, responsiveness and contingency. We rated the interactions of fifty-five toddlers and their family day care home providers on this adult play scale. The family day care homes were assessed with the Harms and Clifford Family Day Care Rating Scale (FDRC) which consists of thirty-three items of childcare quality ranging from basic care through developmentally appropriate activities (Harms & Clifford 1984). The ratings of adult play were strongly associated with a composite measure of day care quality consisting of the FDRC plus child:adult ratio, number of caregivers and number of children.

The results of several early studies suggest that children who enter day care as infants may be less compliant with adults than children in families not using day care (Schwartz, Strickland and Krolick 1974; Rubenstein, Howes and Boyle 1981; Finkelstein 1982). A number of studies also suggest that children's compliance varies as a function of parent-child interaction (Minton, Kagan and Levine 1971; Lytton 1977; Schaffer and Crook 1979; Holden 1983; McLaughlin 1983). Howes and Olenick (1986) examined variations in caregiver-child interaction and compliance. Eighty-nine families with toddler age children participated in the study. Thirty-two families had a child enrolled in a high-quality centre (maximum child:adult ratio of 1:4 for infants; caregivers with formal training in child development; no more than two primary teachers over the year). Twenty-five families had a child enrolled in a low-quality centre (higher child:adult ratios; no formally trained caregivers; more than two primary teachers over the year) and thirty-two families did not use day care. We observed compliance and control situations in the child's home, in day care and in a laboratory setting. Caregivers in high-quality centres were more appropriately sensitive, responsive and contingent during compliance and control situations than caregivers in low-quality centres and children enrolled in high-quality centres were more likely to be appropriately compliant and able to self-regulate. As kindergarteners, children who had experienced high-quality toddler care received higher teacher ratings for appropriate school adjustment (Howes 1990).

In summary it is possible to assess adult-child interactions in day care using the constructs of sensitivity, responsiveness and contingency. Children with more sensitive, responsive and contingent caregivers have more positive patterns of development. Caregivers who work in day care settings with fewer children and optimum conditions of caregiving as well as caregivers with formal training are better able to be sensitive, responsive and contingent to the children in their care.

Attachments to adult caregivers

Sensitive, responsive and contingent mothers predict securely attached infants (Ainsworth *et al.* 1978; Belsky *et al.* 1984). Do children in day care become securely attached to sensitive, responsive and contingent caregivers? Several studies have assessed caregiver-child attachment and concluded that secure as well as insecure patterns of attachment to child caregivers do occur (Anderson, Nagle, Roberts and Smith 1981; Krentz 1983; Ainslie and Anderson 1985; Howes, Rodning, Galluzzo and Myers 1988; Colin 1986). Although theoretically we can conclude that the process of forming attachments would be identical for all significant caregiving adults (Bretherton 1985), there are no studies that specifically examine caregiver-child interactions preceding attachment patterns.

If we assume similar pathways to secure attachments with mothers and with caregivers then the same features of day care environments that predict sensitive, responsive and contingent adult-child interaction in day care – particularly small groups of small children for each adult caregiver and training in child development – should predict secure attachment relationships. We have only begun to test these assumptions. In my laboratory we are conducting two longitudinal studies in tandem.

One sample consists of 115 children enrolled in the study at birth. At 12 months of age all of these children were seen in the Ainsworth Strange Situation for the assessment of attachment (Ainsworth *et al.* 1978) with their mothers. When the children were 18 months old 44 children in the larger sample were enrolled in day care arrangements which included at least one non-familial peer. This sub-sample of children were observed in their day care arrangement. We assessed security of attachment to caregiver with the Waters and Deane Q-Sort for attachment (Waters and Deane 1985). The second sample consists of sixty infants enrolled in childcare arrangements that include non-familial peers before their first birthdays. These children were observed in their childcare arrangements at six month intervals beginning at 18 months. We used the Q-Sort to assess security of attachment to caregiver and to parents. In both samples of children the child:adult ratio was smaller (fewer children per adult) for children securely attached to their caregivers as opposed to children insecurely attached to their caregivers (Howes *et al.* 1988).

If a secure attachment to caregiver is based on an adult's sensitive and responsive behaviours to infants then it makes sense that secure attachments are associated with smaller groups of children. It is probably impossible for one adult, no matter how adept, to provide individualised sensitive care to more than three or four babies. When there are more than four babies per caregiver the mechanics of feeding and diapering alone make it difficult to individualise care.

It is probably more difficult to intuitively understand why training in child development is associated with sensitive, contingent and responsive caregiving and thus with secure attachments. Training in child development provides caregivers with knowledge of developmental stages and of developmentally appropriate activities. Therefore the trained caregiver knows that it is important to respond to the baby's coos and gurgles, and tentative smiles. Of course most mothers have a hard time not responding to these social signals (Schaffer 1984). Therefore some argue that any motherly person would do a good job as a childcare caregiver. There are essential differences between the jobs of mother and of childcare provider that make such an assumption false. The emotional bond between a mother and her baby is stronger than that between an alternative caregiver and the baby. The caregiver may respond to the baby because she is a trained professional and a warm person while the mother may respond from her deep love of the child. Moreover caregivers must simultaneously respond appropriately to several different babies, meeting the needs of the group as well as the child she may be holding. A caregiver must balance the needs of the child's family as well as her own needs. For example she must provide excellent care to the baby without supplanting the mother or contributing to the mother's sense of guilt or inadequacy.

In summary, children in day care appear to form attachments to their caregivers. The security of the attachment relationship is most likely dependent on the sensitivity and responsiveness of the caregiver. Smaller groups of children per adult and training in child development facilitate a caregiver being more sensitive and responsive.

Interactions with peers

One of the major differences between most infants and toddlers enrolled in day care and infants and toddlers at home with their mothers is the intensity and diversity of the children's peer experiences. Infants and toddlers in day care eat, sleep and are toilet trained with a small group of children who are not only unrelated to them but may be representative of several different sub-cultures within the United States. Moreover the children construct their peer interactions and relationships in the absence of parents.

A body of literature describing early peer relationships and friendships corresponds to the increase in infant-toddler day care (see Hay 1985; Brownell 1986; Howes 1987a for reviews of this literature). Infants and toddlers form friendships and engage in complex play interactions earlier than our previous research and theory predicted. Moreover children who began day care as infants or toddlers appear more socially competent than their age mates who began peer contact as older children (Howes 1988b, in press).

There is a smaller body of research examining features of day care associated with social competence with peers. I recently reviewed this research and will summarise it below (Howes 1987b). These features include both characteristics of the adult caregivers and characteristics of the peer group.

Children who form secure attachment relationships with their mothers are more socially competent in their relationships with peers (Lieberman 1977; Waters, Wippman and Sroufe 1979; Pastor 1981; Sroufe 1983; Sroufe, Fox and Pancake 1983; La Frenière and Sroufe 1985; Jacobson and Wille 1986). Therefore we would expect children who form secure attachments to their caregivers to be more competent with peers. We examined this hypothesis in the longitudinal samples discussed above (Howes *et al.* 1988). Children who were rated as securely attached both to their caregivers and to their mothers were observed to be more competent in their interactions with peers. Children who were rated as insecurely attached to their caregivers or to both their caregiver and their mother were less competent in their peer interaction.

Day care caregivers receive very low wages and have low status in the United States (Whitebook and Phillips, in press). The lack of status and low pay contribute to high turnover rates. Therefore it is not unusual for an infant or toddler to experience multiple caregivers in succession. Two studies suggest that infants and toddlers are sensitive to caregiver stability. Cummings (1980) compared infants responses to stable and unstable day care caregivers in both a strange situation and during morning reunions between caregiver and child. Children used the stable but not the unstable caregivers as attachment figures. Rubenstein and Howes (1979) observed toddlers in day care and reported that the toddlers differentiated their social initiations between stable and less stable caregivers. The child who experience a series of unstable caregivers may lose interest in and motivation to engage in the social world. Since social interest in the partner is a fundamental part of social competency with peers, the child who experiences caregiver instability may be at risk for poor peer relationships.

Caregivers may influence children's relationships with peers through their patterns of socialisation of peer contacts. There is virtually no research on caregiver mediation of peer contacts. However we would expect infant and toddler peer interaction to flourish when a caregiver values such contact. Caregivers can place babies in proximity, direct their attention to a peer, and structure early turn-taking interactions. A skilled caregiver will observe and monitor early and fragile peer contacts. An unskilled caregiver will unknowingly interrupt such contacts.

In one study we were able to examine relations between caregiver training and one form of peer interaction. Social pretend play in day care children emerges between 18 and 24 months (Howes 1985) and serves as a marker of competent peer interaction in the early toddler period (Howes 1987a). We compared the social pretend play of toddlers in day care centres with and without formally trained staff (Howes and Unger 1989). Children with caregivers trained in child development were more sophisticated in their social pretend play.

Characteristics of the peer group also contribute to children's peer interactions and relationships. Children that remain in more stable (composed of the same children) peer groups develop more long-term friendships and competent patterns of play (Field, Vega-Lahr and Jagadish 1984; Howes 1988b). If children transfer to new classes or new schools with friends they suffer fewer physiological and behavioural manifestations of stress than if they transfer without friends (Field *et al.* 1984).

Peer groups composed of six to eight children as opposed to larger groups appear to support the development of peer interaction skills in infants and toddlers (Mueller and Vandell 1979). Groups of six to eight children are large enough for the children to have choices for partners yet small enough to protect peer contacts from over-stimulation and interruption.

Same-age and mixed-age peer groups can fulfil different functions (Hartup 1983). In mixed-age groups older children serve as models for the interaction of younger children. Older children may also incorporate younger children into more complex forms of interaction than they would be able to sustain with an age mate (Howes and Farver 1987). In same-age groups children practice and perfect new skills, perhaps fascinating to an age mate and boring to an older partner (Howes and Rubenstein 1981; Rothstein-Fisch and Howes 1988).

In summary, day care settings provide infants and toddlers with varied and intense opportunities for interaction with peers. Infants and toddlers form friendships and engage in complex peer interaction. Secure attachments with caregivers, stable caregivers and peer groups, trained caregivers who skilfully mediate peer interaction and relatively small groups of peers facilitate the development of social competence with peers. Interactions with same-age and mixed-age peers are both beneficial.

Interactions between home and day care characteristics

All infants and toddlers in day care by definition experience discontinuity between home and day care. Caregivers do not act like parents because that is not the nature of their role or of their relationship to the child and children act differently with parents and with caregivers (Long and Garduque 1987). Long and Garduque (1987) suggest that when parents and caregivers agree on important values, discontinuity in behavioural interactions and role expectations between day care and home may be beneficial. Such discontinuity may help children learn to adjust to social demands in the wider social world.

What happens when caregivers and parents are in discord? Unfortunately a series of studies on the caregiver-parent relationships suggests that discord may be common (Joffe 1977; Gipps 1982; Zigler and Turner 1982; Innes and Innes 1984; Kontos 1984, 1987). A particular problem area is caregivers' negative judgements of children and families. A series of studies by Kontos (Kontos, Raikes and Woods 1983; Kontos 1984; Kontos and Wells 1986) suggests that when caregivers perceive some of the children's parents as poor parents the identified group of parents is different in marital status (more likely to be divorced), childrearing attitudes (more likely to value conformity), and communications with caregivers (less likely to communicate) from other parents. Furthermore, while the children of these parents have similar experiences in day care, they may exhibit lower cognitive, language and social skills.

Negative caregiver evaluations of parents may occur because of the structural difficulties of the relationship. Caregivers need parents to be on time, to be reliable in their payments, to communicate information about the child and to not bring the child when she is sick. Parents need the caregiver to be available when they have to work late or when they get caught in traffic, to understand when they can't pay on time and to care for their child when she is a little bit sick and the mother can't miss work. Caregivers and parents meet when either when the parent is rushing off to work in the morning or at night when the caregiver is tired and ready to go home to her own children. Moreover parents may be experiencing separation anxiety while the caregiver is resentful of the higher pay and status of the mother's career. Both the parent and the caregiver may truly believe that only she really understands this baby. We need more research to understand the complexities of the parent-caregiver relationship and its influence on the development of infants and toddlers in day care.

There is another body of research that examines interactions between family characteristics and day care selection. Unlike the research on specific caregiver-parent continuity these studies examine structural relations between families and day care and the effects on children. This research suggests that, in general, good caregiving situations tend to go together. Stressed parents (Howes and Stewart 1987), parents who lead more complex lives (Howes and Olenick 1986), lack social supports (Howes and Stewart 1987) and are less developmentally appropriate in their childrearing values and behaviours (Howes and Olenick 1986; Howes and Stewart 1987) are more likely to enrol their child in low quality day care arrangements rather than high quality arrangements. Not surprisingly children who are enrolled in less than optimal day care arrangements and have less than optimal family care are less competent than children enrolled in more optimal day care and with more optimal family situations (Howes and Olenick 1986; Howes and Stewart 1987; Howes 1988c).

Recently in the United States the scholarly community has conducted a heated debate regarding the amount of risk associated with infant day care (see Phillips, McCartney, Scarr and Howes 1987; Belsky 1988; Clarke-Stewart 1988; Richters and Zahn-Waxler 1988; Thompson 1988). The debate arose from two recent studies (Barglow, Vaughn and Molitor 1987; Belsky and Rovine 1988) reporting elevated rates of insecure maternal attachments in infants whose mothers were employed full time. Neither of these studies examined the features of the day care environments used by these mothers. The material reviewed in this chapter, especially the complex relations between families, day care and children's development suggest that additional research is necessary to fully understand the meaning of the child's experience in day care.

References

Ainsworth, M., Blehar, M., Waters, E. and Wall, S. (1978) *Patterns of Attachment*, Hillsdale, NJ: Erlbaum.

Ainslie, R. and Anderson, C. (1984) 'Daycare children's relationships to their mothers and caregivers', in R.C. Ainslie (ed.) *Quality Variations in Day Care*, New York: Praeger.

Anderson, C., Nagle, R., Roberts, W. and Smith, J. (1981) 'Attachment to substitute caregivers as a function of center quality and caregiver involvement' *Child Development* 52: 53–61.

Bakeman, R. and Brown, J. (1980) 'Early interaction: consequences for social and mental development at three years', *Child Development* 51: 437–47.

Barglow, P., Vaughn, B. and Molitor, N. (1987) 'Effects of maternal absence due to employment on the quality of infant-mother attachment in a low risk sample', *Child Development* 58: 945–54.

Beckwith, L. and Cohen, S. (1983, April) 'Continuity of caregiving with preterm infants', paper presented at the Biennial Meeting of the Society for Research in Child Development, Detroit, Michigan.

Belsky, J. (1988) 'The "effects" of infant day care reconsidered', *Early Childhood Research Quarterly* 3: 235–72.

Belsky, J. and Rovine, M. (1988) 'Nonmaternal care in the first year of life and attachment security', *Child Development* 59: 945–54.

Belsky, J., Rovine, M. and Taylor, D. (1984) 'The Pennsylvania Infant and Family Development Project III: The origins of individual differences in infant-mother attachment', *Child Development* 55: 718–28.

Bradley, R., Caldwell, B. and Elardo, R. (1979) 'Home environment and cognitive development in the first two years', *Developmental Psychology* 15; 246–50.

Bretherton, I. (1985) 'Attachment theory: retrospective and prospect', in I.J. Bretherton and E. Waters (eds) *Growing Points in Attachment Theory, Monographs of the Society for Research in Child Development*, 50: 41–65.

Brownell, C. (1986) 'Convergent developments: cognitive-developmental correlates of growth in infant-toddler peer skills', *Child Development* 57: 275–86.

Carew, J. (1980) 'Experience and the development of intelligence in young children', *Monographs of the Society for Research in Child Development* 45 (6–7, Serial No. 187).

Clarke-Stewart, A. (1988) 'The "effects of infant day care reconsidered" reconsidered: risks for parents, children, and researchers', *Early Childhood Research Quarterly* 3: 293–318.

Cochran, M. (1977) 'A comparison of group day and family child rearing patterns in Sweden', *Child Development* 48: 702–7.

Colin, V. (1986) 'Hierarchies and patterns of infant's attachments to employed mothers and to alternative caregivers', paper presented at the International Society for the Study of Behavioural Development.

Cummings, E. (1980) 'Caregiver stability and daycare', *Developmental Psychology* 16: 31–7.

Easterbrooks, A. and Goldberg, W. (1984) 'Toddler development in the family: the impact of father involvement and parenting characteristics', *Child Development* 55: 740–52.

Field, T., Vega-Lahr, N. and Jagadish, S. (1984) 'Separation stress of nursery school infants and toddlers graduating to new classes', *Infant Behavior and Development* 7: 227–84.

Finkelstein, N. (1982) 'Aggression: is it stimulated by day care?' *Young Children* 37: 3–9.

Gipps, C. (1982) 'Nursery nurses and nursery teachers II: Their attitudes towards pre-school children and their parents', *Journal of Child Psychology and Psychiatry* 23: 255–65.

Golden, M., Rosenbluth, L., Grossi, M., Policare, H., Freeman, H. and Brownlee, J.M. (1978) *The New York City Infant Day Care Study*, New York: Medical and Health Research Association of New York City.

Harms, T. and Clifford, R. (1984) *The Family Day Care Rating Scale*, unpublished manuscript.

Hartup, W. (1983) 'The peer system', in P. Mussen (ed.) *Handbook of Child Psychology*, New York: Wiley.

Hay, D. (1985) 'Learning to form relationships in infancy: Parallel attainments with parents and peers', *Developmental Review* 5: 122–61.

Holden, G. (1983) 'Avoiding conflict: mothers as tactician in the supermarket', *Child Development* 54: 233–40.

Howes, C. (1983) 'Caregiver behavior in center and family day care', *Journal of Applied Developmental Psychology* 4: 99–107.

— (1985) 'Sharing fantasy: social pretend play in toddlers', *Child Development* 56: 1253–8.

— (1987a) 'Social competence with peers in young children: developmental sequences', *Developmental Review* 7: 252–72.

— (1987b) 'Social competency with peers: contributions from child care', *Early Childhood Research Quarterly* 2: 155–67.

— (1988a) 'Relations between early childcare and schooling', *Developmental Psychology* 24: 53–7.

— (1988b) 'Peer interaction in young children', *Monographs of the Society for Research in Child Development*, 53 (1, Serial No. 217).

— (1990) 'Can the age of entry and the quality of infant child care predict behaviors in kindergarten?' *Developmental Psychology* 26: 292–301.

— (in press) 'Antecedents of social competence in middle childhood', *Journal of Applied Developmental Psychology*.

Howes, C. and Farver, J. (1987) 'Social pretend play in 2-year-olds: effects of age of partner', *Early Childhood Research Quarterly* 2: 305–15.

Howes, C. and Olenick, M. (1986) 'Childcare and family influences on toddler's compliance', *Child Development* 57: 202–16.

Howes, C. and Rubenstin, J. (1981) 'Toddler peer behavior in two types of day care', *Infant Behavior and Development* 4: 387–93.

— (1985) 'Determinants of toddlers' experiences in day care: age of entry and quality of setting', *Childcare Quarterly* 14: 140–50.

Howes, C. and Stewart, P. (1987) 'Child's play with adults, toys, and peers: an examination of family and child-care influences', *Developmental*

Psychology 23: 423–30.

Howes, C. and Unger, O. (1989) 'Play with peers in childcare settings', in M. Block and A. Pelligrini (eds) *The Ecological Context of Children's Play*, Norwalk, NJ: Ablex.

Howes, C., Whitebook, M. and Pettygrove, W. (1986) *Variations in Recruitment and Retention of Qualified Staff*, final report to the California Policy Seminar.

Howes, C., Rodning, C., Galluzzo, D. and Myers, L. (1988) 'Attachment and childcare: relationships with mother and caregiver', *Early Childhood Research Quarterly* 3: 403–16.

Innes, R. and Innes, S. (1984) 'A qualitative study of caregivers' attitudes about childcare', *Early Child Development and Care* 15: 133–48.

Jacobson, J.L. and Wille, D.E. (1986) 'The influence of attachment pattern on developmental changes in peer interaction from the toddler to the pre-school period', *Child Development* 57: 338–47.

Jennings, K.D., Harmon, R.J., Morgan, G.A., Gaiter, S.L. and Yarrow, L.J. (1979) 'Exploratory play as an index of mastery motivation', *Developmental Psychology* 15: 386–94.

Joffe, C. (1977) *Friendly Intruders: Childcare Professionals and Family Life*, Los Angeles: University of California Press.

Kontos, S. (1984) 'Congruence of parent and early childhood staff perceptions of parenting', *Parenting Studies* 1: 5–10.

—— (1987) 'The attititudinal context of family-day care relationships', in D.L. Peters and S. Kontos (eds) *Continuity and Discontinuity of Experience in Childcare*, Norwood, NJ: Ablex.

Kontos, S. and Wells, W. (1986) 'Attitudes of caregivers and the daycare experiences of families', *Early Childhood Research Quarterly* 1: 47–68.

Kontos, S., Raikes, H. and Woods, A. (1983) 'Early childhood staff attitudes towards their parent clientele', *Childcare Quarterly* 12: 45–58.

Krentz, M. (1983) 'Differences between mother-child and caregiver-child attachments of infants in family day care', paper presented at Biennial Meeting of the Society for Research in Child Development.

La Frenière, P. and Sroufe, L.A. (1985) 'Profiles of peer competence in preschool: inter-relations between measures, influence of social ecology, and relation to attachment theory', *Developmental Psychology* 21: 56–69.

Lieberman, A. (1977) 'Preschoolers competence with a peer: relations with attachment and peer experience', *Child Development* 48: 1277–87.

Long, F. and Garduque, L. (1987) 'Continuity between home and family day care: caregivers' and mothers' perceptions and children's social experiences', in D. Peters and S. Kontos (eds) *Continuity and Discontinuity of Experience in Childcare*, Norwood, NJ: Ablex.

Lytton, H. (1977) 'Correlates of compliance and the rudiments of conscience in two-year-old boys', *Canadian Journal of Behavioral Science* 9: 242–51.

McLaughlin, B. (1983) 'Child compliance to parent control techniques', *Developmental Psychology* 19: 667–73.

Minton, C., Kagan, J. and Levine, J. (1971) 'Maternal control and obedience in the two-year-old', *Child Development* 42: 1873–94.

Mueller, E. and Vandell, D. (1979) 'Infant-infant interaction: a review', in J.D. Osofsky (ed.) *Handbook of Infant Development*, New York: Wiley.

Pastor, D. (1981) 'The quality of mother-infant attachment and its relationship to toddler initial sociability with peers', *Developmental Psychology* 17: 326–35.

Phillips, D.A., McCartney, K., Scarr, S. and Howes, C. (1987) 'Selected review of infant day care research: a cause for concern', *Zero to Three* 8: 18–21.

Richters, J. and Zahn-Waxler, C. (1988) 'The infant day care controversy: current status and future directions', *Early Childhood Research Quarterly* 3: 319–36.

Rothstein-Fisch, C. and Howes, C. (1988) 'Toddler interaction in mixed age groups', *Applied Developmental Psychology* 9: 211–18.

Rubenstein, J. and Howes, C. (1979) 'Caregiving and infant behavior in day care and in homes', *Developmental Psychology* 15: 1–24.

— (1983) 'Socio-emotional development of toddlers in day care: the role of peers and individual differences', in S. Kilmer (ed.) *Advances in Early Education and Day Care*, San Francisco: JAI Press.

Rubenstein, J., Pedersen, F. and Yarrow, L. (1977) 'What happens when mother is away: a comparison of mothers and substitute caregivers', *Developmental Psychology* 13: 529–30.

Rubenstein, J., Howes, C. and Boyle, P. (1981) 'A two year follow-up of infants in community based daycare', *Journal of Child Psychology and Psychiatry* 22: 209–18.

Ruopp, R., Travers, J., Glantz, F. and Coelen, C. (1979) *Children at the Center*, Cambridge, MA: ABT Books.

Schaffer, H.R. (1984) *The Child's Entry into a Social World*, New York: Academic.

Schaffer, H.R. and Crook, C. (1979) 'Maternal control techniques in a directed play situation', *Child Development* 50: 989–96.

Schwartz, J., Strickland, R. and Krolick, G. (1974) 'Infant day care: behavioral effects at preschool age', *Developmental Psychology* 10: 502.

Skinner, E.A. (1986) 'The origins of young children's perceived control: Mothers' contingent and responsive behavior', *International Journal of Behavioral Development* 9: 359–82.

Sroufe, A. (1983) 'Infant-caregiver attachment and patterns of adaptation in preschool', in M. Perlmutter (ed.) *Minnesota Symposium in Child Psychology*, Minnesota: University of Minnesota Press.

Sroufe, A., Fox, N. and Pancake, V. (1983) 'Attachment and dependency in developmental perspective', *Child Development* 54: 1615–27.

Thompson, R. (1988) 'The effects of infant day care through the prism of attachment theory: a critical appraisal', *Early Childhood Research Quarterly* 3: 273–82.

Waters, E. and Deane, K.E. (1985) 'Defining and assessing individual differences in attachment relationships: methodology and the organization of behaviors in infancy and childhood', in I.J. Bretherton and E. Waters (eds) *Growing Points in Attachment Theory and Research, Monographs of the Society for Research in Child Development* 50: 41–65.

197

Waters, E., Wippman, J. and Sroufe, A. (1979) 'Attachment positive affect and competence in the peer group', *Child Development* 50: 821–9.

Whitebook, M. and Phillips, D. (in press) 'The childcare provider: pivotal player in the child's world', in S. Chehrazi (ed.) *Balancing Working and Parenting: Psychological and Developmental Implications of Day Care*, New York: American Psychiatric Press, Inc.

Zigler, E. and Turner, P. (1982) 'Parents and day care workers: a failed partnership', in E. Zigler and E. Gordon (eds) *Day Care: Scientific and Social Policy Issues*, Boston: Auburn House.

Chapter eleven

Current and future issues in policy and research

Edward C. Melhuish and Peter Moss

Social context and day care

The experience of the five countries discussed in this book illustrates how societal factors such as ideology and labour markets influence social policy and hence social institutions such as day care facilities. Ideology and labour markets can act directly on childcare; the extent to which young children experience day care is largely influenced by levels of maternal employment, which reflect the demands of the labour market as well as attitudes about the acceptability of women with young children going out to work (though the two probably interact, changes in labour market demand and attitudes going hand-in-hand).

The extent of day care can also be influenced directly by policy. The development of paid post-natal leave in Sweden and the GDR has meant that children in these countries now enter day care settings usually after one year of age. The time Swedish children spend in day care has fallen, partly due to the introduction of a right for parents to work part-time, while another entitlement may have led to children spending more time at home when they are not well.

Social policy also directly determines the day care environments experienced by young children. In the US and UK most children receive private day care, mostly from relatives and childminders, with the remainder coming from 'nannies' and private nurseries, the latter form of care having grown rapidly in the US over the last 20 years and being likely to do so in the near future in the UK. In France, despite more extensive publicly funded services, private provision continues to predominate, in particular relatives and private childminders. A distinctive feature of the French situation is the large number of 2-year-olds in nursery school settings, a consequence of the almost universal provision of nursery education and the admission policy of nursery schools.

At the opposite extreme, in the GDR nearly all children are cared for in publicly-funded nurseries, with private provision by relatives and childminders having a marginal role. More children in Sweden are with relatives and private childminders – but most are in publicly-funded services; while these include a substantial contribution from organised childminding schemes, nursery provision is more widespread. With the government's commitment to publicly-funded childcare for all children over 18 months by 1991, the proportion of children in these public services and in nurseries will continue to increase.

The increasingly insignificant role of private childminders and relatives in the GDR and Sweden must partly be in response to the increase in publicly-funded services in both countries. But it may also reflect other developments, for example increasing employment rates among women of all ages reducing the number of female relatives able or willing to offer care. It also seems clear that, where some form of public childminding system exists, most women interested in this form of work opt for the public system, either because the pay, conditions and support are better or because it is harder to make a living as a private minder.

Policy can also affect children's environments in other ways – for example, the concentration of large numbers of disturbed and handi-capped children in public nurseries in the UK, or the age segregation of children where nurseries only take children under 3 or where nurseries divide children into narrow age groupings.

While these differences of environment must affect children's daily experience, it is not possible to be certain about the exact relationship between social context and quality of care, quality being defined in terms of children's actual experience. While we lack the data to be able to say with certainty that children in one country receive better or worse quality care than children in another country, it is highly probable that quality of care is more consistent and better on average in countries like the GDR and Sweden, which have developed or are developing national systems of publicly-funded and relatively well resourced services, than in countries like the UK and US where private arrangements are para-mount and where, in any case, the level of both public services and the regulation of private services depends heavily on decisions made by individual states or local authorities. Where private arrangements are dominant and variations in quality substantial, it might be expected that children from disadvantaged families would be more likely to experi-ence poorer quality care.

Day care research in five countries

Day care in the UK is diverse in type and variable in quality, largely dependent on private arrangements, with little input from public re-sources. The research reported by Edward Melhuish illustrates how, in these circumstances, children's experience in different types of care varied markedly, particularly their experience of interaction with others, a central aspect of quality of care. There was evidence that this 'between type' variation in children's experiences could influence both language development and socio-emotional development. While there were substantial social class differences in the use of different types of care, the 'type of care' effect acted independently of social class.

The French research described by Geneviève Balleyguier also shows 'between type' differences; between 9 months and 2 years of age, temperamental differences emerged between children cared for at home, by childminders or in nurseries. However, by the time the children are in nursery school at 3½ years these differences had mostly disappeared. This research also revealed considerable variations in childrearing between different types of childcare which showed some associations with child development. The last French study reported illustrates 'within type' differences. The variations that can occur within one type of day care (nurseries) in the nature of adult-child interactions influenced child behavior (and potentially development) substantially. This study reveals the sensitivity of young children to the quality of the day care environment and the problems that can be created by inadequate adult-child interactions.

Within the large research literature from the USA, Carollee Howes has concentrated on research which has analysed factors that contribute to the quality of day care, and can create 'within type' and 'between type' differences. Various organisational factors have been found to be associated with (though not guarantees of) positive experiences for children; for example, better child:adult ratios, better working conditions for caregivers (for example, shorter hours and less housework), safer environments, better caregiver training and more stability amongst caregivers. These factors seem likely to affect adult interactions with children, in particular sensitive contingent responsiveness. Thus better child:adult ratios are related to better caregiver-child attachments probably because better ratios lead to increased adult responsiveness.

Swedish day care is carefully regulated, relatively homogeneous, with central government taking a lead in setting targets for quantity and quality and providing resources to ensure these targets are met. Consequently provision appears to be of a high standard, or at least to display those organisational factors often associated with positive experiences for children. The day care received by young children in Sweden is probably more consistent and of superior quality to that received by young children in the UK, USA or even France. In these circumstances the research reported by Philip Hwang, Anders Broberg and Michael Lamb found that the quality of home care was most predictive of developmental variation between children; by contrast, quality of day care had little impact, being only weakly associated with some personality differences between children. Home care is part of the total care environment of children and the impact of variation in quality of home care found in the Gothenburg project emphasises how the quality of care can affect children's development, wherever it occurs or whoever gives it. The lack of day care effects in Sweden may reflect uniformly high standards of provision, or, at least, that most day care services reach some threshold point, above which, variation between or within type becomes less significant for children's experience or development. It is also the case that most Swedish children now do not enter day care until after one year of age, and variations in quality, or variations above a threshold point, may be less significant as children get older.

Day care in the GDR is also carefully regulated, as in Sweden, but is even more extensive and apparently homogeneous; nursery care is now an almost universal part of the upbringing of children from one year of age. In such circumstances, research comparing the effects of different types of care is both impractical and irrelevant. Research, instead, has become closely integrated with day care policy and practice, to a greater degree than in any of the countries in this book. In particular, research has become targeted on improving the quality of care within nurseries and, consequently, removing 'within type' differences. Particular emphasis has been placed on developing a pedagogical orientation within nurseries, and moving away from a previous emphasis on health and physical care. The research reported by Irina Weigl and Christine Weber shows how the educational and developmental possibilities offered by nurseries are being explored and exploited, through the integration of research, policy and practice, and how specific changes in specific aspects of care can influence the language, play and artistic abilities of young children.

The research from all five countries illustrates how childcare environments – whether in the home or in day care – can affect children's well-being and development. While some of the studies show differences between different types of care, more importantly, other studies illustrate that large differences can occur within the same type of day care, with large variations possible between, for example, nurseries. Moreover, it seems likely that these within-type differences are more important than between-type differences, and that between-type differences are likely to diminish where within-type differences are tackled positively to produce uniformly high quality, as in the case of Sweden and the GDR. The fact that such differences can be tackled, and are not just inherent features, emphasises the significance of social context in creating particular day care environments and establishing the quality of those environments.

Some specific issues

Responsibility for day care for children under 3

Governments in all five countries accept responsibilities for day care for children under 3 – but to varying degrees. In both the UK and USA, children and their care are assumed to be private issues; public intervention in the provision or subsidising of services requires a powerful justification, and is limited very largely to families who are poor, inadequate or deviant. At the same time, the USA has introduced a system of general tax relief on day care costs, which has favoured better-off families; however this arises less from an acceptance of social responsibility for day care, than from a perception that these costs are an ordinary and necessary business expense. The same attitude to children and their care contributes to the USA offering no employment rights to parents and the UK offering only a limited entitlement to maternity leave.

By contrast, governments in France, Sweden and the GDR accept a general responsibility for children and their care. Childcare is viewed as a social issue and responsibility, to which society should contribute. This is reflected in universal employment rights for parents and publicly-funded day care services open to all parents, or at least to all those who are employed. In all three countries, the development of these services is the responsibility of local and regional authorities. But where as in Sweden and the GDR central government has set national targets – essentially provision for all parents who want it – and ensured funding is available for these targets to be achieved locally, no such target has been set by central government in France, where the level and pace of development depends on local and regional authorities.

Most day care for young children is required because parents are employed. The UK government, in response to the growing demand for women's employment, has emphasised the importance of employers providing direct or indirect day care support for their employees, and sees such provision as a major component in a private market response to the growing demand for day care; currently, many employers are showing great interest in day care. What the end result of this will be in practice is difficult to predict; despite similar interest in the USA, Deborah Phillips concludes that 'employers are not a major source of childcare support'. The same is currently true of the other countries. In both France and the GDR there are some services attached to particular workplaces, though many of these are integrated into the main public day care system, receiving public funding in return for allocating some places to local children. The few workplace nurseries in Sweden were taken over by local authorities in the 1960s, again with a proportion of places going to local children.

The current emphasis in the UK on employers providing day care raises the question of the balance between workplace and neighbourhood day care – should children be looked after where they live or where their parents work? (though in practice employers can support neighbourhood services by, for example, subsidising parents' costs rather than subsidising a nursery on or near the workplace). In those countries which have well developed publicly-funded services – Sweden, the GDR, but also Denmark – there has been a clear preference for neighbourhood provision, though in some cases with a limited amount of workplace provision. The arguments involve the problems of linking day care to a job (which ties workers, increases the risk of discontinuity of care for children, places the onus for taking and collecting children on one parent and can create transport problems especially in large cities), and the threat to the well-being of local communities by removing from them children and services and opportunities for parents and children to develop or sustain local social networks.

In both Sweden and France however employers do contribute to the development of day care services through social insurance contributions – in Sweden part of this contribution (just under 3 per cent of payroll) is earmarked for day care and covers the cost of central government's contribution to local services, while in France the growing role of CAFs in supporting day care services has channelled part of the employers' CAF contribution to this end. In both countries therefore employers support day care, but as part of a compulsory and general system intended to benefit the general workforce rather than employees of particular companies.

In all countries, whatever the policy of governments or the extent of public provision, parents are assumed and expected to have major responsibility for their children and their care. This means in practice that mothers have most of the work and responsibility entailed. Only Sweden has addressed this gender issue seriously at a national level. That men should more equally share family responsibilities has been widely discussed and accepted in Sweden – though there is some way to go before this becomes reality. A central objective of equality policy for some years has been to increase men's involvement in childcare as a necessary corollary of women's increased involvement in employment. This objective is reflected in the employment rights available for parents – paternity leave is an obvious example, but also parental leave and leave to care for sick children, which is equally available to mothers and fathers and offers virtually full compensation for lost earnings for the parent taking leave (parental leave in most other countries is, as in France, either unpaid or paid at a low flat rate; this acts as a major economic disincentive to men taking leave given that in most families fathers still earn more than mothers). Although only a minority of fathers take any period of parental leave, the Swedish commitment to increasing men's involvement in childcare continues; a goal of the government's Equality Policy is to increase fathers' take-up of parental leave and the right to part-time employment.

The function of childcare services for young children

In most countries, the earliest day care services for young children were provided for poor and needy families, either to protect children from their home environments or to help poor women go out to work; the tradition has been a welfare one, with the institutions oriented towards children's health, nutrition and other aspects of physical care. This tradition and orientation remains dominant in both the US and UK, though in both cases the need for a more educational or developmental orientation has begun to be recognised. In many other countries, including Sweden, the GDR and France, there have been more significant changes. Publicly-funded services have developed into general services open to all working parents. The same trend can be seen in other countries. Nurseries in Belgium were exclusively for low income families where the mother worked, and they received state funds on this basis; a change in funding arrangements in 1970 opened them to all parents. In Denmark, nurseries were seen as a preventive measures with funding tied to priority being given to low income families; in 1964, in response to a rapid increase in women's employment, legislation scrapped the link between funding and low income families and initiated a rapid increase of provision open to all parents. Similar developments occurred in Italy, following legislation in 1971 which recognised the right of any mother to use nurseries and which transferred responsibilities for nurseries to local and regional authorities away from a state organisation whose original brief had been to provide for 'abandoned or needy mothers and to children from very poor families'.

These changes have been matched by a growing emphasis on nurseries adopting a more educational or pedagogical approach. This trend is apparent in Sweden and the GDR, and to a lesser extent in France, as well as in other countries. This in turn raises the question of the relationship between nurseries and the education system, in particular educational provision for children under school age, and the inconsistencies between nurseries and this educational provision; for example, nurseries usually are the responsibility of health or welfare agencies, nursery workers have lower levels of training, pay and conditions than workers in nursery schools or kindergartens and parents usually have to make some contribution to the cost of nurseries, while nursery schooling is usually free. These inconsistencies are particularly obvious in a situation where nurseries and nursery education both provide for the same age group (for example, 2-year-olds in France, 3- and 4-year-olds in the UK). Solutions in the long term may involve bringing all services within education, or putting all services before compulsory school age into a separate department, with matching changes in the conditions and training of workers and so on.

Equity and equality

In most countries, publicly-funded services are unequally distributed between different areas; access to services therefore depends considerably on where a family lives. Similar disparities can occur in the regulation and support of private services, and also, as the example from Los Angeles quoted by Deborah Phillips illustrates, in the availability of private services. This situation, or at least that part of it concerned with public agencies, reflects differing resources and priorities among local authorities and a reluctance by central governments to establish clear targets and guidelines, matched, where necessary, with funding.

The issue of equity also arises elsewhere. As publicly-funded services expand, higher income families make increasing use of them, sometimes to the point of using them proportionately more than lower income families. This may be for several reasons – for example, higher income families being more able to 'work' the system and get a place, or lower income families being less attracted to nursery care and preferring to use care by relatives or local, private childminders. Whatever the reasons, the consequences are that during this phase of service development, higher income families get a disproportionate share of the subsidy going to services, while lower income families using relatives or private childminders get no subsidy at all.

Lower income families are also liable to do less well in a system based mainly or wholly on private services. Systems of tax relief on day care costs tend to benefit higher income families, who in any case are likely to have access to a wider variety of services (for example nannies, for-profit nurseries) and better quality provision. Furthermore, parents in higher skilled jobs are more likely to receive some support for day care from their employer, since it is this group of workers that employers will most need to recruit and retain. The end result is likely to be a two-(or more) tiered system, with large inequalities related to family income.

Choice and diversity

There are two dimensions of choice that are particularly relevant. First, choice for parents in how they combine work with family responsibilities. This is often put in terms of giving mothers a choice between going out to work and staying at home. Alternatively, it can be defined in terms of giving mothers and fathers more choice about what hours they work and when they work them, together with the opportunity to stop employment for a period. This begs many questions. How much choice should parents have? For how long should they have choice? What conditions produce equal choice for all parents? How can a policy of choice be developed that does not reinforce existing gender inequalities in employment and the home?

Of the five countries covered in this book, Sweden has gone furthest in tackling these questions. Swedish policies assume that parents will be employed for most of the time they have children – and to that extent consciously limit choice between employment and non-employment – but offer an increasingly substantial break after birth. There is considerable flexibility in how that break may be taken – for example, when parental leave is extended to 18 months in 1991, parents will be able to take their leave at any time until their child is 8, dividing the leave up into several periods if they choose; and all or part of the leave can be taken part-time. Underpinning the leave is nearly full compensation for lost earnings. A further right to work a 6-hour day until a child starts school also increases parents' choice, albeit without compensation for lost income. Access to good quality, subsidised childcare completes the package – though a guaranteed place will only be available to children over 18 months, reducing the choice available to parents with younger children. By contrast, France emphasises choice in how parents organise employment and family responsibilities, but has failed to develop matching supportive policies. Day care provision for children under 3 is limited, and parental leave, though long, is mostly unpaid and relatively inflexible. As a consequence, real choice is very constrained except perhaps for some high income families.

The other aspect of choice concerns type of day care. The GDR has gone for comprehensive public provision, but offers no choice – all care is in nurseries. Both Sweden and France offer nurseries and organised childminding schemes, though the degree to which parents are free to make a choice depends on the amount and mix of provision in each area – where supply is less than the demand, parents will be under pressure to take what is offered, while many areas either have a preponderance of nurseries or childminding. Both French and Swedish policies also allow the possibility of diversity of providers, with funds available to parent groups or voluntary organisations, as well as local authorities.

Another approach to increasing choice, within the context of a system using public funds, is to subsidise parents' day care costs – either through tax relief or cash allowances – so freeing them, in theory at least, to choose the provision they want and ensuring that all parents, including for example lower income parents using relatives, are assisted. While this approach may offer greater choice and flexibility, it may have other consequences which need to be taken into account in deciding whether to adopt it in preference to the supply-subsidy approach. It may, for example, lead to greater inequalities in provision, with higher income families being more able to supplement an allowance or tax relief with private funding.

Both approaches – supply- and demand-subsidy – have potential advantages and disadvantages, an assessment of which must depend on each reader's values. The point to be emphasised is that a substantial degree of choice and diversity in day care for young children is feasible under either system (or even some combination of the two, under which, for example, parents could have access to subsidised services or, under certain conditions, a cash allowance to contribute to alternative arrangements). It is also important to emphasise that research findings do not suggest that any one type of provision – nursery care or childminding – is so much better that that type alone should be funded, or so much worse that funding should be withheld from it. In these circumstances it appears not only feasible but desirable to cater for diversity of parental choice.

Regulating the private sector

No countries attempt to regulate the whole range of private day care arrangements. Typically, for example, care provided in a child's own home by a nanny or babysitter is exempt from any control. A number of countries, including Sweden and the GDR, also exempt childminders, although four American states also have no official interest in this form of care. In addition some American states only register childminders, without any attempt to inspect them or apply conditions, and most exempt childminders with less than three children. In all countries where childminders are supposed to be registered, many do not do so and operate illegally. Certainly in the UK, and possibly elsewhere, the resources put into regulating childminders, and the thoroughness with which the task is done, varies between local authorities. The same is true for the regulation of private nurseries and in both the UK and some US states certain private nurseries are exempted from any form of regulation.

The case for regulating private services rests not with improving quality – for in the private market, that should rest primarily with market forces – but more basically in the need to protect children, and especially young children, against possible harm or abuse. The case also assumes such basic protection is so important that it must be a social responsibility, assumed by the state or its agents, and not left entirely to parents. As such, regulation should cover all types of day care, with the possible exception of close relatives, and with no exemptions. Clear guidelines need to be laid down detailing what children should be protected from and how this is done, and these guidelines applied uniformly. Adequate resources need to be available to ensure that regulation can be conducted thoroughly and regularly, to a uniform standard in all areas.

In the private market the only mechanism available to foster the development of good quality day care is parental choice. With sufficient knowledge of the characteristics of the day care available and a reasonable degree of choice then the parents' own values will determine what childcare is used and presumably good quality care will be chosen and prosper. In the two countries in this book which rely almost totally on the private market for the provision of day care, the USA and the UK, this mechanism does not seem to have been working well. The research suggests that the quality of care in these countries is very variable with much day care apparently being of distinctly poor quality.

Childcare workers

The training, status, pay and conditions of childcare workers caring for young children is usually low compared to workers with older children; workers with children under 3 come below workers in nursery schools or kindergartens who, in turn, come below school teachers, who themselves often have a hierarchy related to the age of children taught. At the bottom of the pile come private childminders and women who care for children in the children's own home.

Day care is one example of a process by which skilled jobs are treated as unskilled because they are undertaken almost entirely by women. In other words, it is difficult to see any objective justification for the low position in the occupational hierarchy occupied by these workers. This low position is unlikely to be conducive to developing and sustaining high quality work – it contributes to high turnover among workers and may adversely affect the calibre of potential recruits for the work and the motivation of those already doing the work. One reason why this situation has developed is because of the limited employment opportunities open to women elsewhere, as well as stereotypical views about appropriate jobs for women. As these conditions change, the supply of women prepared to undertake the care of young children – or indeed other types of caring work – may well decrease, unless at least pay and other conditions improve. Faced by increasing demand, shortages may develop or the cost of services, private and public, may increase.

Quality of childcare

One conclusion which comes through clearly from research in the five countries considered in this book is the importance of the quality of childcare as a mediating factor affecting child development. What is meant by the quality of childcare? The position taken here is to define good quality childcare in terms of experiences which foster children's development and well-being. Quality of care must therefore be defined in terms of children's experiences which affect development and well-being. Research on child development points to several aspects of the young child's experience as having potential developmental consequences. These aspects of experience should be regarded as equivalent to the quality of care, and would include adult-child interaction, peer interaction, interpersonal relationships, activities fostering learning and development, healthy and safe conditions and emotional climate or happiness. Carollee Howes with evidence from the USA and Edward Melhuish in a UK study consider the first three of these aspects of quality of care. Irina Weigl and Christine Weber discuss how research in the GDR has led to a consideration of all these aspects in developing work in nurseries. Often in considerations of the quality of care the notion of happiness is glossed over. Even if there were no research evidence linking happiness to developmental outcomes, such an aspect of care should be considered essential on purely humanitarian grounds, but there are research data offering empirical support as well, for example, Meng (1989) has found that infants' emotions affect learning.

There are a number of associated factors which correlate with quality of care in that they are likely to contribute to positive experiences and good developmental outcomes. They facilitate good quality care but do not guarantee it. Carollee Howes mentions several – child:adult ratio, group size, caregiver training, curriculum (developmentally appropriate activities) and status and salary of caregivers. There are others such as assigning specific caregivers to children (to stabilise relationships), staff turnover, stability of care, equipment and accommodation. Such factors are largely determined by the social context and are potentially open to manipulation and/or legislation to improve the quality of care.

One component which comes through as central to good quality care is experience of interactions providing sensitive responsiveness, i.e. responding appropriately to the children's communications. The importance of this is seen in all five countries. In the USA, research on childcare both within the home and in day care settings reflects this; in Sweden the greater variability of home care than out-of-home care meant that variations in HOME scores (a measure of responsiveness and stimulation for the child in the child's own home) were the best predictors of intellectual outcomes; in Britain the differential effects of type

of care can be explained by variations between types of care in responsiveness and stimulation for the child; in France similarly the variation
in stimulation and responsiveness between nurseries affected children as
did variation between and within other types of care. In the GDR this
aspect of sensitive responsiveness is reflected in the programme introduced in nurseries where the importance of caregiver-child interactions
is continually emphasised; the Programme for Educational Work in
Nurseries gives guidance to nursery workers both at the level of guiding
principles and specific recommendations for good practice.

The relationship between the quality of care provided at home and
out-of-home is likely to be the decisive factor in whether home versus
day care effects on child development occur. Where the quality of
out-of-home care is superior to that provided at home then children
receiving day care are likely to show beneficial effects as reported for
studies of children from disadvantaged families receiving day care (e.g.
Ramey and Mills 1977; Golden *et al.* 1978; O'Connell and Farran
1982). However, where the quality of out-of-home care is inferior to that
of home care then detrimental effects may occur (e.g. Melhuish *et al.*, in
press). Hence both positive and negative effects for day care are to be
expected as a function of the relationship between the quality of home
and out-of-home care, with no day care effects where there is approximate equivalence in quality of care in the settings compared. A corollary of this point is that the same day care may have different effects for
different groups of children depending upon the relative quality of home
care available.

Age and day care

How old should young children be before experiencing day care?
Belsky (1988) argues that children who start full-time (more than 20
hours per week) day care before one year of age are at increased risk for
forming an insecure attachment to the mother. As mentioned in the
chapter by Carollee Howes, this resurrection of an old proposition has
caused substantial controversy. As the relevant studies cited by Belsky
did not examine the characteristics of the care experienced by the
children explanations in terms of quality of care rather than separation
from the mother cannot be discounted. Belsky's arguments hold that the
increased risk of insecure attachment will lead to longer-term detrimental effects as secure attachment to the mother is postulated to
mediate several developmental processes. Therefore, whenever children
spend a substantial period of their first year in full-time non-parental
care an increased risk of developmental problems, particularly socio-
emotional, is predicted. Belsky has thoroughly discussed the evidence in
favour of this proposition. However, the issue is disputed (e.g. Richters

and Zahn-Waxler 1988). Clarke-Stewart (1988, 1989), while accepting the increased (8–15 per cent) risk of insecure attachment associated with full-time day care under one year of age, argues that such an effect is more likely to reflect other aspects of the total ecology of maternal employment and not the effect of day care itself. Such aspects include possible differences in the attitudes, behaviour toward the child or stress of employed and non-employed mothers, or the differential validity of the assessment procedure for children who do or do not experience substantial day care.

Not all data are readily compatible with Belsky's view. Andersson (1986) and Andersson and Kihlbohm (1989) in Sweden found positive effects at ages 8 and 13 for starting day care in the first year for some aspects of cognitive and social development.

Changes in Sweden – where children now mostly start day care after one year of age – make this study impossible to replicate. Were replication possible, then it would be important to collect data on children and families before admission to day care; the positive effects reported by Andersson may simply reflect pre-day care differences. A similar critique can be, and indeed has been made (Richters and Zahn-Waxler 1988), of Belsky's interpretation of US data. The negative outcomes ascribed by Belsky to early day care experience may be the product of negative child, parent or family factors present before the admission to day care, but associated with an early start in the US context. In a study which does take account of a wide range of antecedent child and family differences in the UK, Melhuish concluded that day care effects were best explained in terms of differences between type of care reflecting quality of care rather than parental versus non-parental care. Also in France, Geneviève Balleyguier did not find the persisting effects for day care which would be anticipated if attachment to the mother were disrupted. Whether admission to full-time day care in the first year involves an enhanced risk of insecure infant-mother attachment and longer-term problems, and, whether this is a general risk or only occurs under certain conditions, remains open to debate. The debate may however be overtaken by events. This has already happened in Sweden and the GDR, where children typically start day care after one year of age due to the extension of parental leave; and similar or even longer extensions of parental leave have occurred in other countries (e.g. West Germany, France, Finland, Hungary). Flexible leave, including part-time employment options, together with compensation for lost earnings may create a situation where norm for most developed countries will be for parents to share 12 months parental leave, taken on either a full-time or part-time basis. While one argument for such developments is that early infancy is the time when it is most difficult to provide good quality non-parental care, it can also be argued for in terms of the quality of life for children, parents and families.

Children's age is, however, a critical variable in considering the quality of care because the needs of children change as they develop and good quality day care needs to take account of this. This aspect of day care is most clearly acknowledged in the GDR where the whole programme in nurseries reflects the changing developmental needs of children. This work, developed over many years and based on both practical experience and the results of research, provides many lessons for those who would aim to improve the quality of day care.

Future directions for research

In all the countries included in this book there has been an increasing trend to focus research on the issue of the quality of day care, and to become less concerned with the issue of whether parental care is better than non-parental care. In those countries where social policy is most involved with day care, particularly Sweden and the GDR, there has been most progress in facilitating the provision of good quality day care, and in these countries increased use of day care has led to more extensive development of day care services to encourage good practice.

The work in the GDR concerned with educational functions that day care can fulfil emphasises that day care for children under 3 can entail educational responsibilities as well as routine care. As attention becomes increasingly focused on the components of good quality care then the developmental needs of children which include the provision of learning opportunities will increasingly guide the nature of day care provision.

A major focus for future research in all countries should be the further development of good quality care in all settings, and several relevant aspects of care have already been mentioned. However, research which has no effect on policy is of limited use; attention needs to be given to developing close relations between research, policy and practice. In this respect the integration of day care research with day care policy and practice in the GDR is particularly striking. Here the questions addressed by researchers are closely tied to the issues relevant to policy and practice, with the research results rapidly assimilated into the formation and execution of social policy. Now undoubtedly the extensive integration of research and policy seen in the GDR is in part a consequence of the political system of that country; but this does not mean that countries with different political systems cannot learn from the GDR's experience or that such integration is not possible for other countries.

Research on improving day care provision will inevitably involve methodologies which require intervention in day care settings and the evaluation of that intervention. Sometimes the term 'action research' is used to characterise this approach. Such intervention strategies are seen in a small way in some of the French research and it is a major model for research in the GDR. Such an approach is well suited to a day care system which includes within it a process of evaluation of the current quality of provision. Indeed one of the future requirements for research in this area is to provide readily applicable measures of the quality of day care, which can be used not only in future research but also in the regular monitoring of day care provision as part of an evaluation strategy. If such measures could be used in different societies, then cross-national comparisons which facilitate learning between countries would obviously be enhanced. It is likely however that, because of the different social contexts of countries, complete comparability would be impossible and such measures would probably consist of elements common to all countries plus elements specific to a particular country.

Finally, future research should, and surely will, see an increasing emphasis on cross-national approaches – ranging from researchers being conversant with work done in other countries to studies spanning two or more countries. Researchers in each country will learn increasingly from their colleagues in other countries, resources will be pooled and better exploited and the results of individual studies (and studies from one country) will be set in context contributing enormously to the interpretation of findings and the quality of conclusions drawn from findings.

References

Andersson, B.-E. (1986) *Home Care or External Care*, Report No. 2 from the Stockholm Institute of Education.
Andersson, B.-E. and Kihlbohm, U. (1989) 'Effects of child care and mother's education on children's development', paper presented to the International Society for the Study of Behavioural Development, Jyvaskyla, Finland.
Belsky, J. (1988) 'The "effects" of infant day care reconsidered', *Early Childhood Research Quarterly* 3: 235–72.
Clarke-Stewart, K.A. (1988) 'The "effects of infant day care reconsidered" reconsidered: risks for parents, children and researchers', *Early Childhood Research Quarterly* 3: 293–318.
— (1989) 'Infant day care: maligned or malignant?', *American Psychologist* 44: 266–73.
Golden, M., Rosenbluth, L., Grossi, M., Policare, H.J., Freeman, N. Jr. and Brownlee, E.M. (1978) *The New York City Infant Day Care Study*, New York: Medical and Health Research Association of New York City.

Melhuish, E.C., Lloyd, E., Martin, S. and Mooney, A. (in press) 'Type of day care at 18 months: relations with cognitive and language development', *Journal of Child Psychology and Psychiatry*.

Meng, Z. (1989) 'The organizational function of emotion on cognitive tasks in infancy', paper presented to the International Society for the Study of Behavioural Development, Jyvaskyla, Finland.

O'Connell, J.C. and Farran, D.C. (1982) 'Effects of day care experience on the use of intentional communicative behaviors in a sample of socio-economically depressed infants', *Developmental Psychology* 18: 22–9.

Ramey, C.T. and Mills, P. (1977) 'Social and intellectual consequences of day care for high-risk infants', in R. Webb (ed.) *Social Development in Childhood: Daycare Programs and Research*, Baltimore: Johns Hopkins University Press.

Richters, J.E. and Zahn-Waxler, C. (1988) 'The infant day care controversy: current status and future directions', *Early Childhood Research Quarterly* 3: 319–36.

215

Name index

216

Subject index

HUMANITIES